EPISODE ONE: FLATLINE

STORY
BILL JEMAS
BRIAN FINKELSTEIN

SCRIPT
BRIAN FINKELSTEIN
MIKE SOVIERO
MICHAEL COAST

LAYOUTS
JULIAN ROWE

PENCILS
MARCO CASTIELLO

COLORS
THOMAS CHU

DAVE LANPHEAR
RICHARD BROOKS

EDITOR
RICHARD BROOKS

MEDICAL CONSULTANT
DR. HARRY HARAMIS

EPISODE TWO: UNDEAD ON ARRIVAL

STORY
BILL JEMAS

SCRIPT
BILL JEMAS
BOBBY STODDARD
MICHAEL COAST

LAYOUTS
STAN CHOU
JULIAN ROWE

PENCILS
STAN CHOU
MARCO CASTIELLO

COLORS
LEONARDO PACIAROTTI
STELLAR STUDIOS

INKS
STELLAR STUDIOS

COVER
JULIAN ROWE

LETTERS
CAROLINE FLANAGAN

EDITOR
CAROLINE FLANAGAN

EPISODE THREE: GRAVEYARD SHIFT

STORY
BILL JEMAS

SCRIPT
BRIAN FINKELSTEIN
BOBBY STODDARD
BILL JEMAS

LAYOUTS
STAN CHOU

PENCILS
STAN CHOU
ANDRES PONCE

COLORS
MARTA MARTINEZ
LEONARDO PACIAROTTI

COVER
MICHAEL MacRAE

LETTERS
CAROLINE FLANAGAN

EDITOR
CAROLINE FLANAGAN

EPISODE FOUR: INTENSIVE SCARE

STORY
BILL JEMAS
MICHAEL COAST
STAN CHOU

SCRIPT
MICHAEL COAST
BRIAN FINKELSTEIN
BILL JEMAS

LAYOUTS
STAN CHOU

PENCILS
STAN CHOU
ANDRES PONCE

COLORS
MARTA MARTINEZ

COVER
CHRIS EHNOT

LETTERS
CAROLINE FLANAGAN
CLAIRE DRANGINIS

EDITOR
CAROLINE FLANAGAN

MEDICAL CONSULTANT
DR. HARRY HARAMIS

EPISODE FIVE: IN STITCHES

STORY
BILL JEMAS
MICHAEL COAST
STAN CHOU

SCRIPT
MICHAEL COAST
BILL JEMAS

LAYOUTS
STAN CHOU

PENCILS
STAN CHOU
ANDRES PONCE

COLORS
MARTA MARTINEZ

COVER
MANUEL GARCIA

LETTERS
CAROLINE FLANAGAN

EDITOR
CAROLINE FLANAGAN

MEDICAL CONSULTANT
DR. HARRY HARAMIS

THEN
NOW

	1966	2015
WORLD POPULATION	3,400,000,000	7,200,000,000
McDonald's		
LOCATIONS	850	36,000
COUNTRIES	1	118
BIGGEST BURGER	1.6oz	5.4oz
AVERAGE MEAL CALORIES	590	1,500
Walmart		
LOCATIONS	24	11,495
COUNTRIES	1	28
PERCENTAGE OF PRODUCTS MADE IN CHINA	0%	70%
NFL		
SUPER BOWL VIEWERS	50,000,000	114,000,000
AVERAGE SALARY	$15,000	$1,900,000
Apple		
LOCATIONS	0	453
iOS DEVICES SOLD	0	1,000,000,000
Prison Industry		
STATE AND FEDERAL PRISON POPULATION	200,000	2,300,000
PERCENTAGE OF FEDERAL PRISON POPULATION: DRUG VIOLATIONS	11%–16%	50%
Health Industry		
COST OF HEALTH CARE	$201 PER CAPITA	$10,000 PER CAPITA
COST OF MEDICARE	$3,000,000,000	$634,300,000,000
Political Industry		
COST OF PRESIDENTIAL CAMPAIGN	$8,800,000	$5,000,000,000

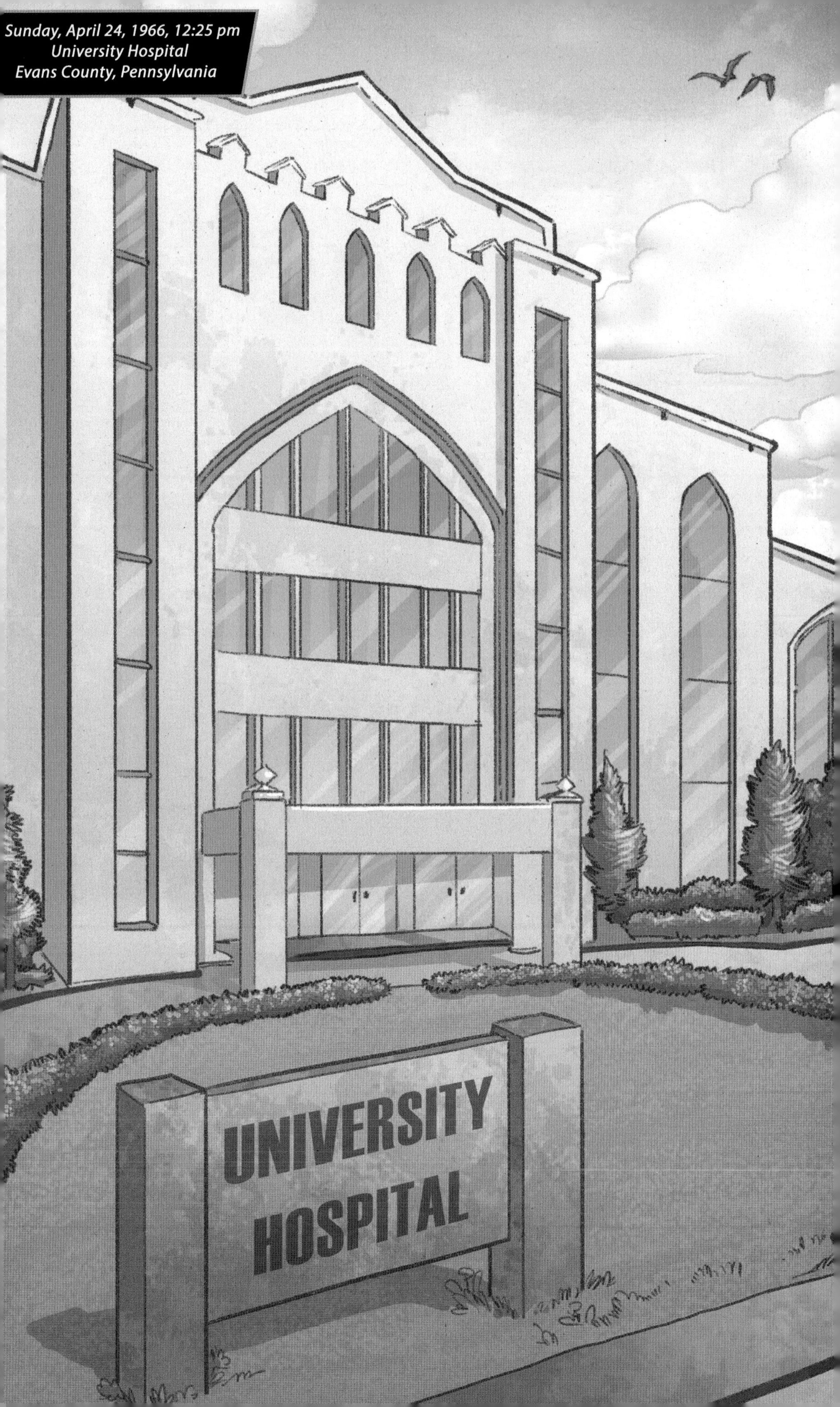
Sunday, April 24, 1966, 12:25 pm
University Hospital
Evans County, Pennsylvania
UNIVERSITY
HOSPITAL

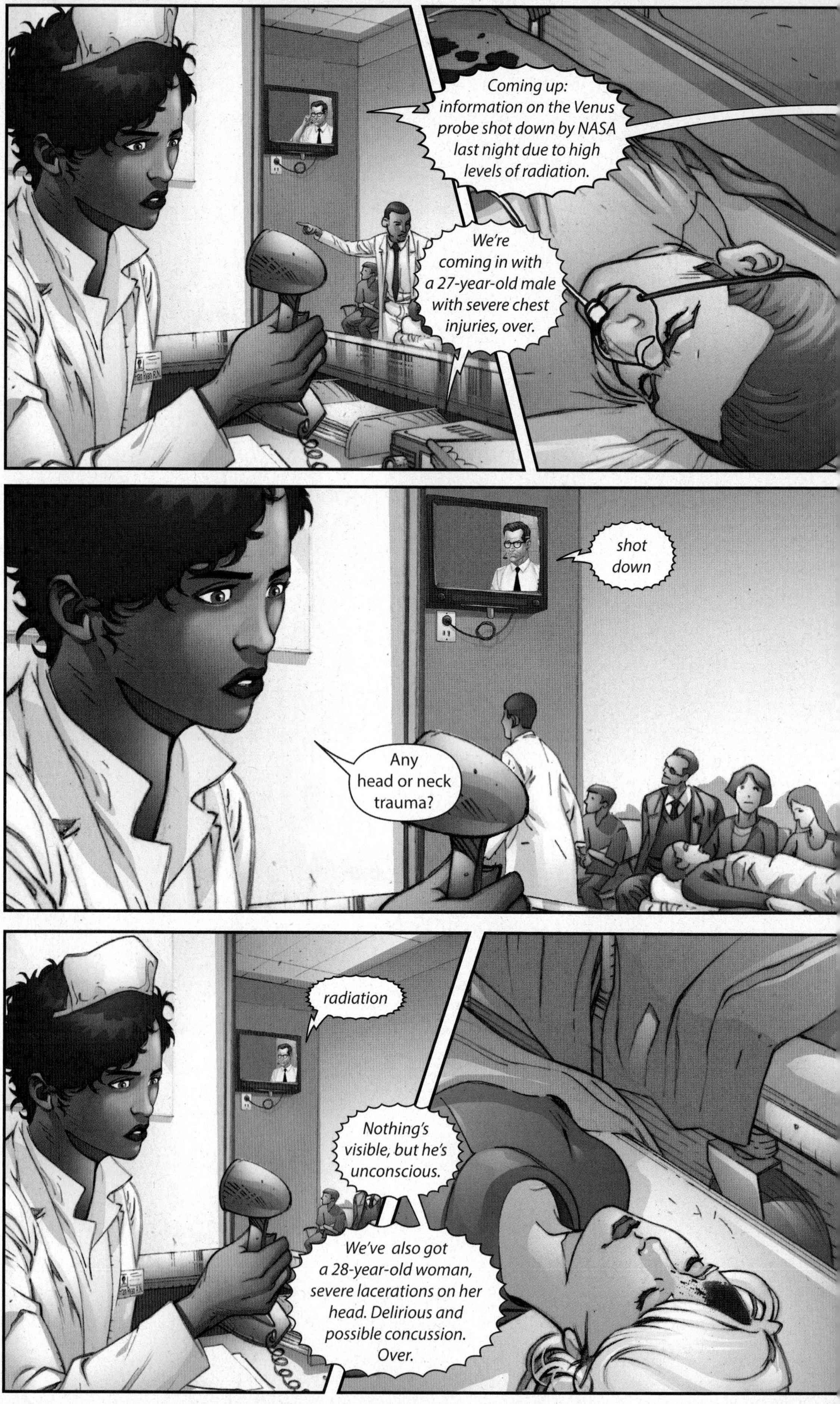
Coming up: information on the Venus probe shot down by NASA last night due to high levels of radiation.
We're coming in with a 27-year-old male with severe chest injuries, over.
shot down
Any head or neck trauma?
radiation
Nothing's visible, but he's unconscious.
We've also got a 28-year-old woman, severe lacerations on her head. Delirious and possible concussion. Over.

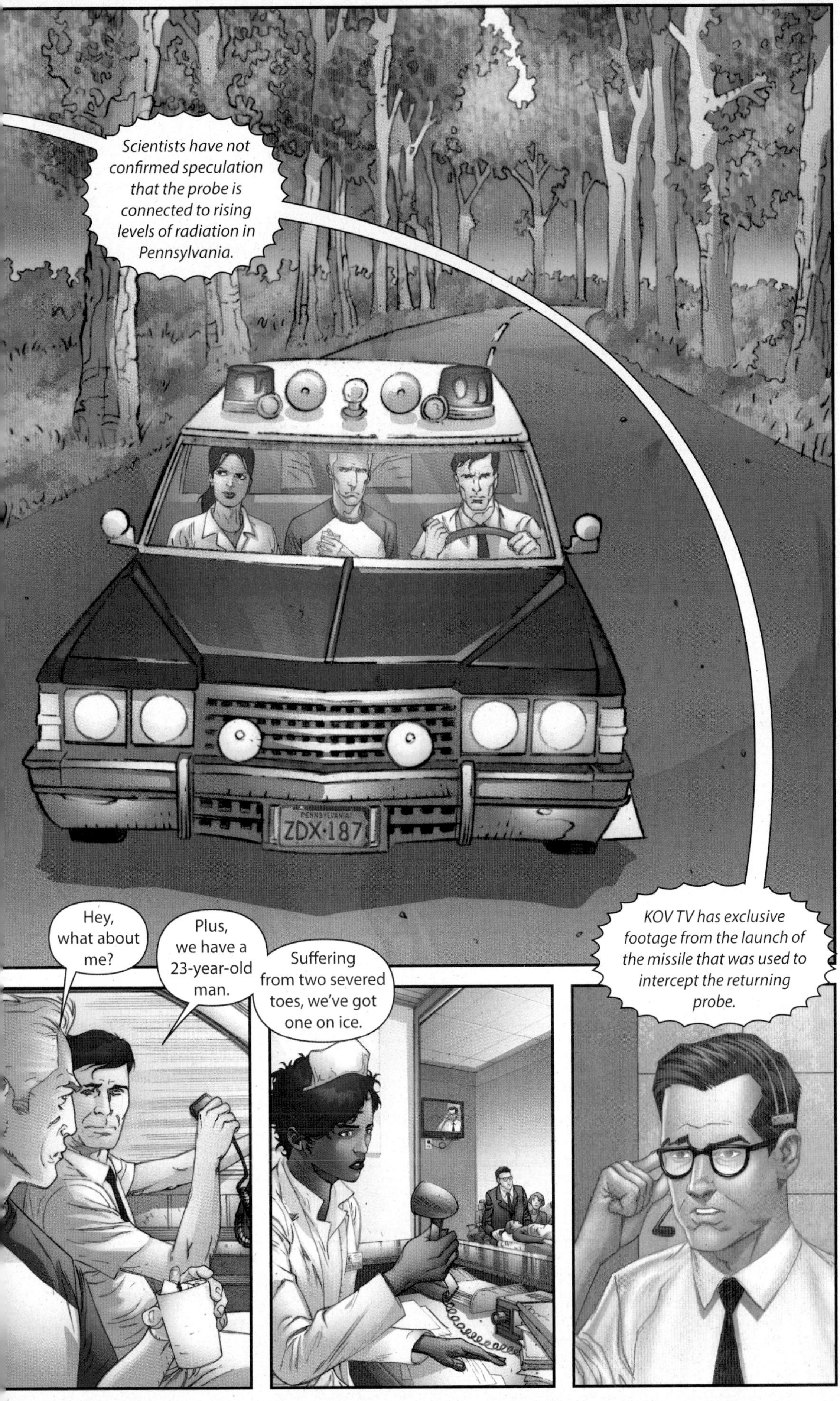
Scientists have not confirmed speculation that the probe is connected to rising levels of radiation in Pennsylvania.
PENNSYLVANIA
ZDX·187
Hey, what about me?
Plus, we have a 23-year-old man.
Suffering from two severed toes, we've got one on ice.
KOV TV has exclusive footage from the launch of the missile that was used to intercept the returning probe.

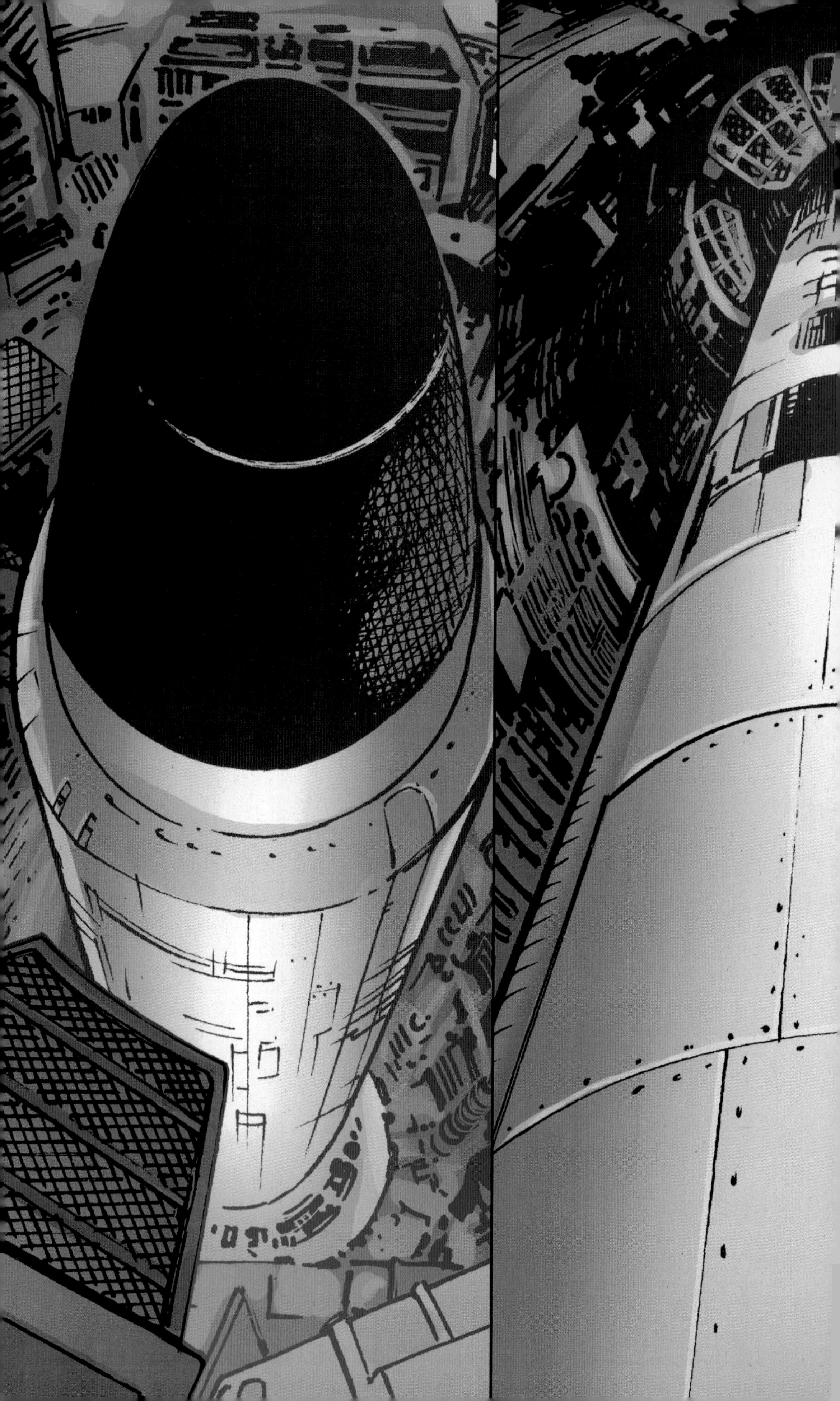

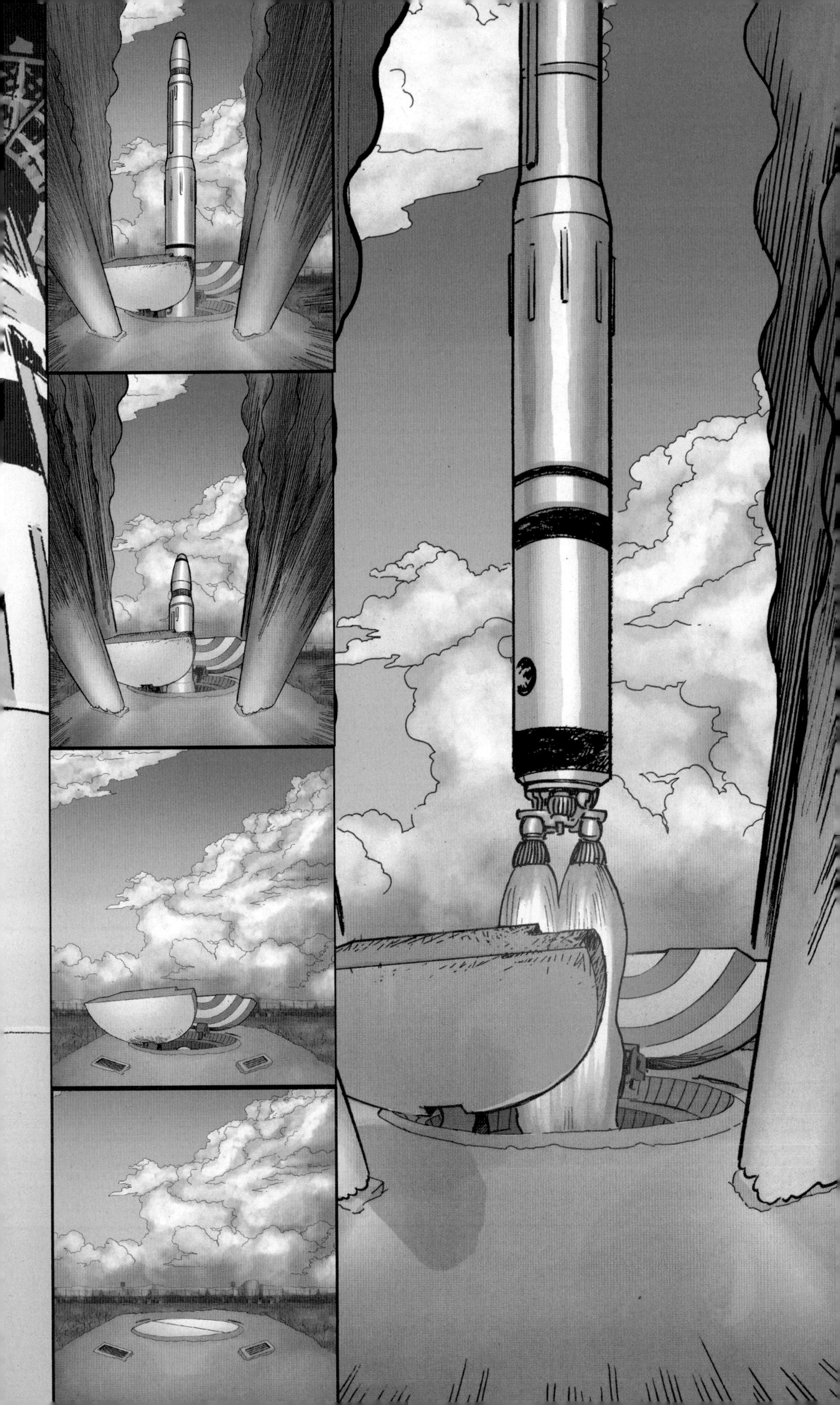

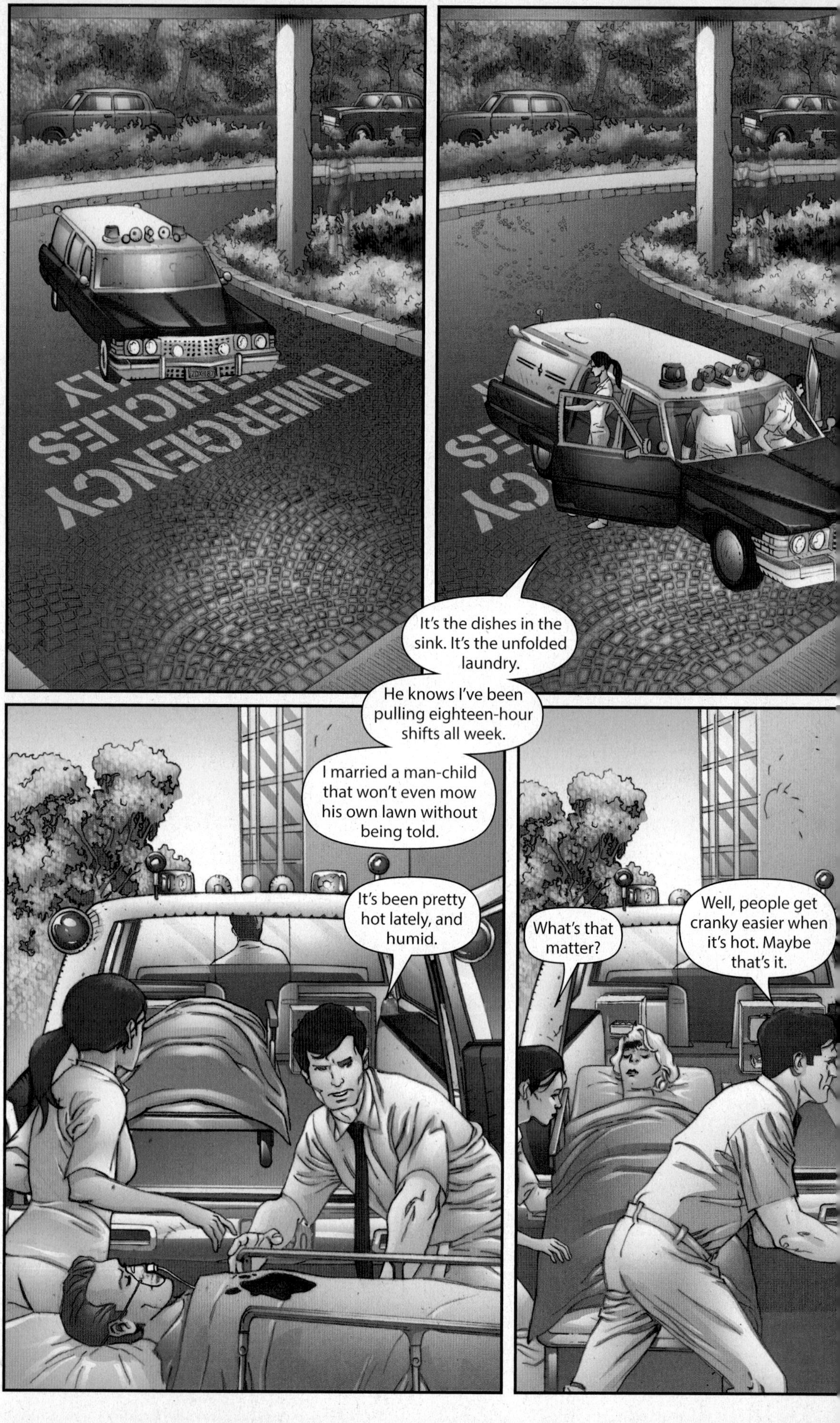
EMERGENCY VEHICLES
It's the dishes in the sink. It's the unfolded laundry.
He knows I've been pulling eighteen-hour shifts all week.
I married a man-child that won't even mow his own lawn without being told.
It's been pretty hot lately, and humid.
What's that matter?
Well, people get cranky easier when it's hot. Maybe that's it.

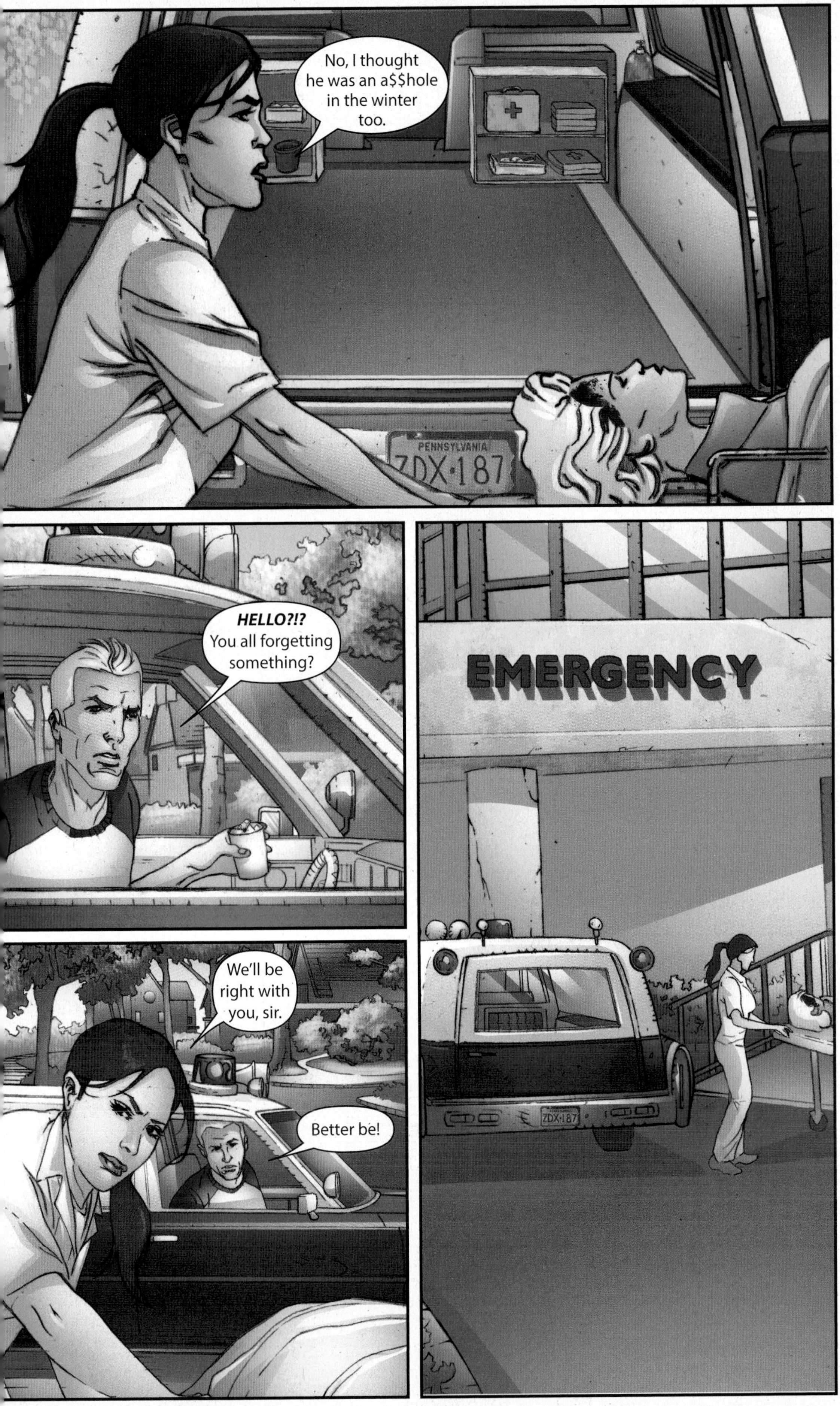
No, I thought he was an a$$hole in the winter too.
PENNSYLVANIA
ZDX•187
HELLO?!? You all forgetting something?
We'll be right with you, sir.
Better be!
EMERGENCY
ZDX•187

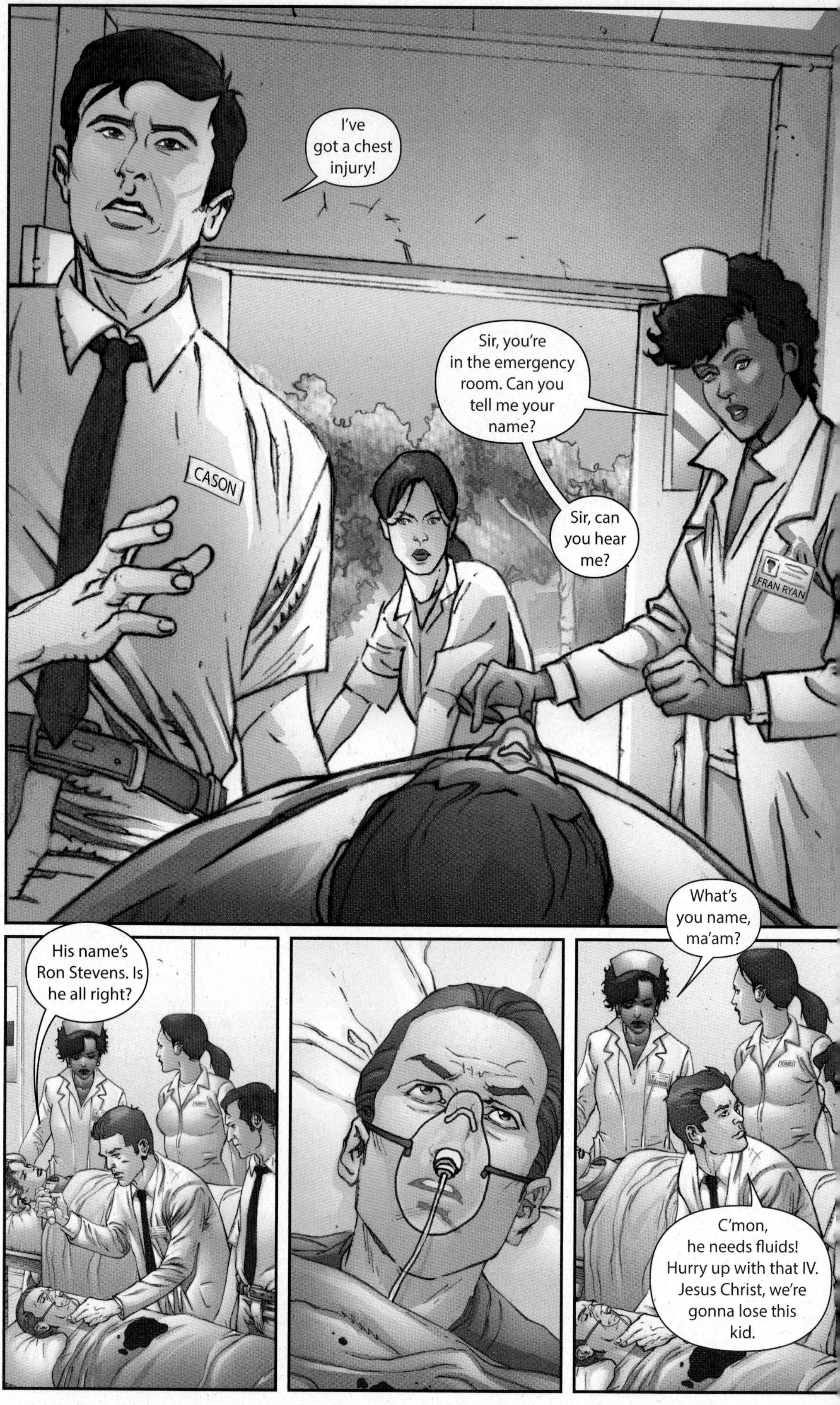
I've got a chest injury!
CASON
Sir, you're in the emergency room. Can you tell me your name?
Sir, can you hear me?
FRAN RYAN
His name's Ron Stevens. Is he all right?
What's you name, ma'am?
C'mon, he needs fluids! Hurry up with that IV. Jesus Christ, we're gonna lose this kid.

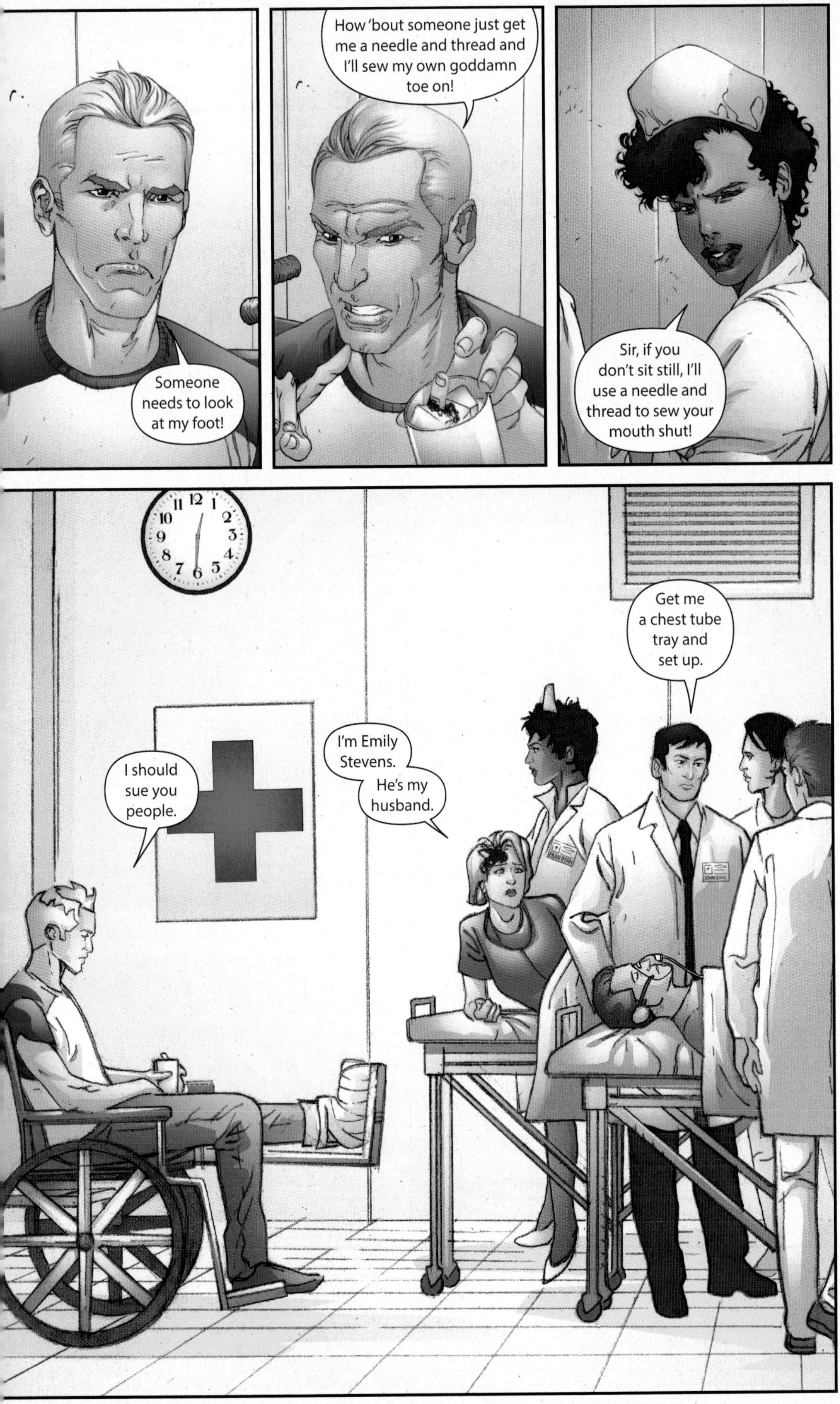
Someone needs to look at my foot!
How 'bout someone just get me a needle and thread and I'll sew my own goddamn toe on!
Sir, if you don't sit still, I'll use a needle and thread to sew your mouth shut!
I should sue you people.
I'm Emily Stevens.
He's my husband.
Get me a chest tube tray and set up.
FRAN RYAN
JOHN SONG

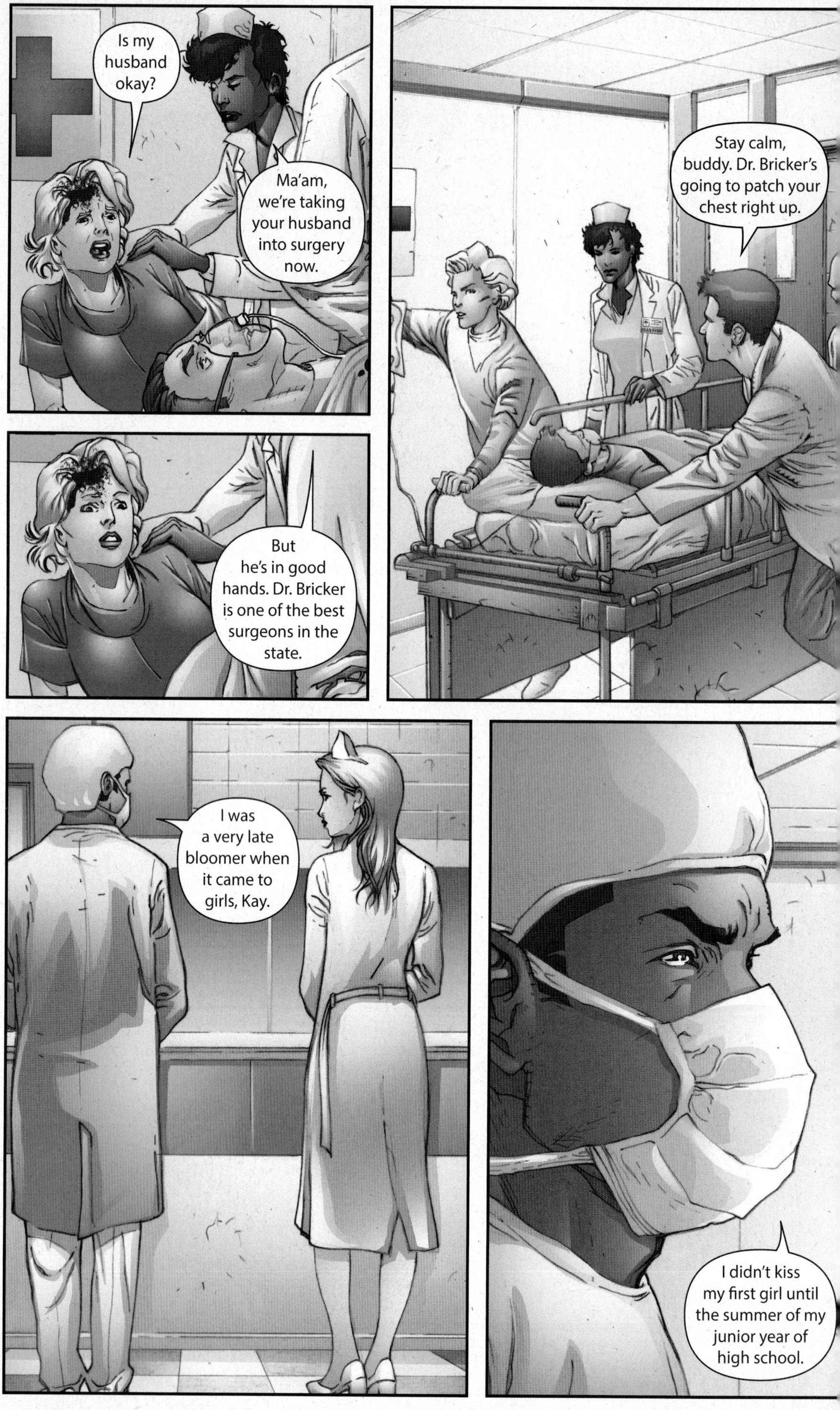
Is my husband okay?
Ma'am, we're taking your husband into surgery now.
Stay calm, buddy. Dr. Bricker's going to patch your chest right up.
But he's in good hands. Dr. Bricker is one of the best surgeons in the state.
I was a very late bloomer when it came to girls, Kay.
I didn't kiss my first girl until the summer of my junior year of high school.

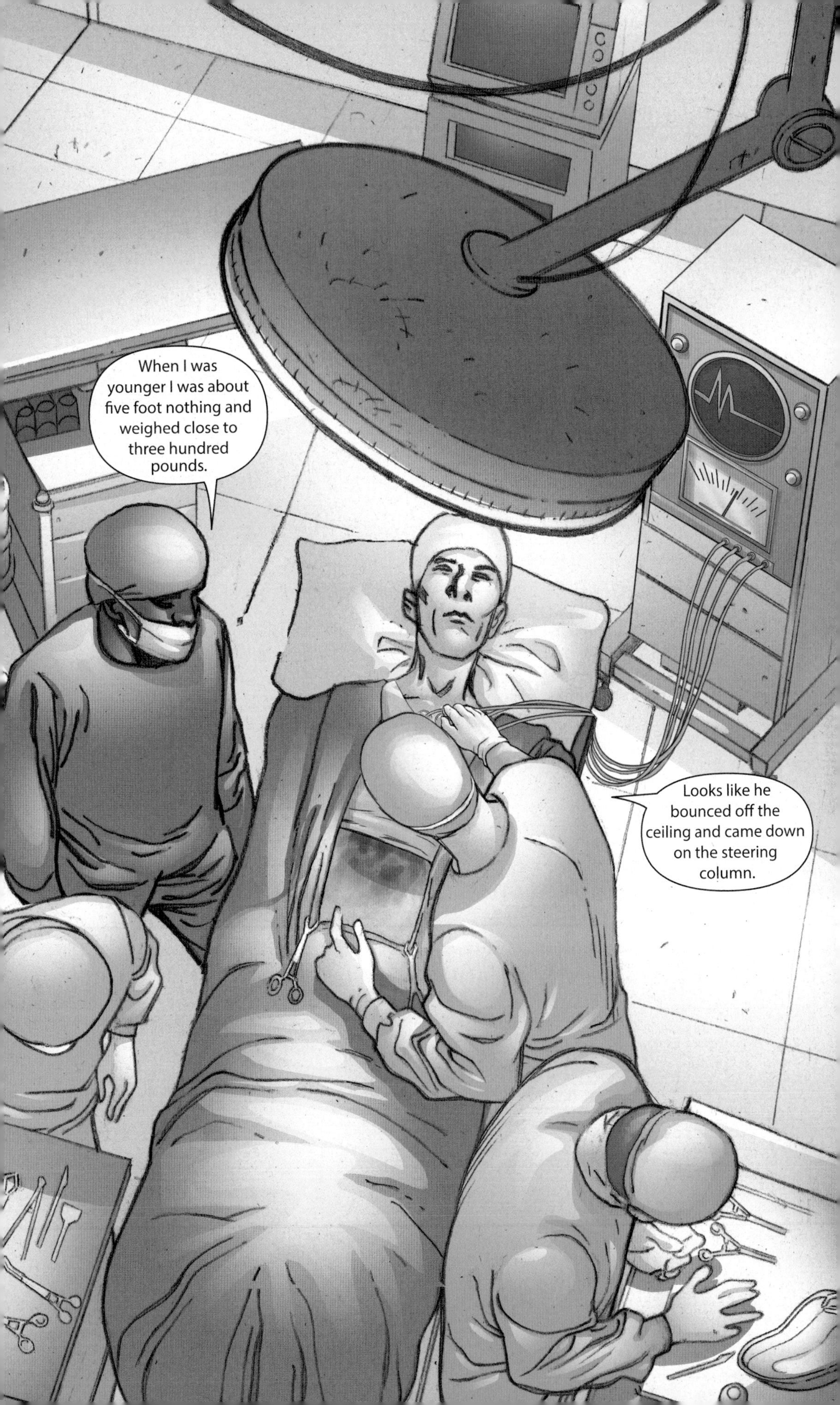
When I was younger I was about five foot nothing and weighed close to three hundred pounds.
Looks like he bounced off the ceiling and came down on the steering column.

I was known as "Plummpy."
No girl wanted to date a "Plummpy."
We've got internal hemorrhaging. Let's open him up right away.
The main reason was the state of New Jersey deemed me mentally challenged.
Now I'm not mentally challenged.
But I do have dyslexia.

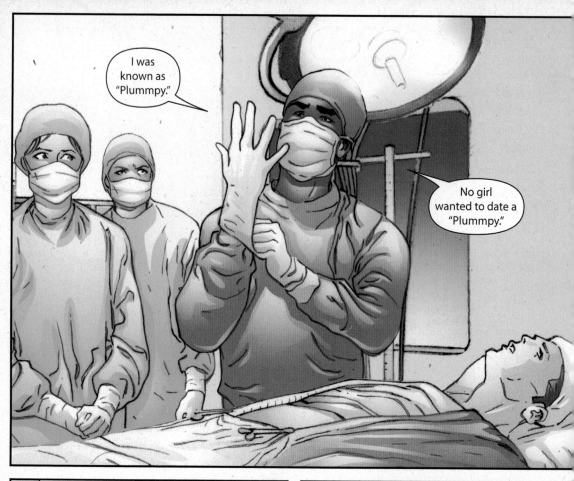

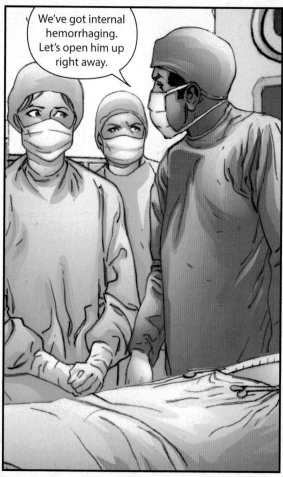

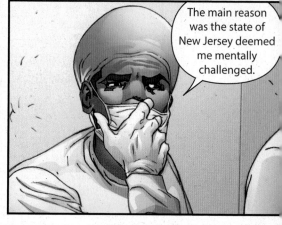

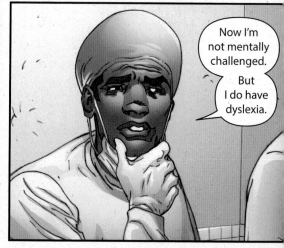

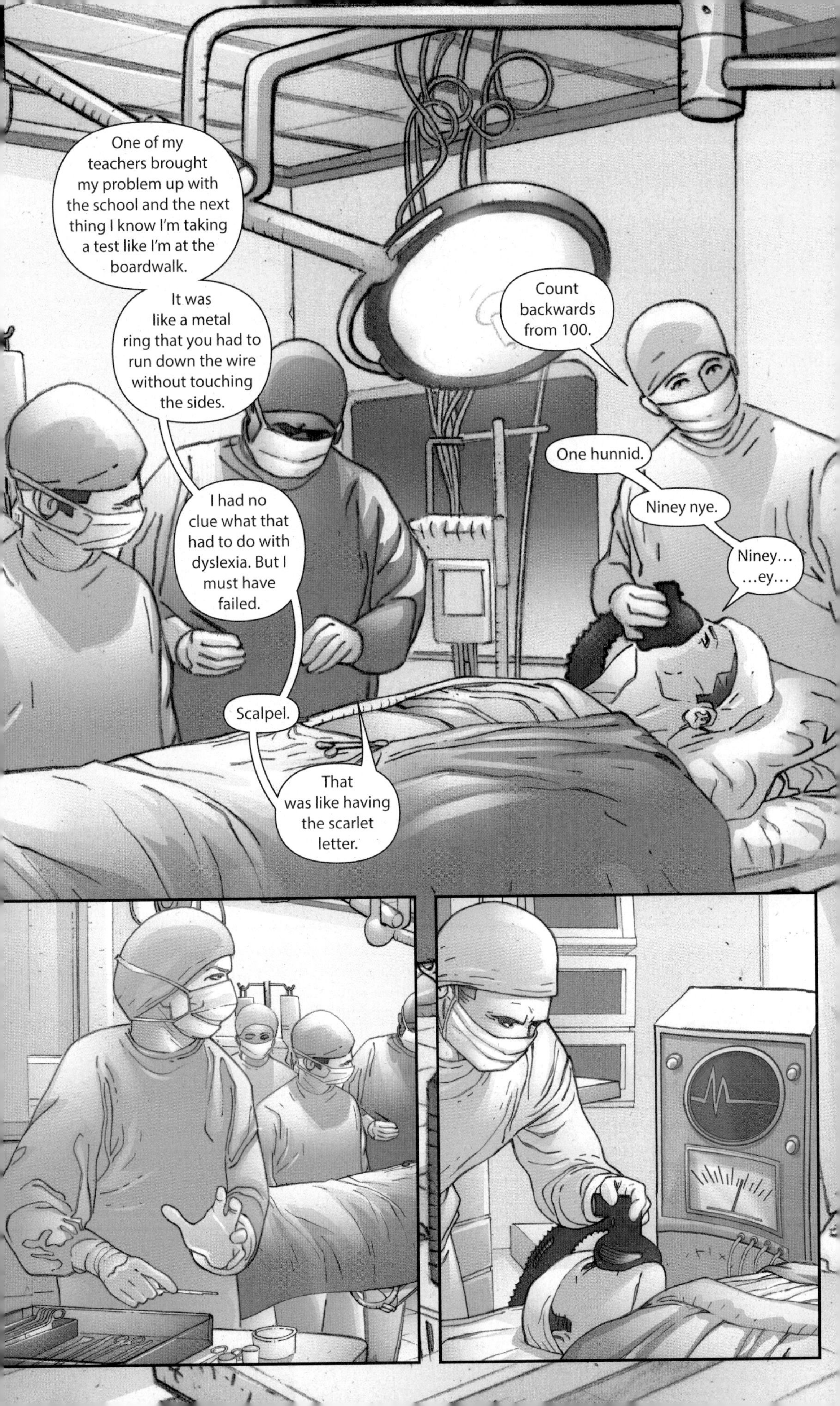
One of my teachers brought my problem up with the school and the next thing I know I'm taking a test like I'm at the boardwalk.
It was like a metal ring that you had to run down the wire without touching the sides.
Count backwards from 100.
One hunnid.
Niney nye.
Niney… …ey…
I had no clue what that had to do with dyslexia. But I must have failed.
Scalpel.
That was like having the scarlet letter.

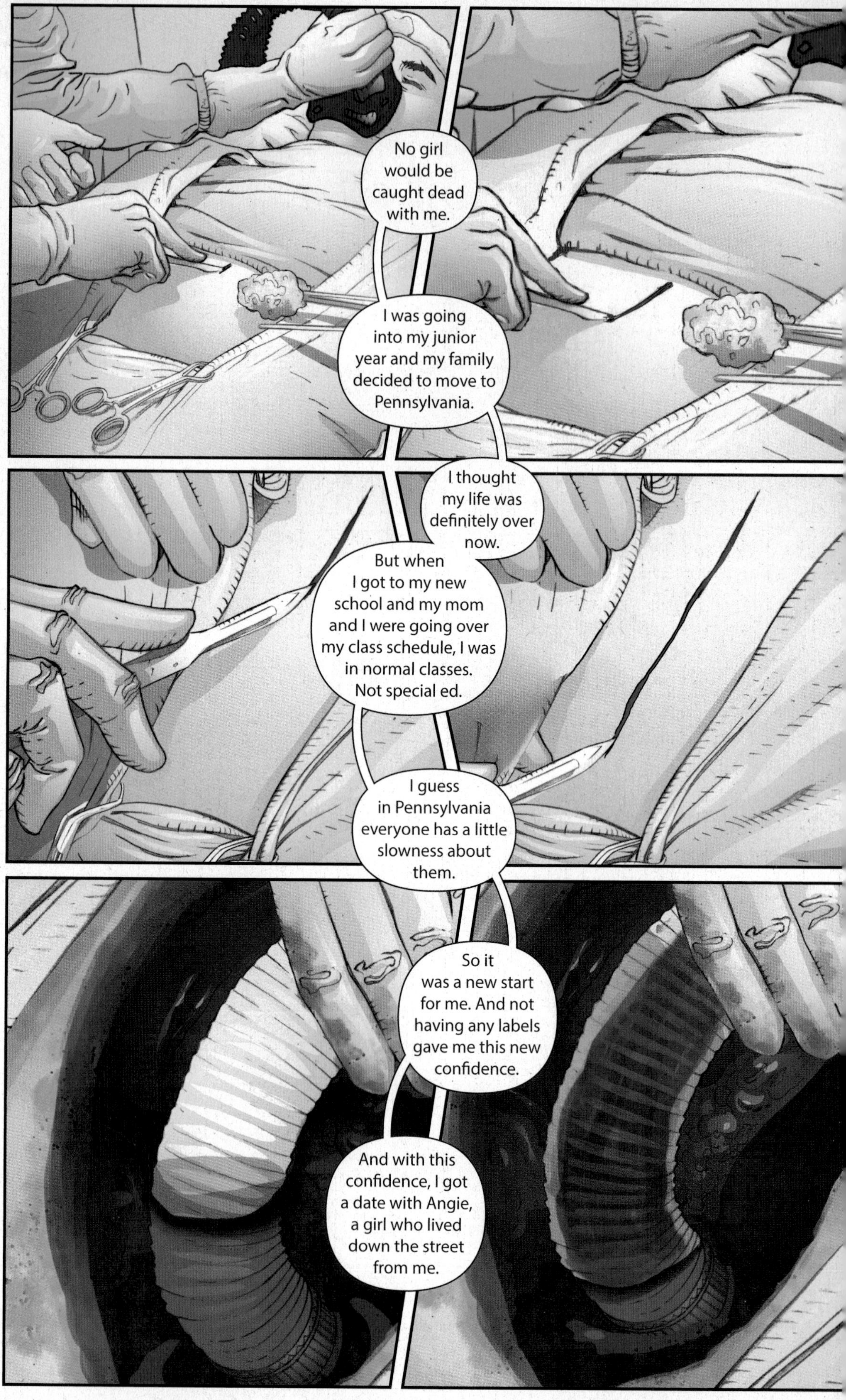
No girl would be caught dead with me.
I was going into my junior year and my family decided to move to Pennsylvania.
I thought my life was definitely over now.
But when I got to my new school and my mom and I were going over my class schedule, I was in normal classes. Not special ed.
I guess in Pennsylvania everyone has a little slowness about them.
So it was a new start for me. And not having any labels gave me this new confidence.
And with this confidence, I got a date with Angie, a girl who lived down the street from me.

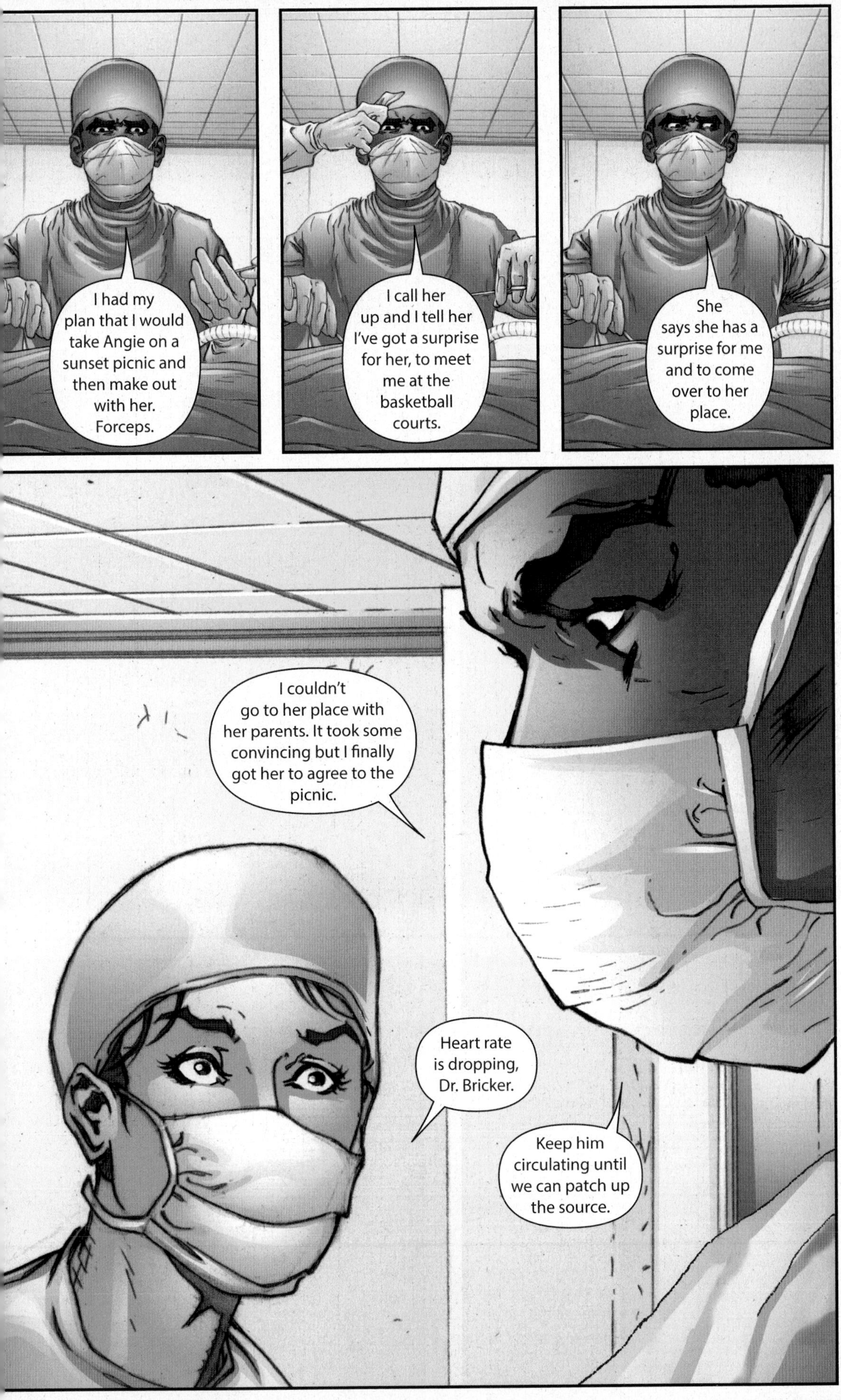
I had my plan that I would take Angie on a sunset picnic and then make out with her. Forceps.
I call her up and I tell her I've got a surprise for her, to meet me at the basketball courts.
She says she has a surprise for me and to come over to her place.
I couldn't go to her place with her parents. It took some convincing but I finally got her to agree to the picnic.
Heart rate is dropping, Dr. Bricker.
Keep him circulating until we can patch up the source.

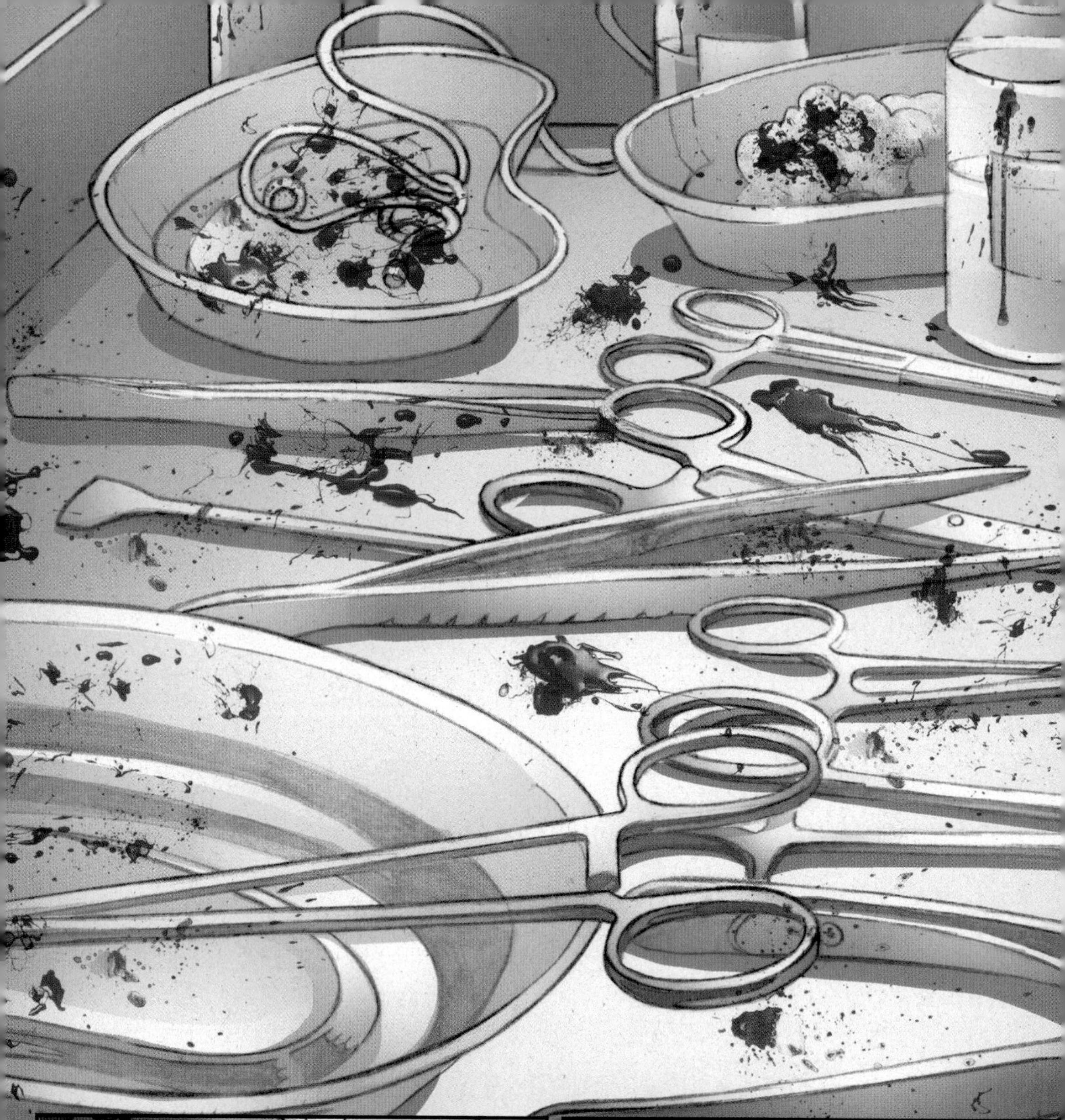

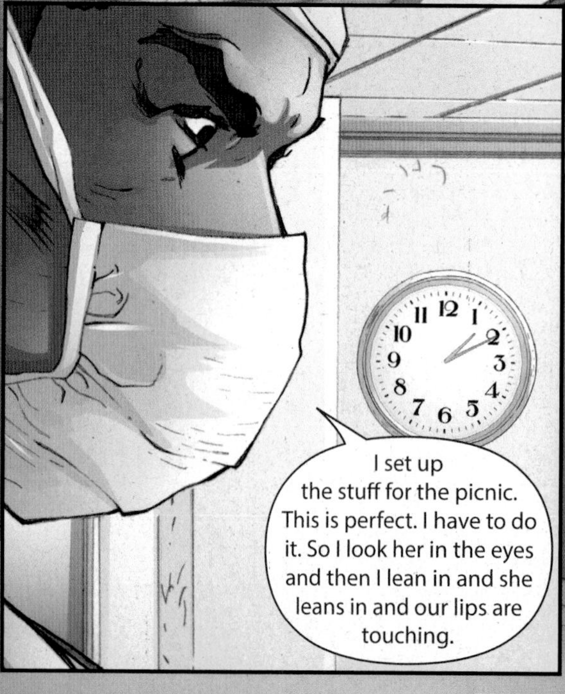
I set up the stuff for the picnic. This is perfect. I have to do it. So I look her in the eyes and then I lean in and she leans in and our lips are touching.

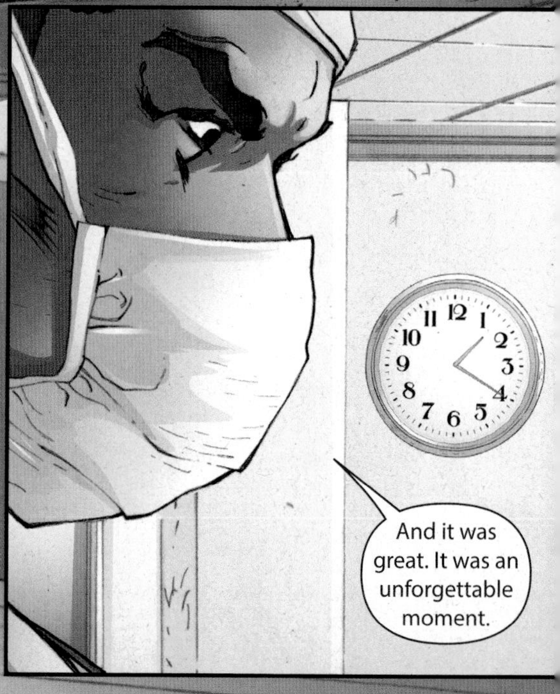
And it was great. It was an unforgettable moment.

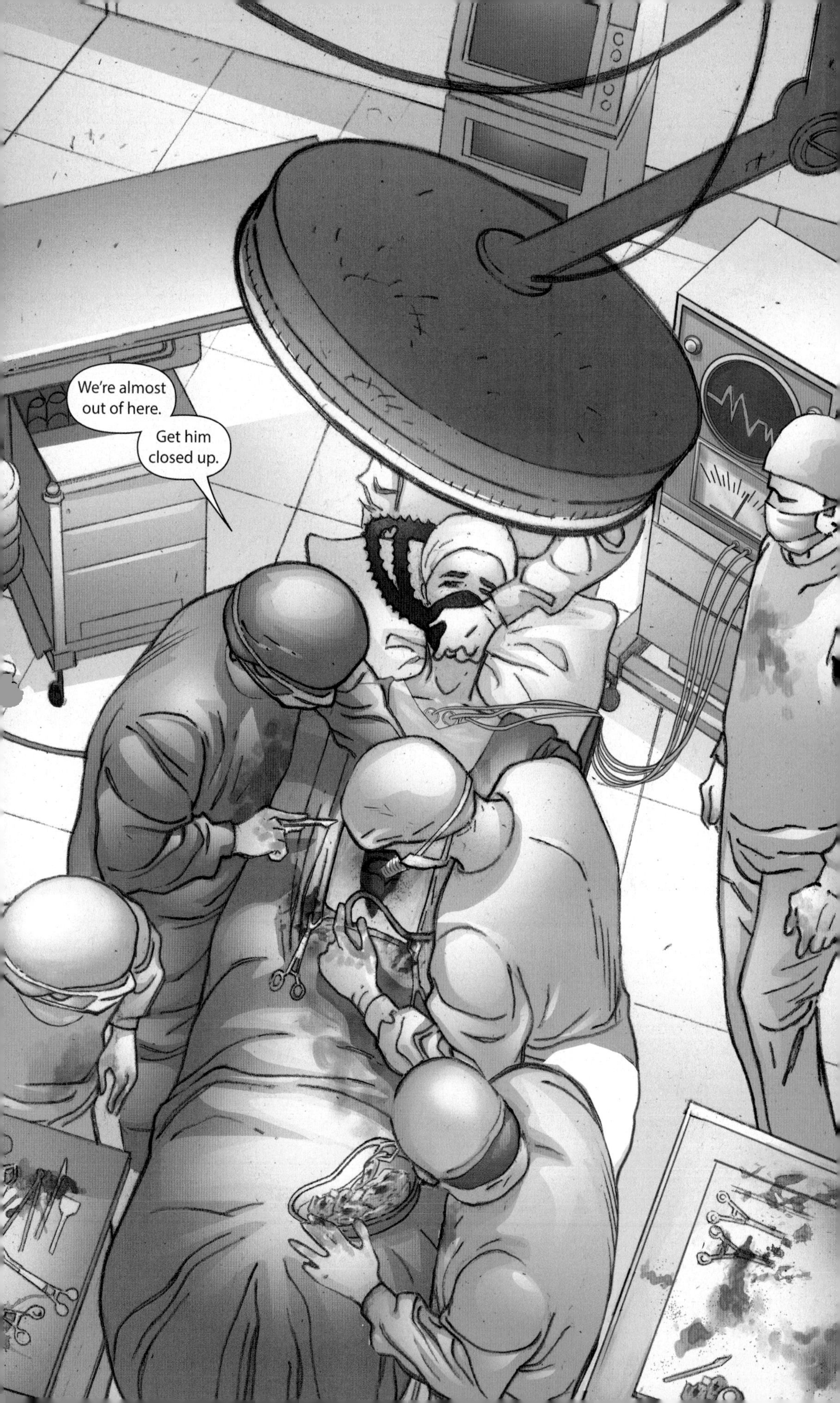
We're almost out of here.
Get him closed up.

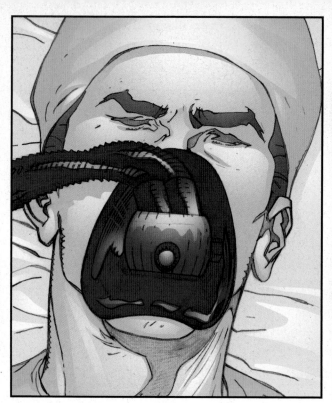

That was amazing, Doctor.

I had a great team.

Another "unforgettable moment?"

The thing about that? We started to walk back to her place and Angie says it's a shame she couldn't give me my surprise.

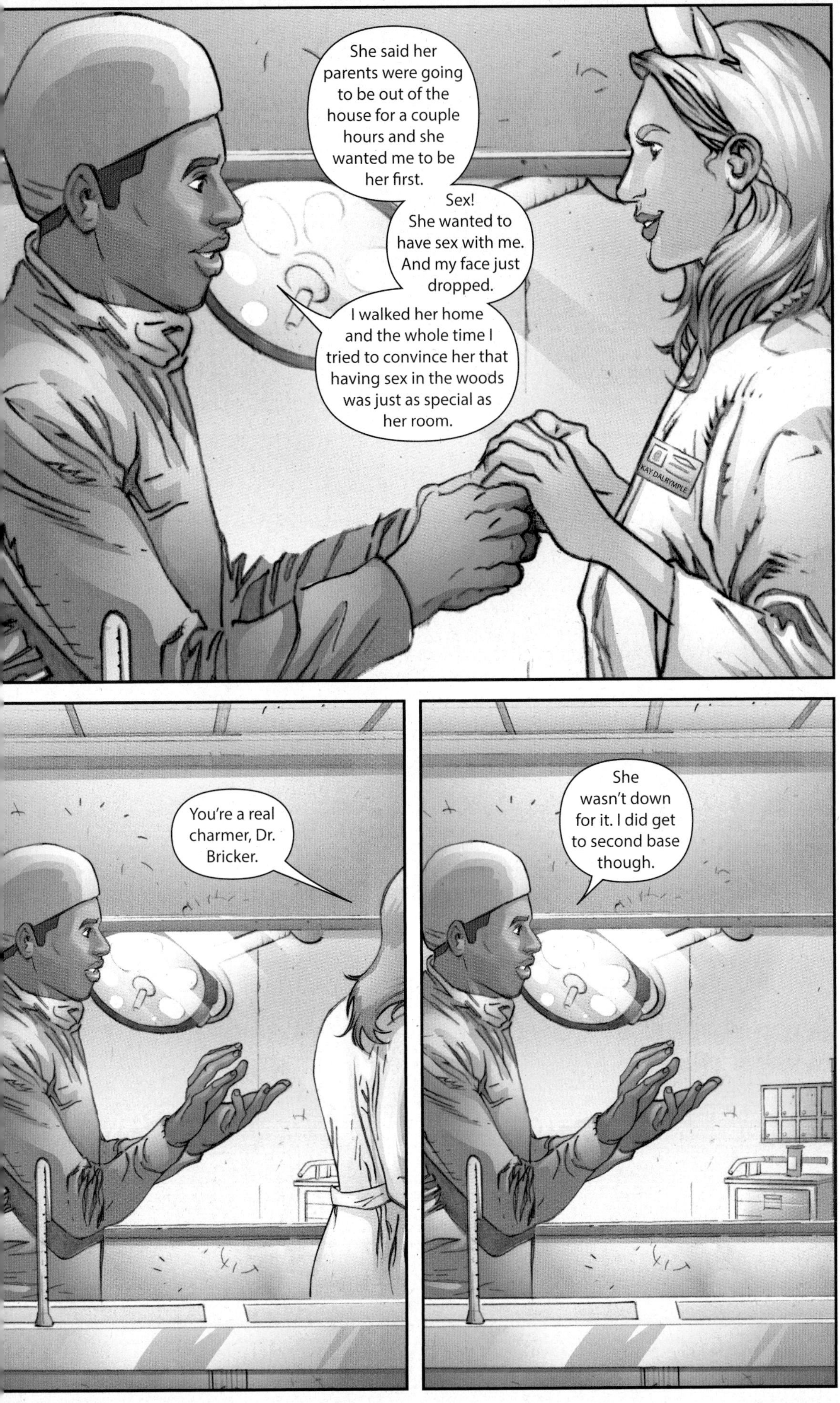
She said her parents were going to be out of the house for a couple hours and she wanted me to be her first.
Sex! She wanted to have sex with me. And my face just dropped.
I walked her home and the whole time I tried to convince her that having sex in the woods was just as special as her room.
KAY DALRYMPLE
You're a real charmer, Dr. Bricker.
She wasn't down for it. I did get to second base though.

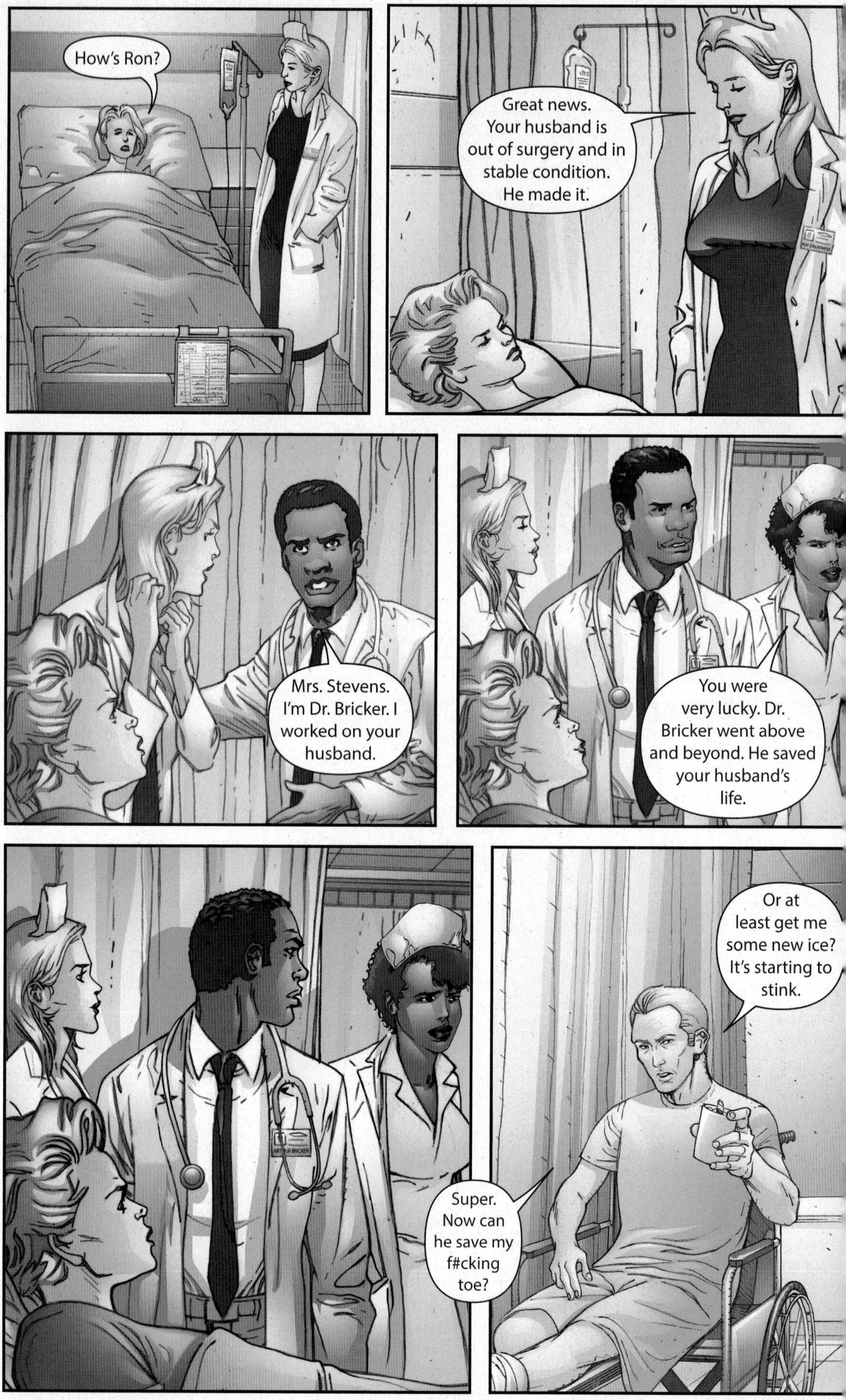
How's Ron?
Great news. Your husband is out of surgery and in stable condition. He made it.
Mrs. Stevens. I'm Dr. Bricker. I worked on your husband.
You were very lucky. Dr. Bricker went above and beyond. He saved your husband's life.
Super. Now can he save my f#cking toe?
Or at least get me some new ice? It's starting to stink.

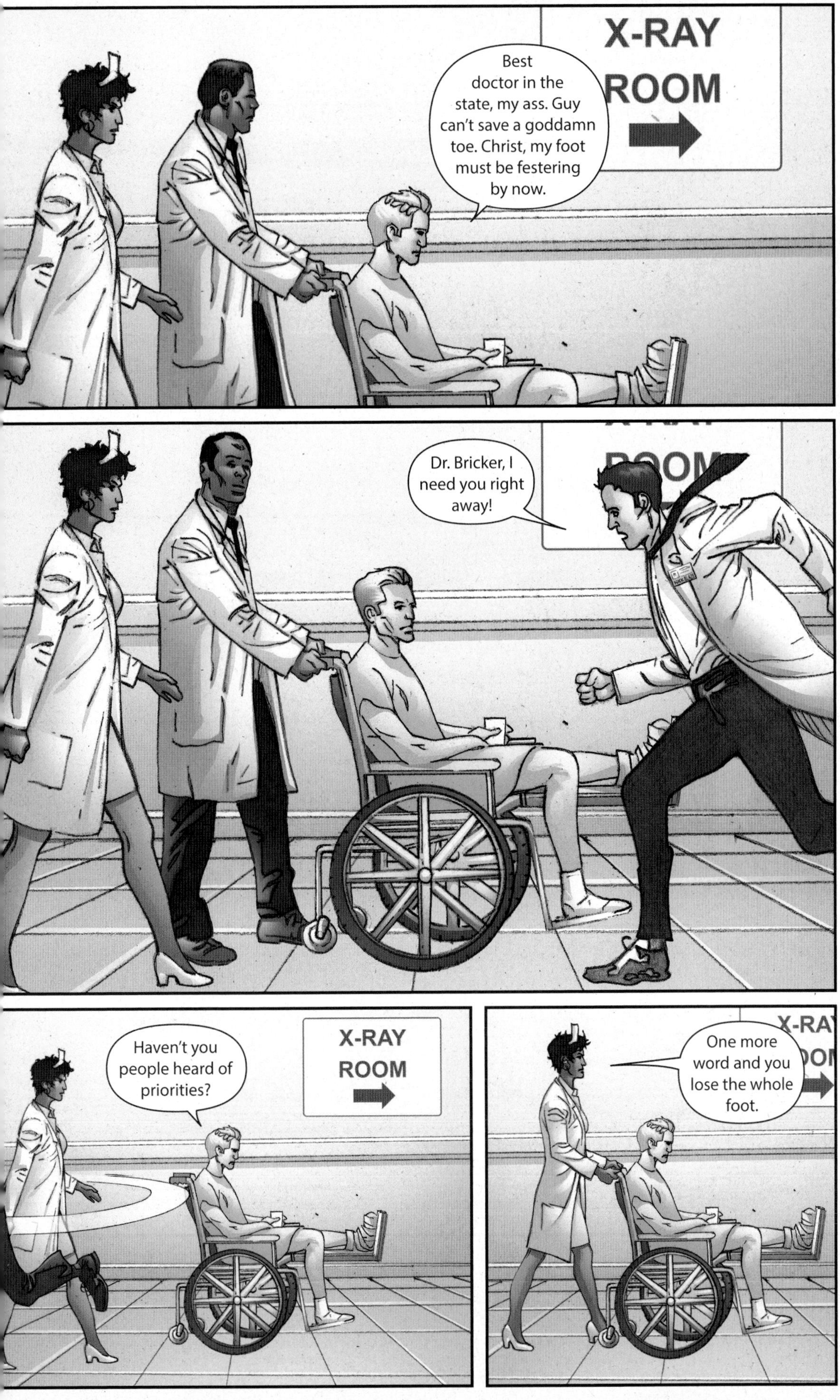
X-RAY ROOM
Best doctor in the state, my ass. Guy can't save a goddamn toe. Christ, my foot must be festering by now.
Dr. Bricker, I need you right away!
Haven't you people heard of priorities?
X-RAY ROOM
One more word and you lose the whole foot.

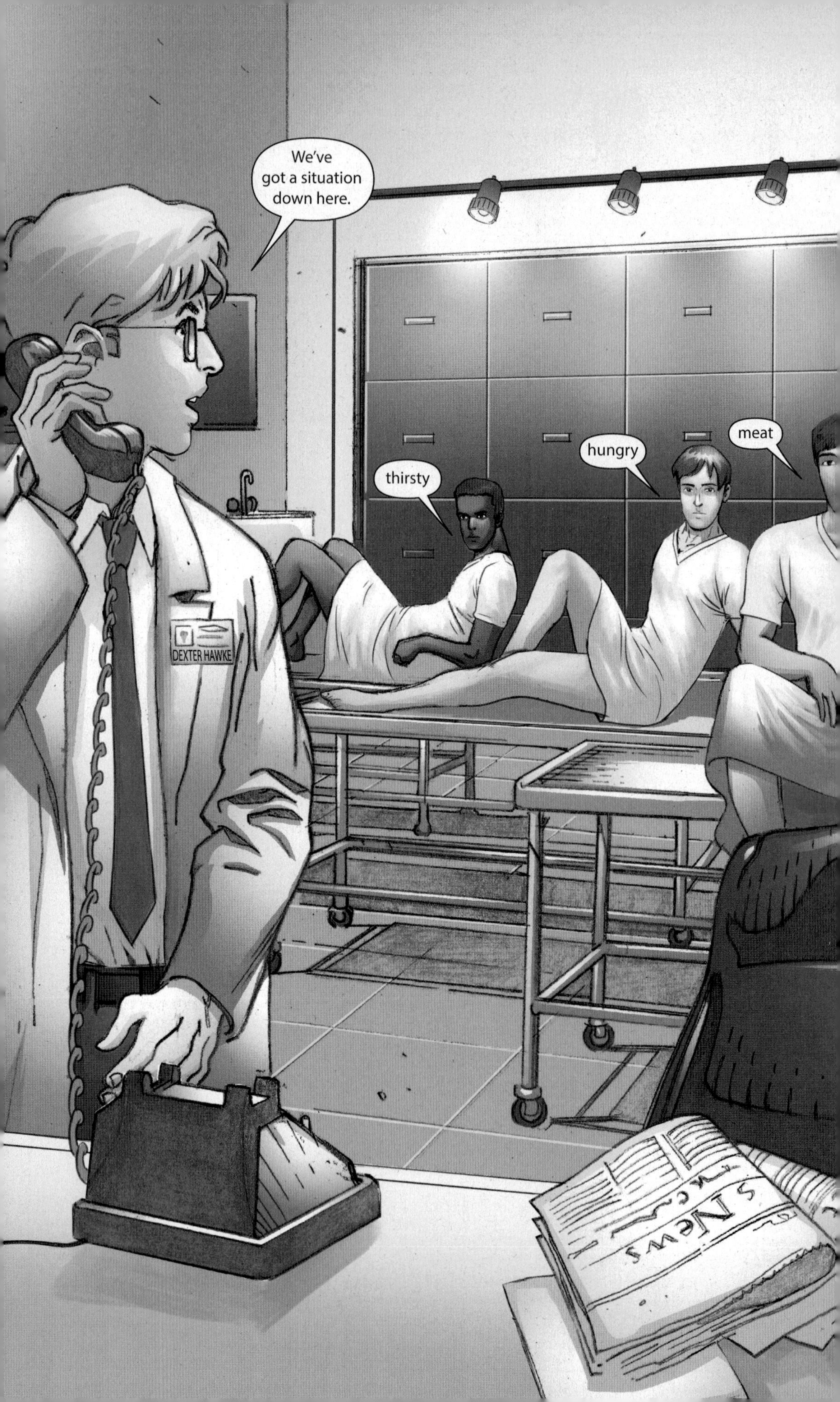
We've got a situation down here.
thirsty
hungry
meat
DEXTER HAWKE
News

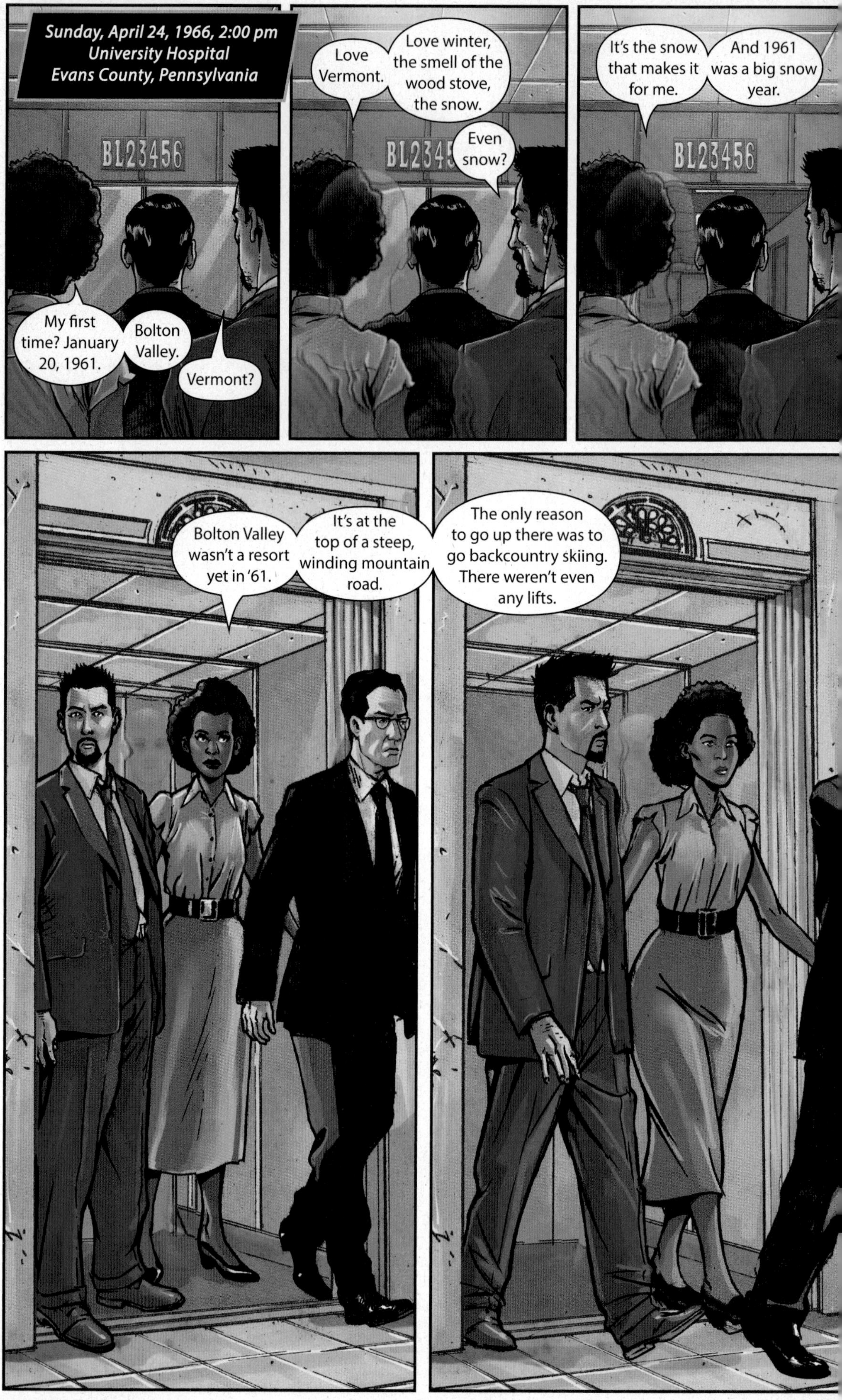
Sunday, April 24, 1966, 2:00 pm
University Hospital
Evans County, Pennsylvania
BL23456
My first time? January 20, 1961.
Bolton Valley.
Vermont?
Love Vermont.
Love winter, the smell of the wood stove, the snow.
Even snow?
It's the snow that makes it for me.
And 1961 was a big snow year.
Bolton Valley wasn't a resort yet in '61.
It's at the top of a steep, winding mountain road.
The only reason to go up there was to go backcountry skiing. There weren't even any lifts.

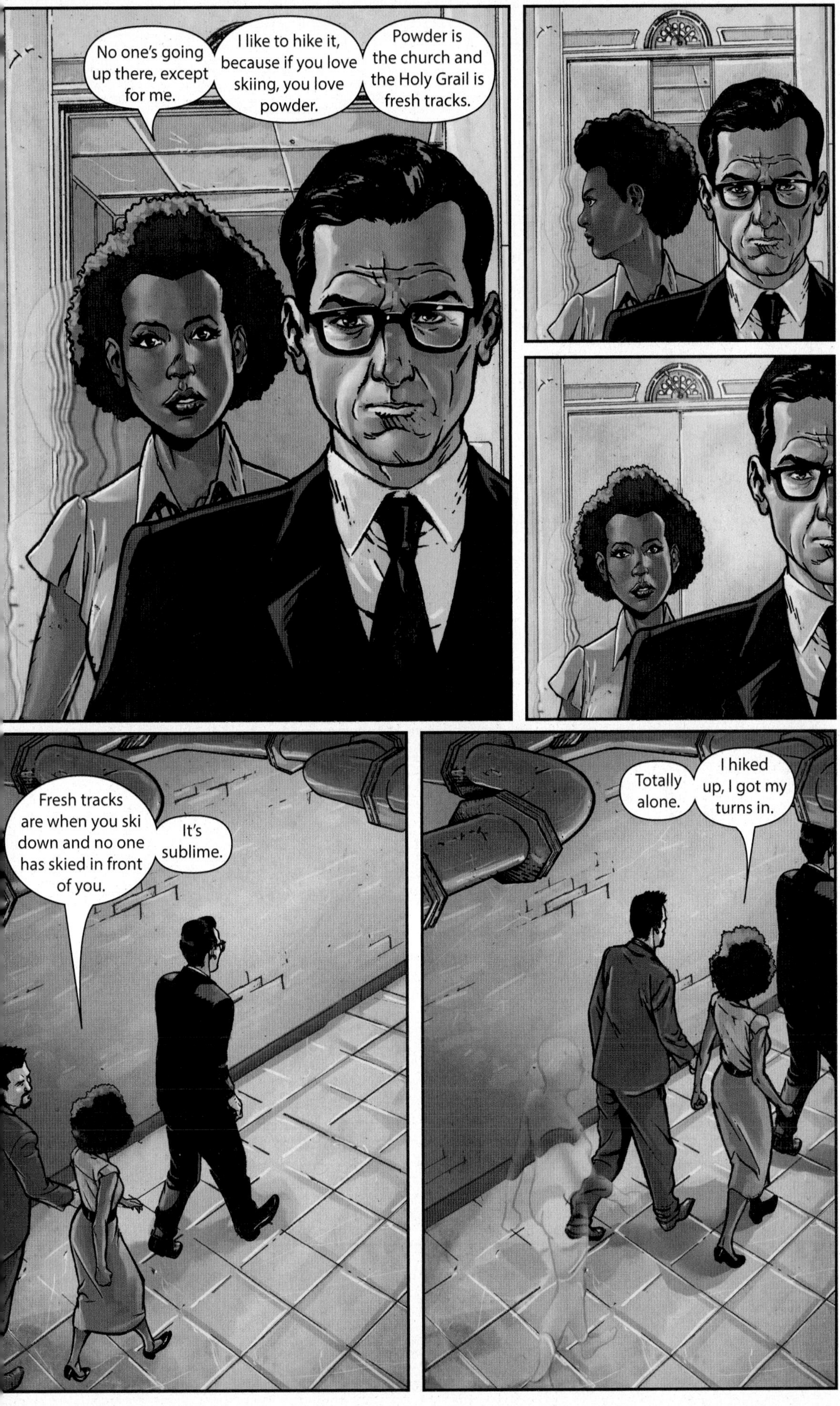
No one's going up there, except for me.
I like to hike it, because if you love skiing, you love powder.
Powder is the church and the Holy Grail is fresh tracks.
Fresh tracks are when you ski down and no one has skied in front of you.
It's sublime.
Totally alone.
I hiked up, I got my turns in.

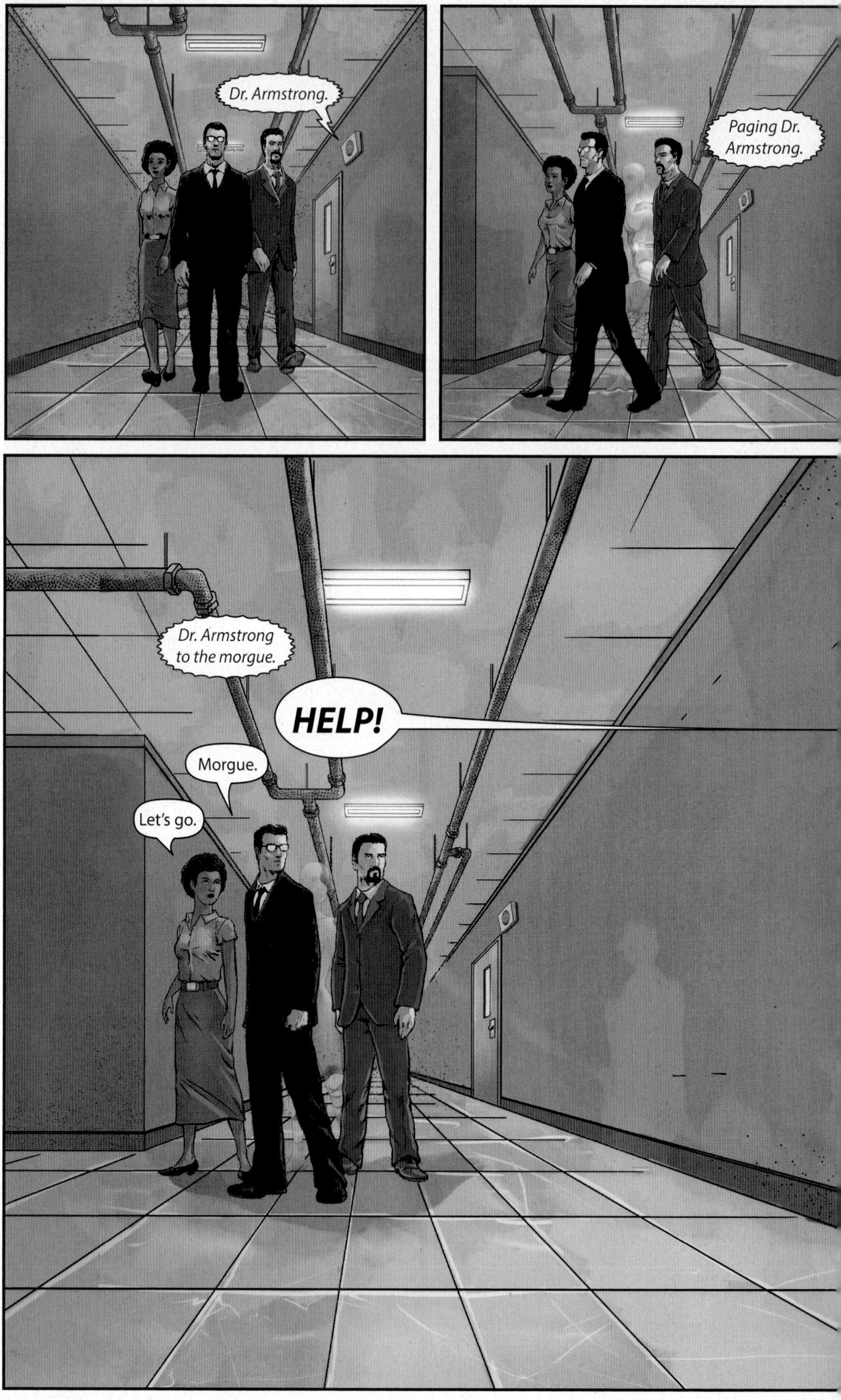
Dr. Armstrong.
Paging Dr. Armstrong.
Dr. Armstrong to the morgue.
HELP!
Morgue.
Let's go.

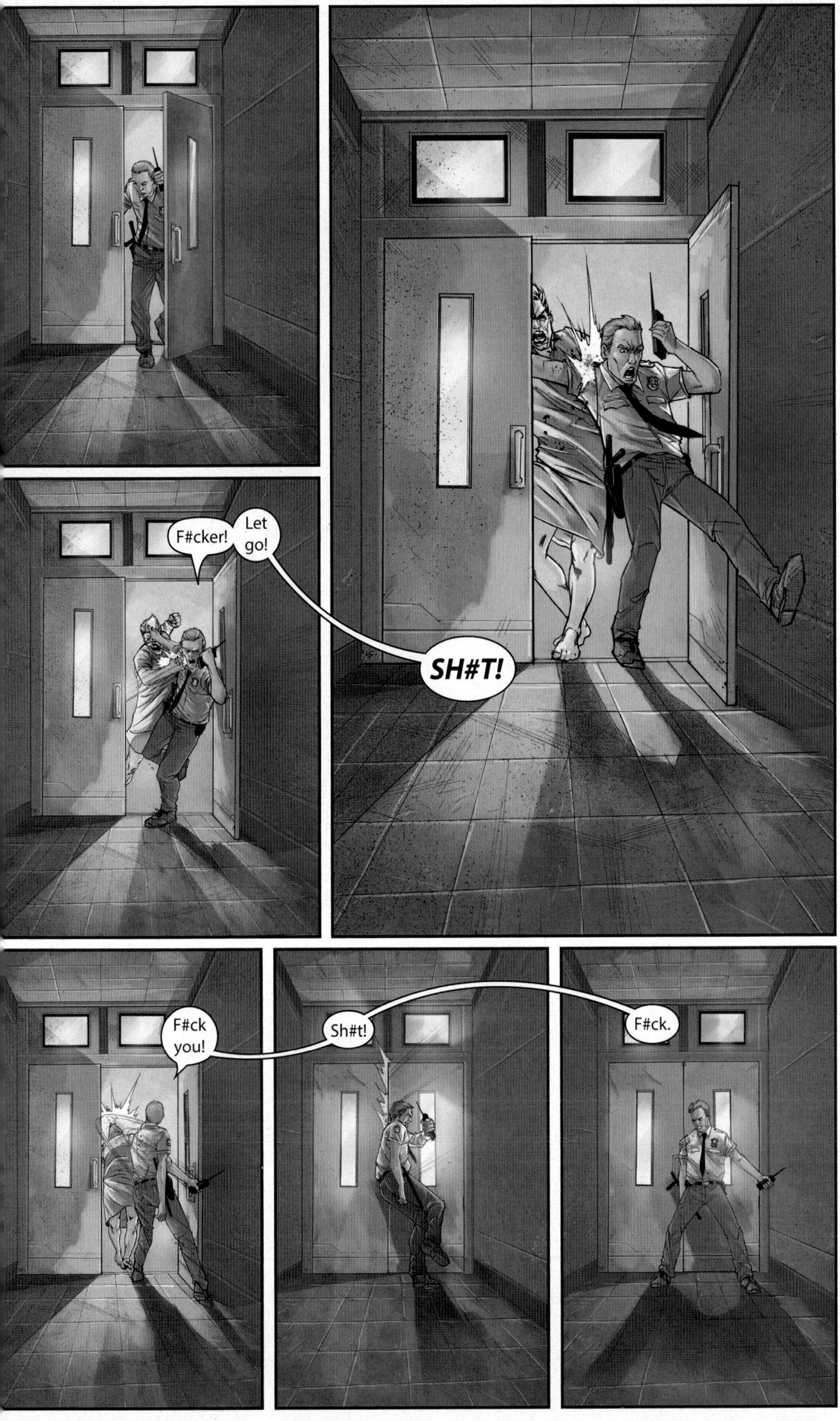
F#cker!
Let go!
SH#T!
F#ck you!
Sh#t!
F#ck.

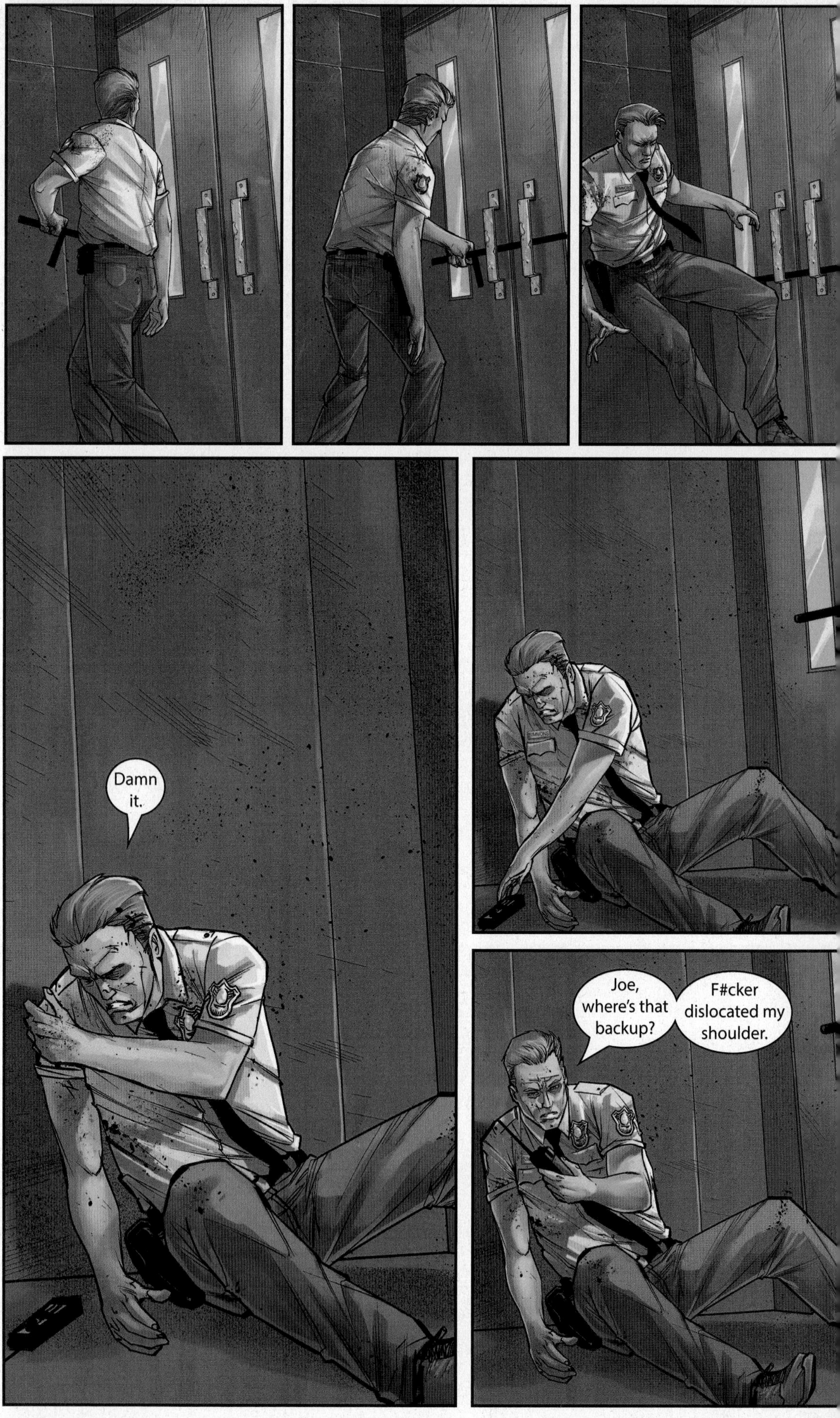
Damn it.
Joe, where's that backup?
F#cker dislocated my shoulder.

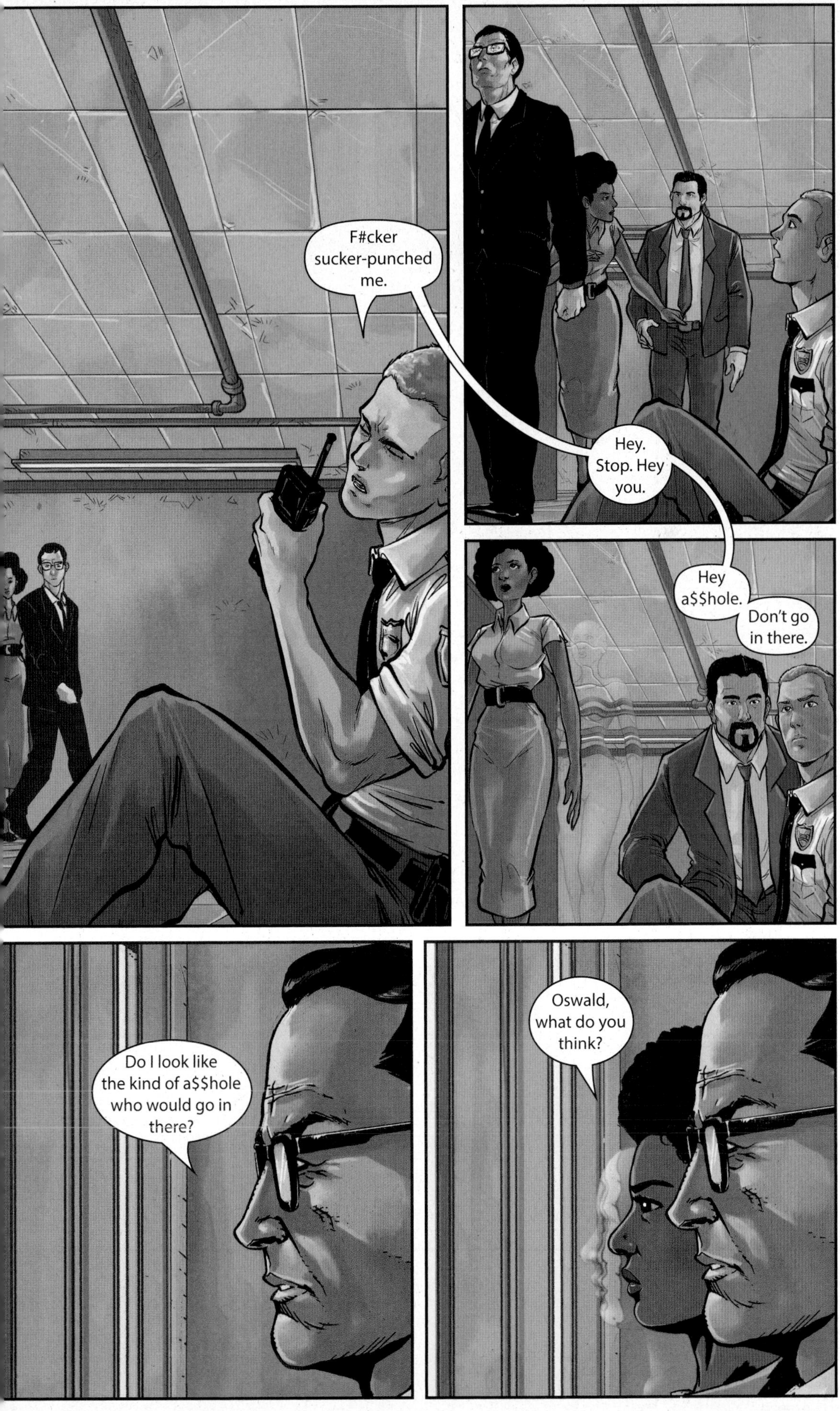
F#cker sucker-punched me.
Hey. Stop. Hey you.
Hey a$$hole.
Don't go in there.
Do I look like the kind of a$$hole who would go in there?
Oswald, what do you think?

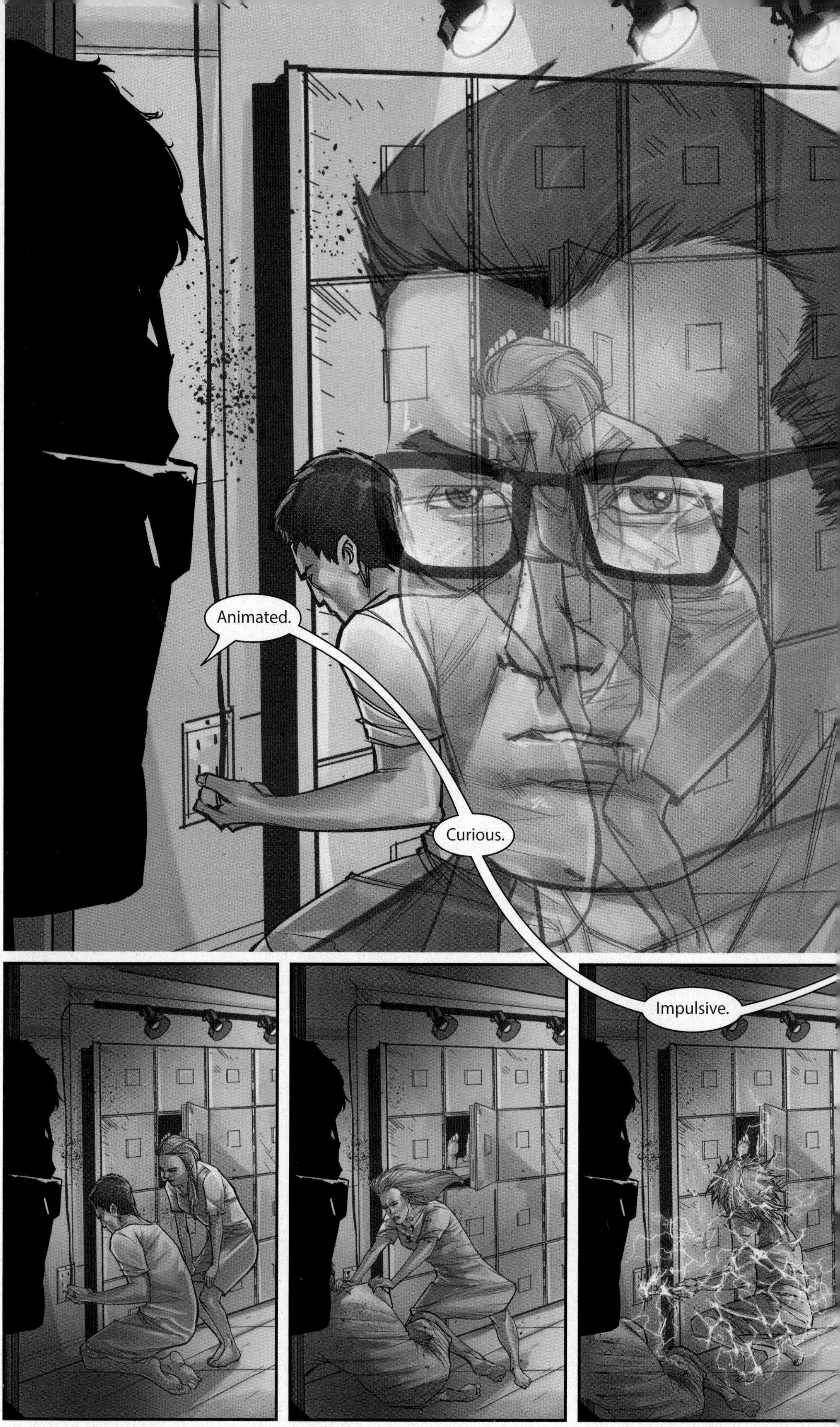
Animated.
Curious.
Impulsive.

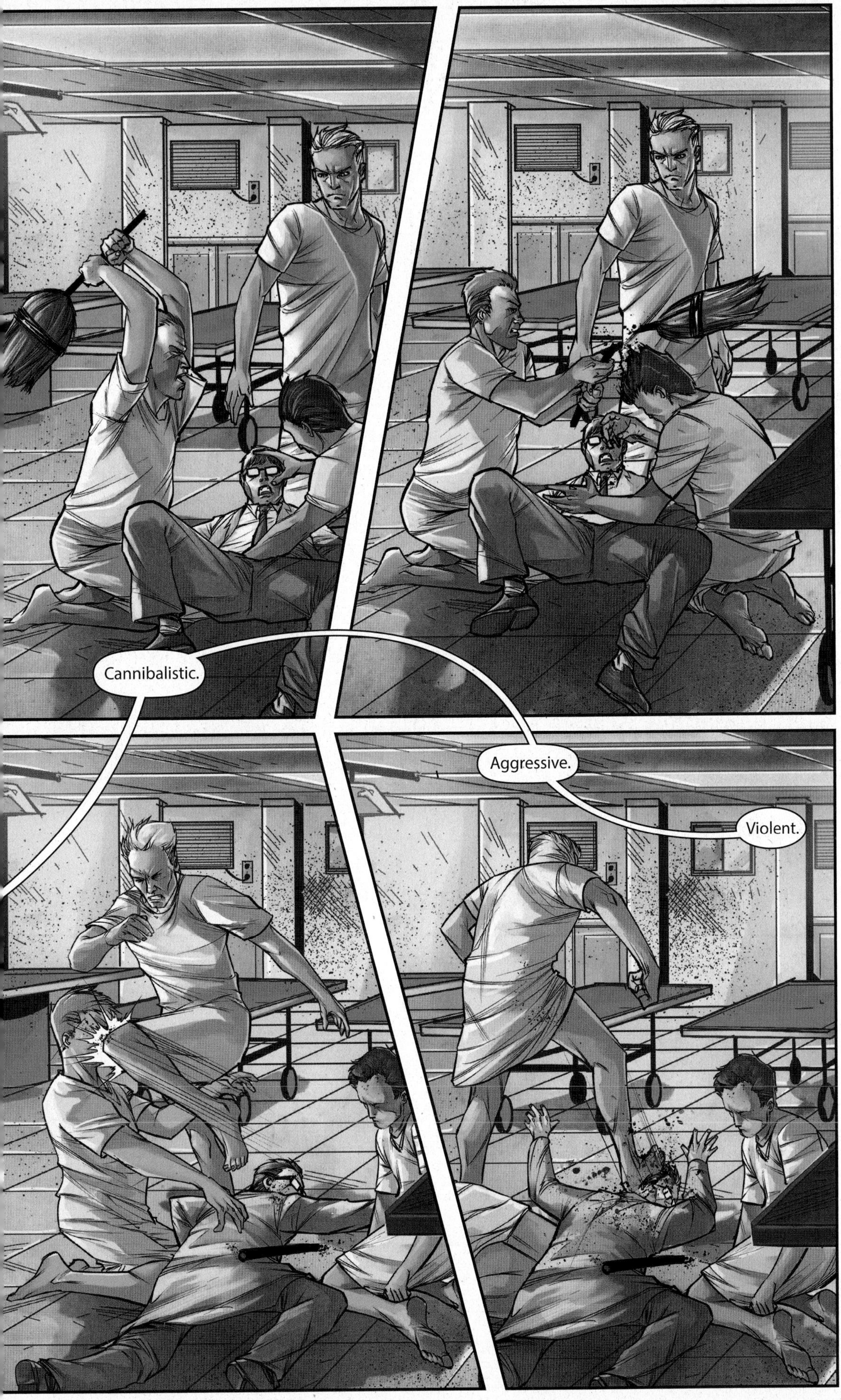
Cannibalistic.
Aggressive.
Violent.

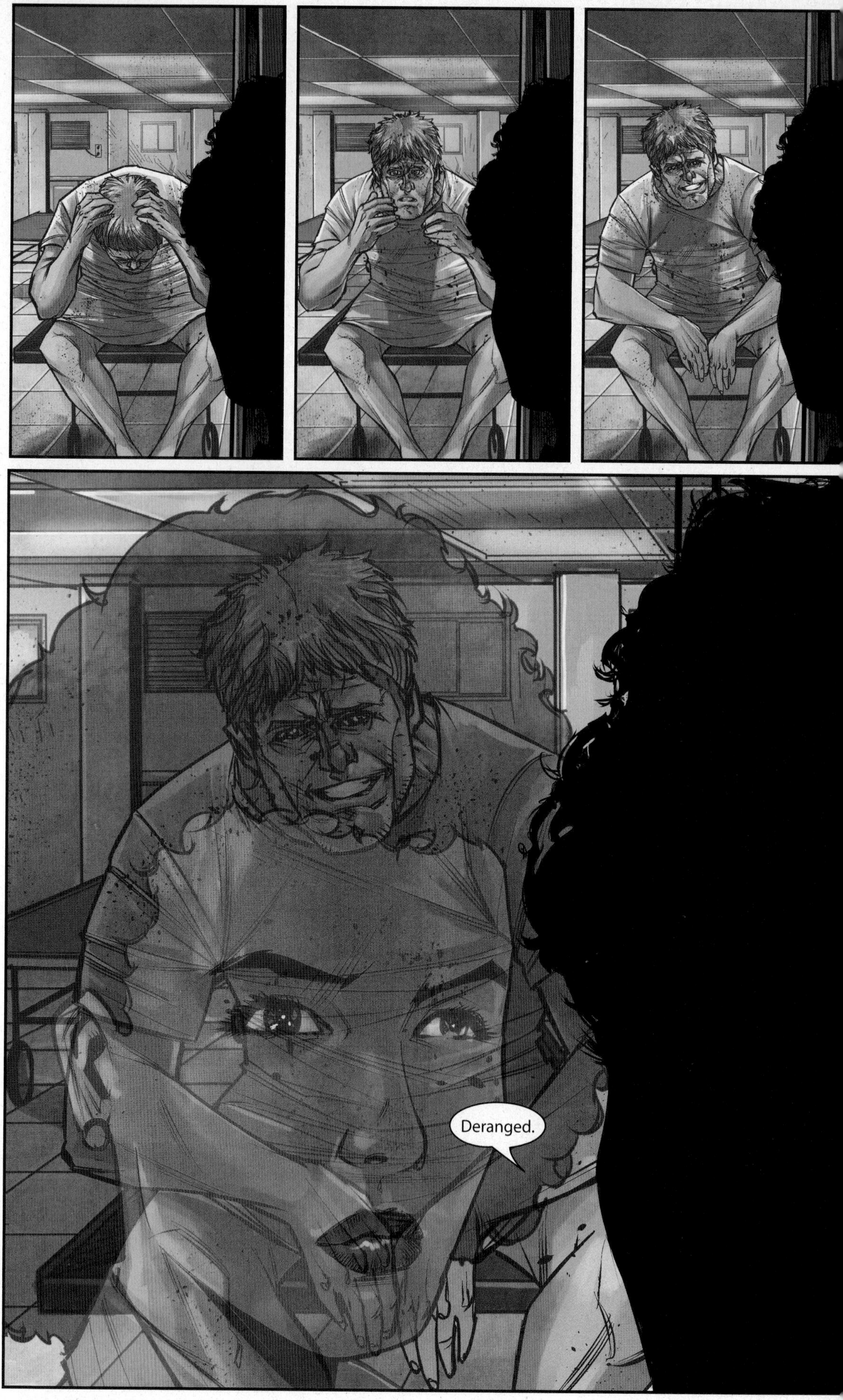
Deranged.

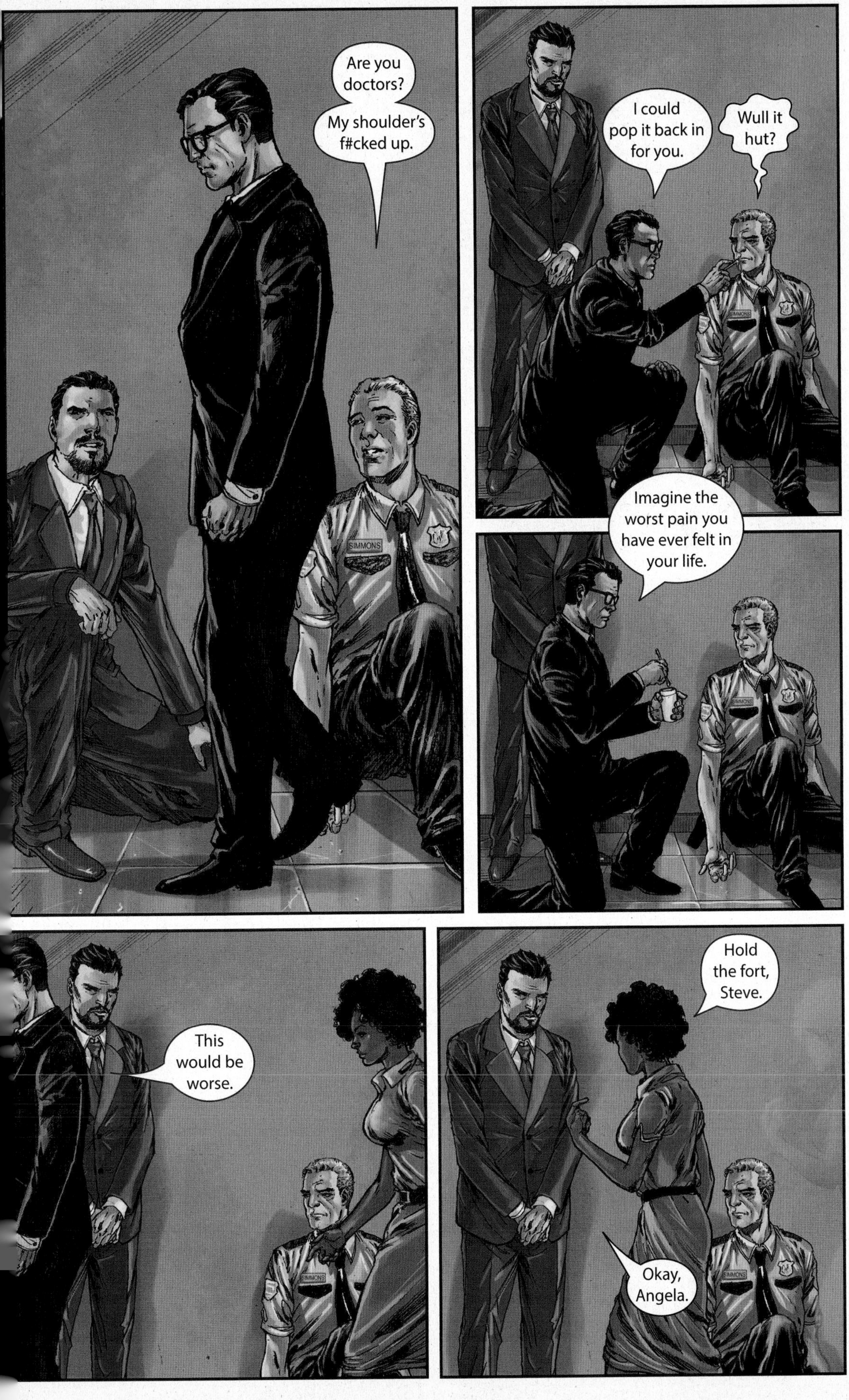
Are you doctors?
My shoulder's f#cked up.
I could pop it back in for you.
Wull it hut?
Imagine the worst pain you have ever felt in your life.
This would be worse.
Hold the fort, Steve.
Okay, Angela.

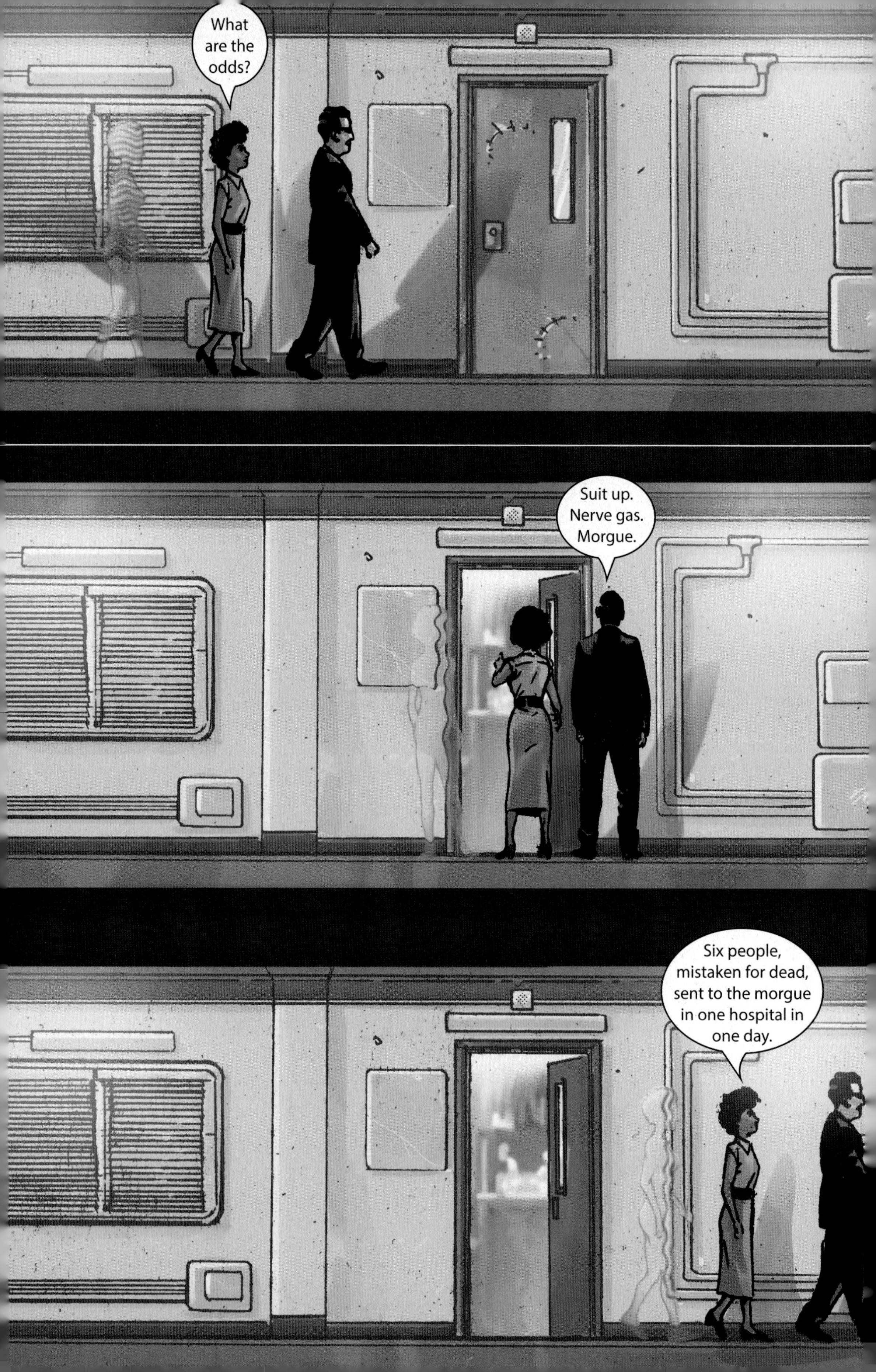
What are the odds?
Suit up. Nerve gas. Morgue.
Six people, mistaken for dead, sent to the morgue in one hospital in one day.

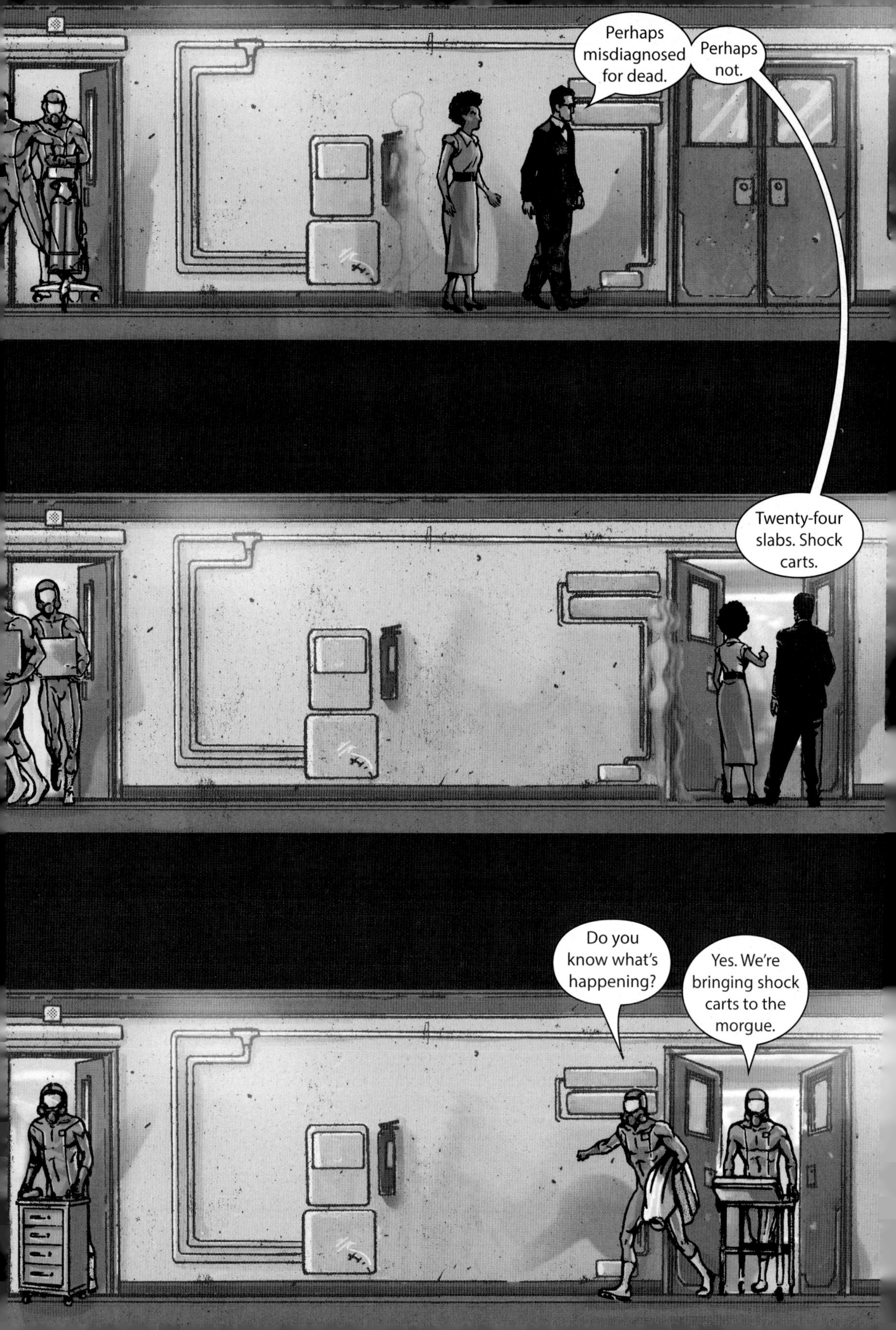
Perhaps misdiagnosed for dead.
Perhaps not.
Twenty-four slabs. Shock carts.
Do you know what's happening?
Yes. We're bringing shock carts to the morgue.

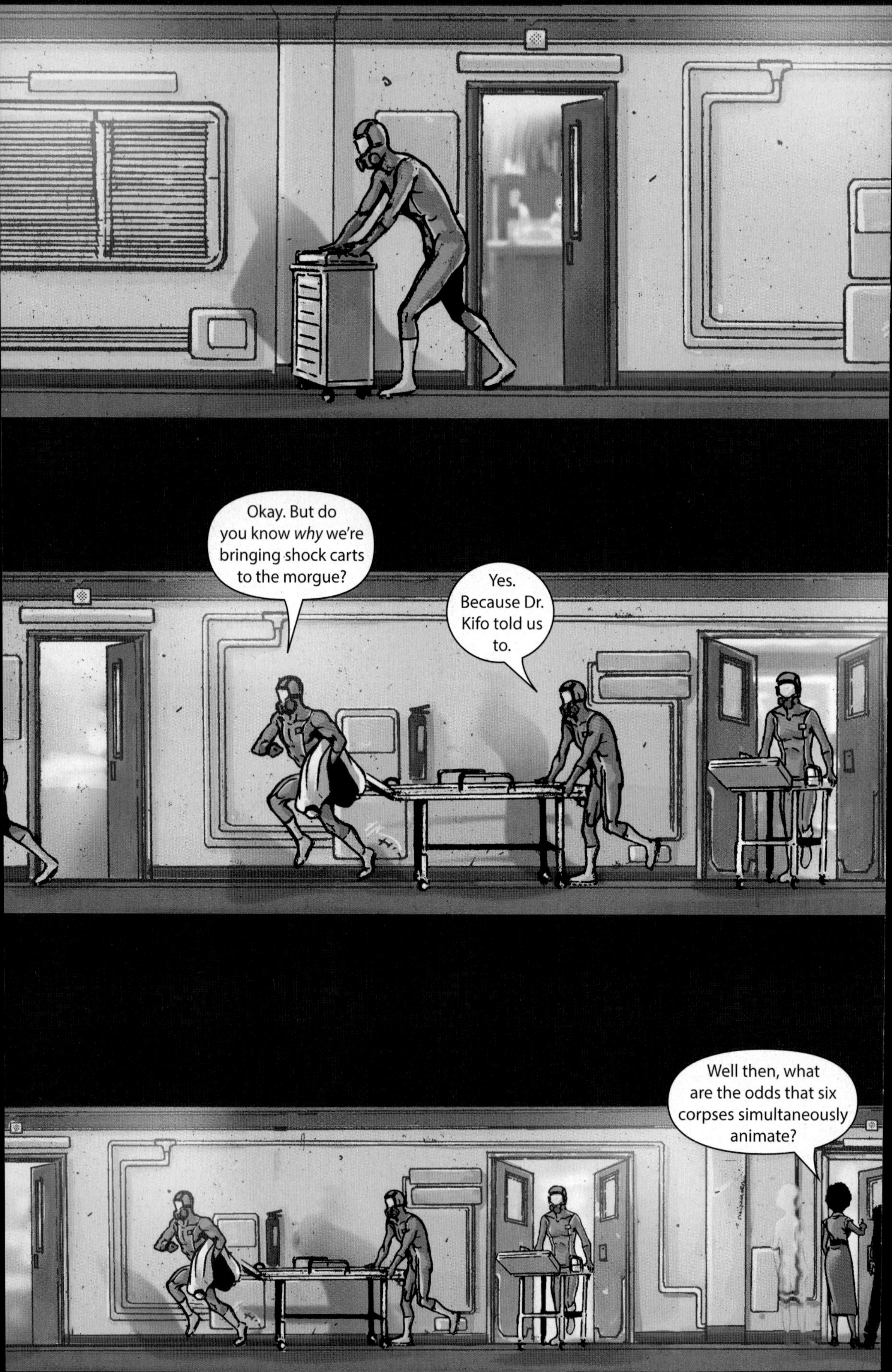
Okay. But do you know *why* we're bringing shock carts to the morgue?
Yes. Because Dr. Kifo told us to.
Well then, what are the odds that six corpses simultaneously animate?

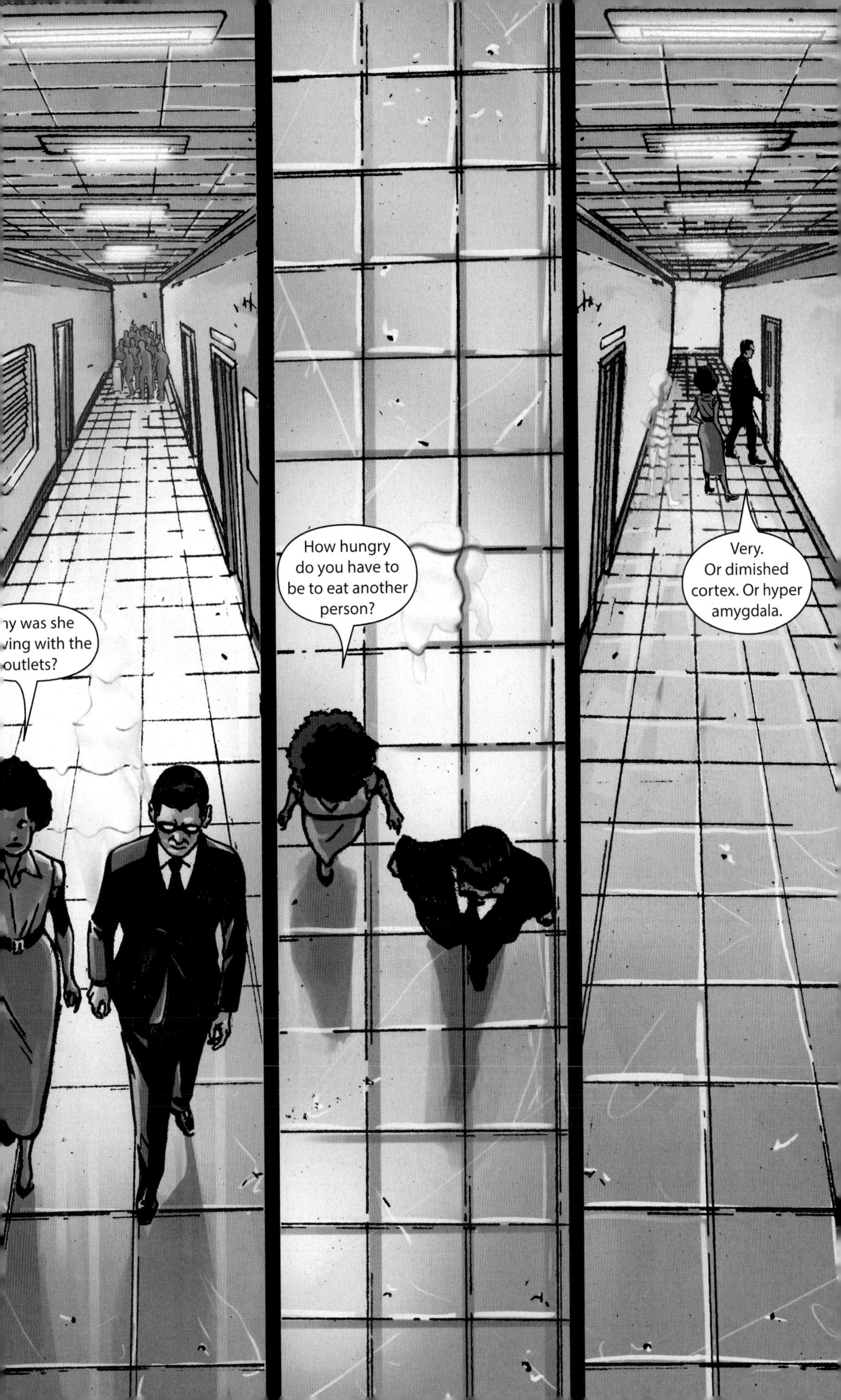

ıy was she
ving with the
outlets?
How hungry do you have to be to eat another person?
Very.
Or dimished cortex. Or hyper amygdala.

Sunday, April 24, 1966, 1:59 pm
University Hospital
Evans County, Pennsylvania

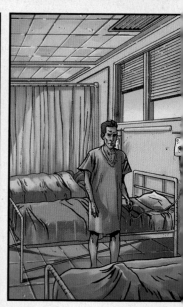

...with the latest news from the station that's first on your dial.

The time is now 2 pm.

American bombers attacked oil deposits and radar sites in the Haiphong area yesterday—

—and eluded six Soviet-made missiles fired by the Communists during raids, the United States command said today.

Carrier-based navy planes hit the Do Sun oil dump 17 miles southeast of Haiphong and pilots reported hits on several storage tanks.

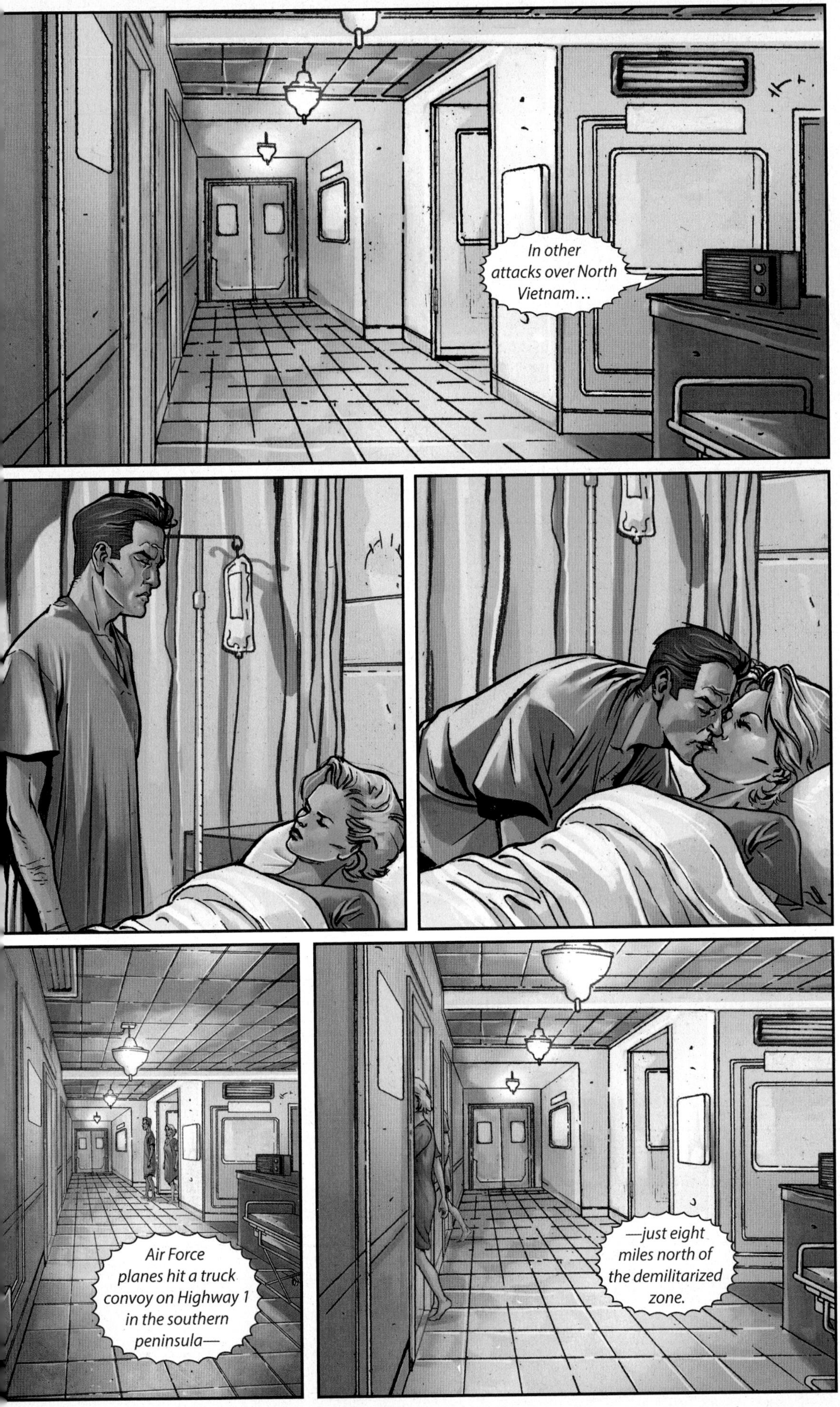
In other attacks over North Vietnam…
Air Force planes hit a truck convoy on Highway 1 in the southern peninsula—
—just eight miles north of the demilitarized zone.

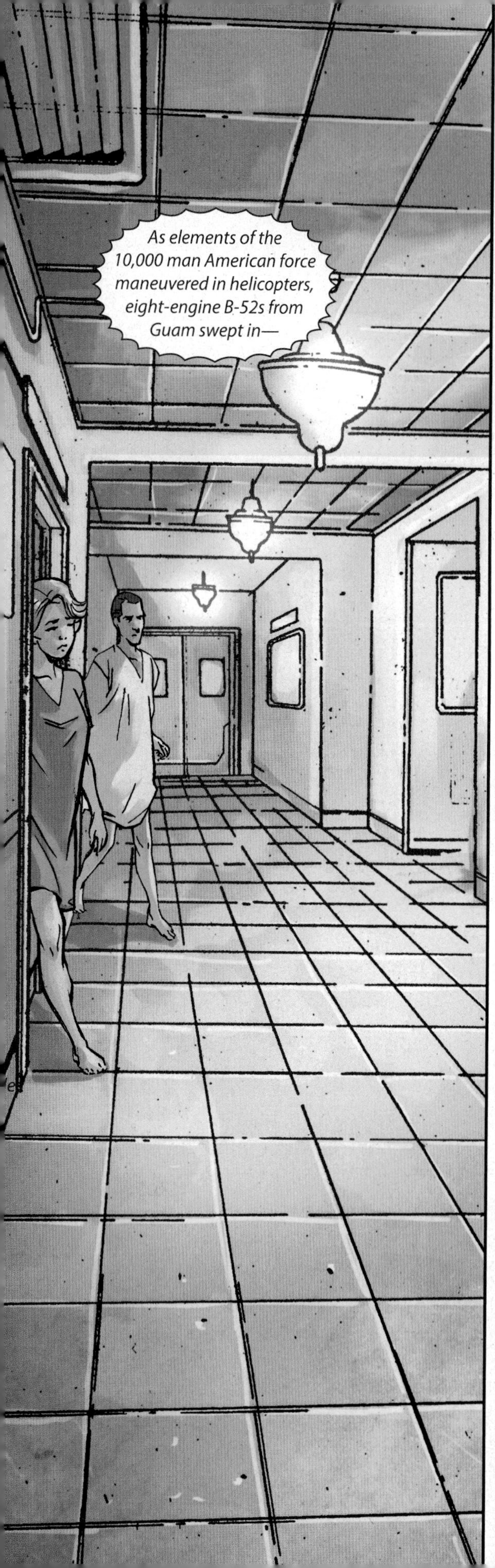
As elements of the
10,000 man American force
maneuvered in helicopters,
eight-engine B-52s from
Guam swept in—

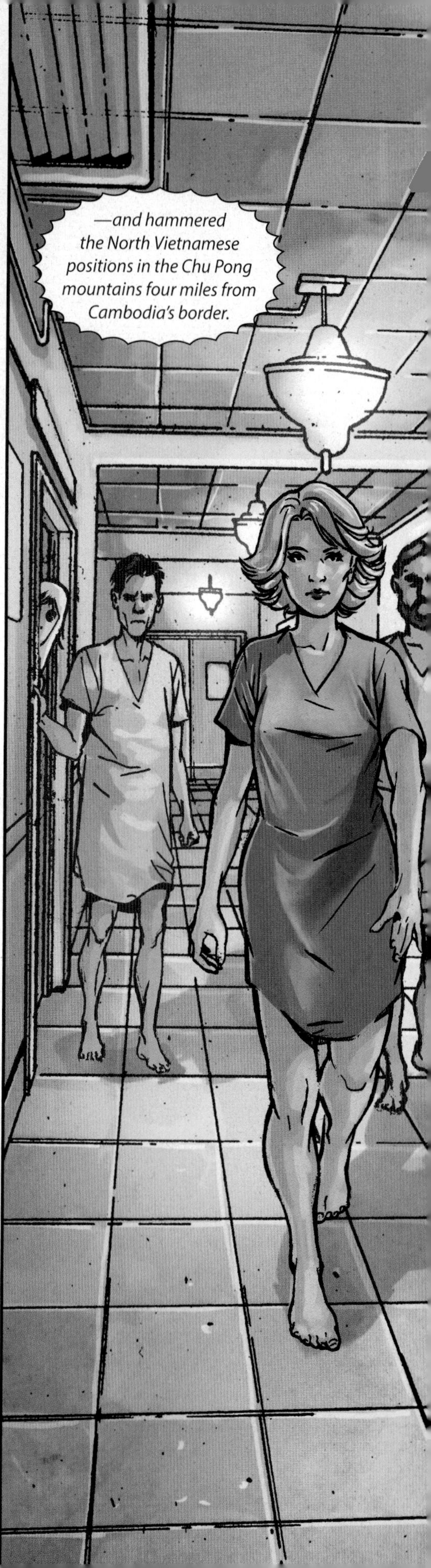
—and hammered
the North Vietnamese
positions in the Chu Pong
mountains four miles from
Cambodia's border.

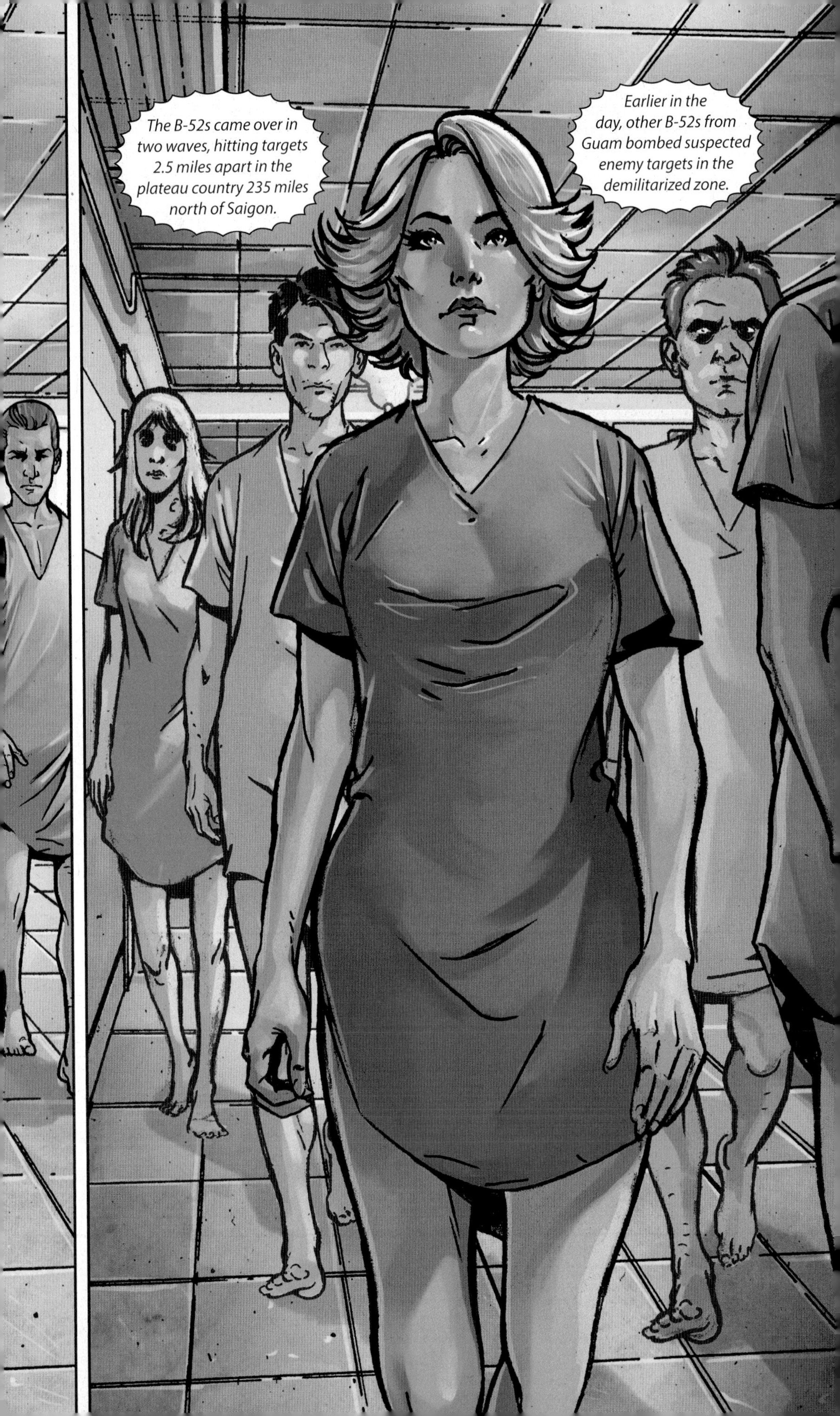
The B-52s came over in two waves, hitting targets 2.5 miles apart in the plateau country 235 miles north of Saigon.
Earlier in the day, other B-52s from Guam bombed suspected enemy targets in the demilitarized zone.

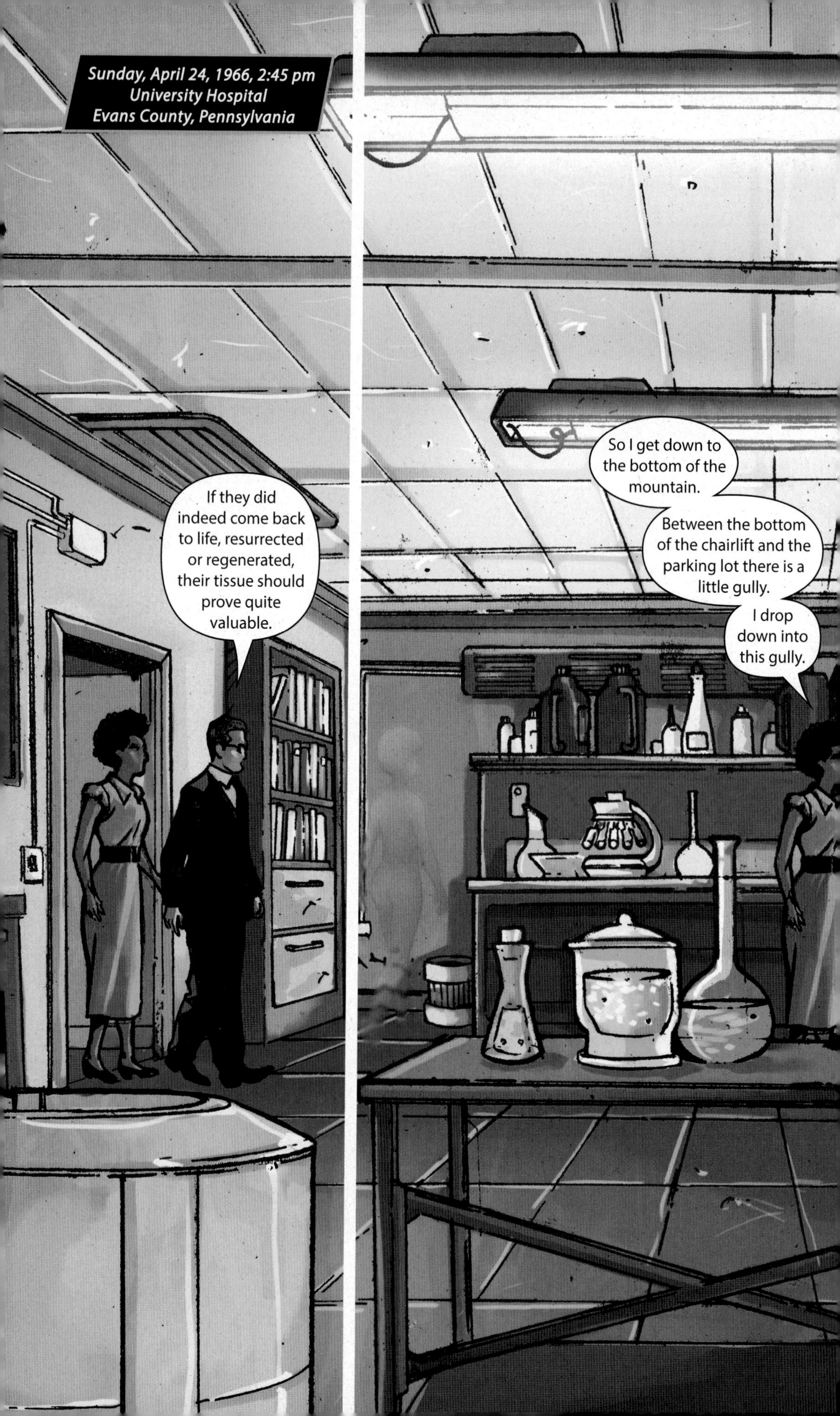
Sunday, April 24, 1966, 2:45 pm
University Hospital
Evans County, Pennsylvania
If they did indeed come back to life, resurrected or regenerated, their tissue should prove quite valuable.
So I get down to the bottom of the mountain.
Between the bottom of the chairlift and the parking lot there is a little gully.
I drop down into this gully.

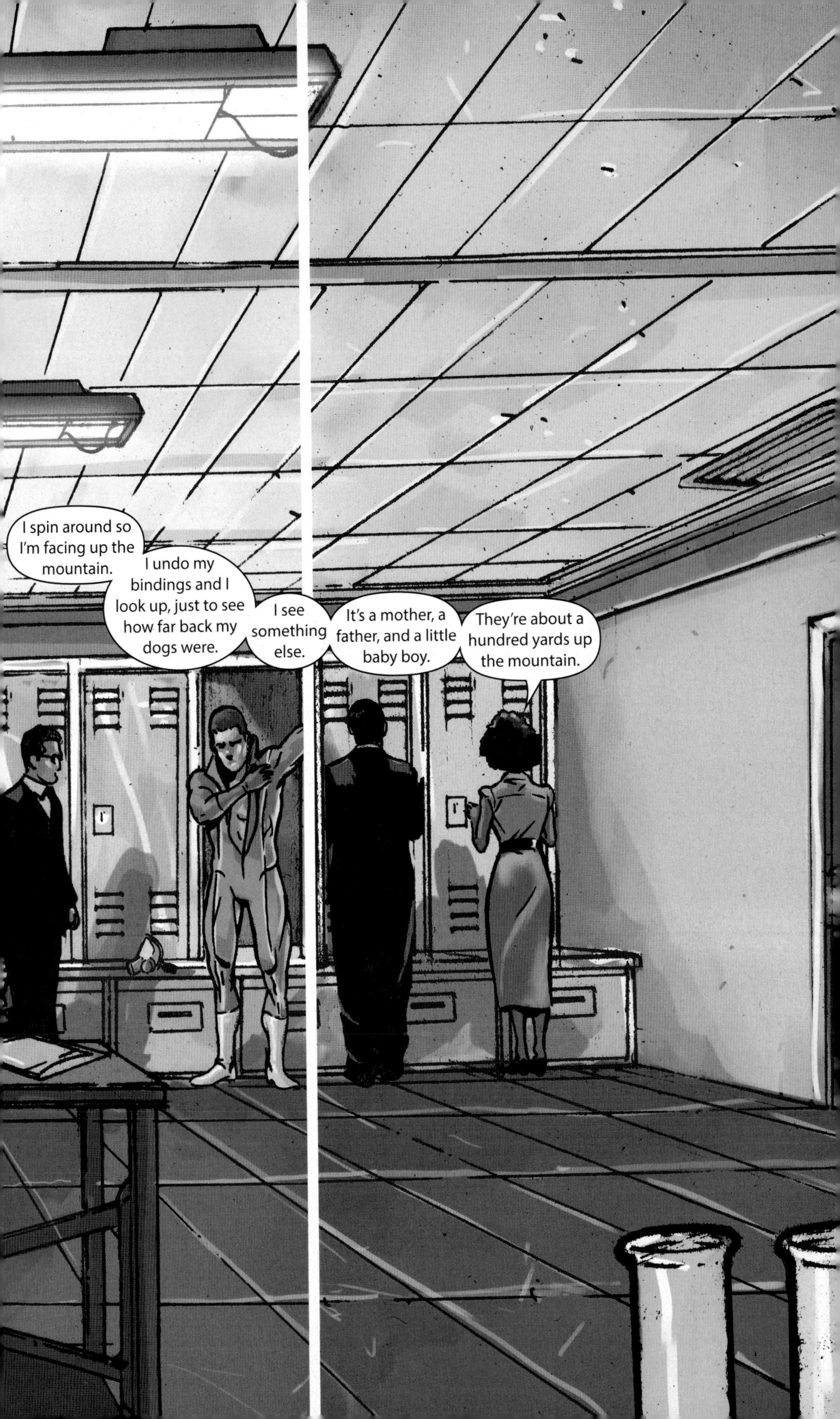
I spin around so I'm facing up the mountain.
I undo my bindings and I look up, just to see how far back my dogs were.
I see something else.
It's a mother, a father, and a little baby boy.
They're about a hundred yards up the mountain.

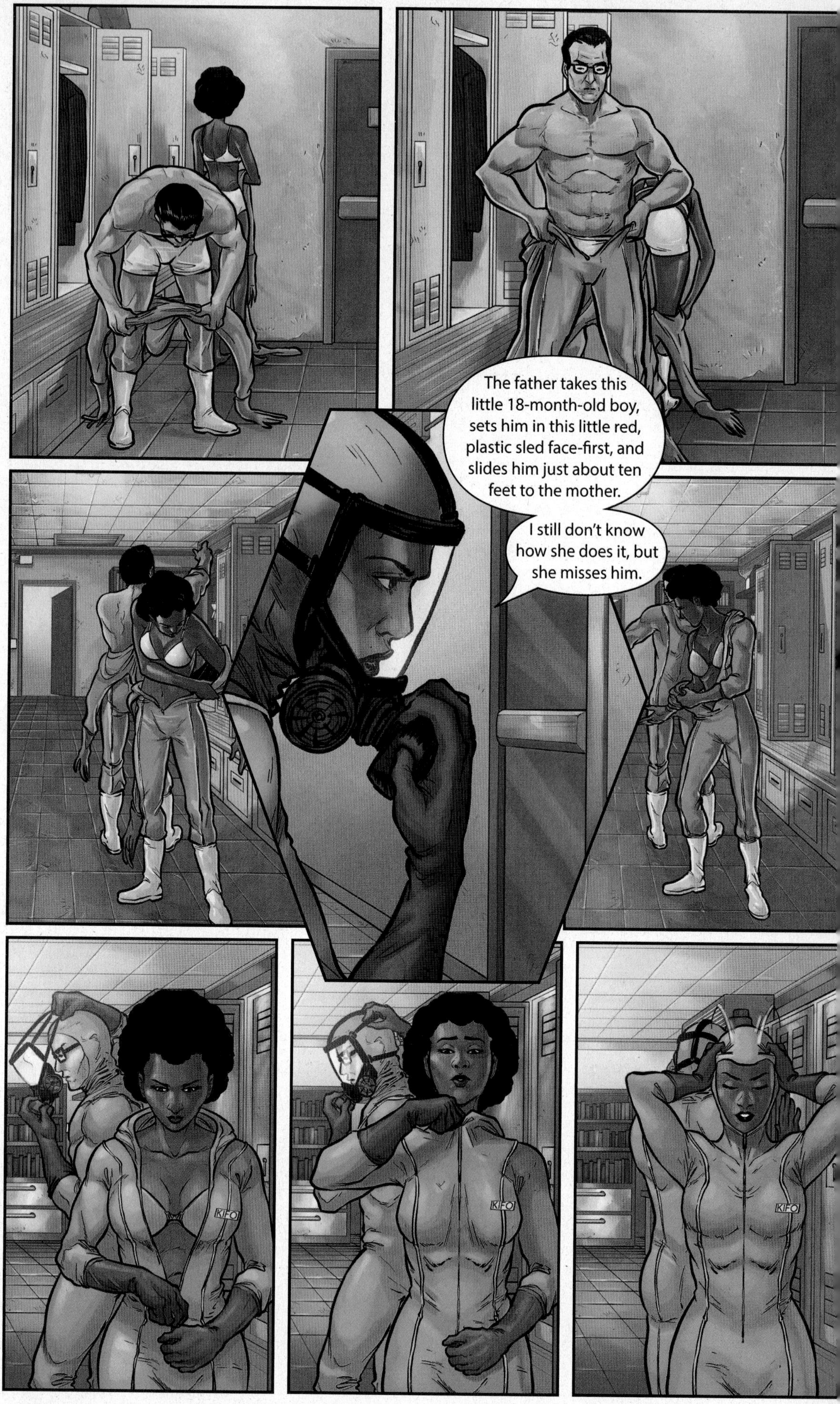

The father takes this little 18-month-old boy, sets him in this little red, plastic sled face-first, and slides him just about ten feet to the mother.
I still don't know how she does it, but she misses him.
KIFO
KIFO
KIFO

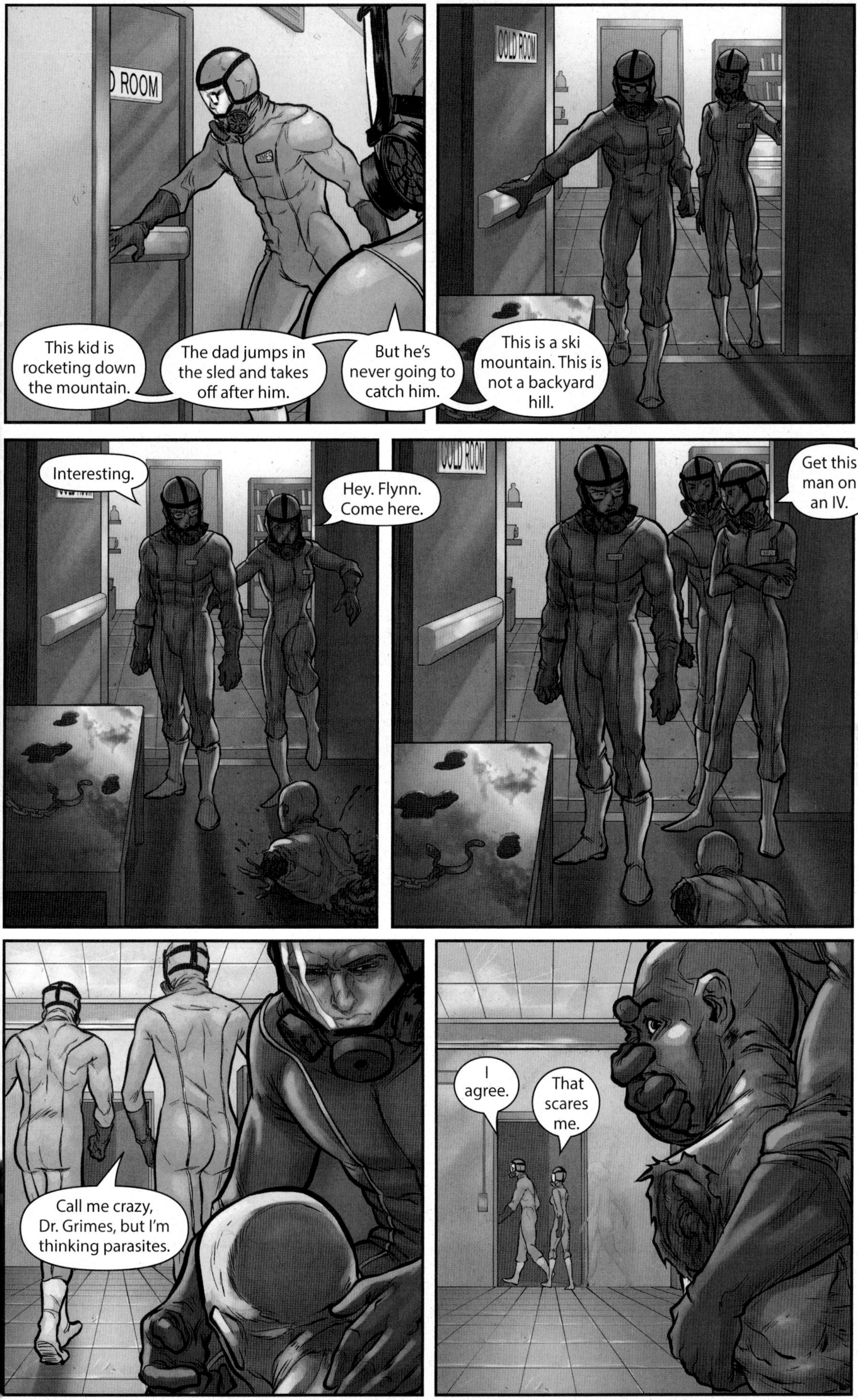

D ROOM
This kid is rocketing down the mountain.
The dad jumps in the sled and takes off after him.
But he's never going to catch him.
COLD ROOM
This is a ski mountain. This is not a backyard hill.
Interesting.
Hey. Flynn. Come here.
COLD ROOM
Get this man on an IV.
Call me crazy, Dr. Grimes, but I'm thinking parasites.
I agree.
That scares me.

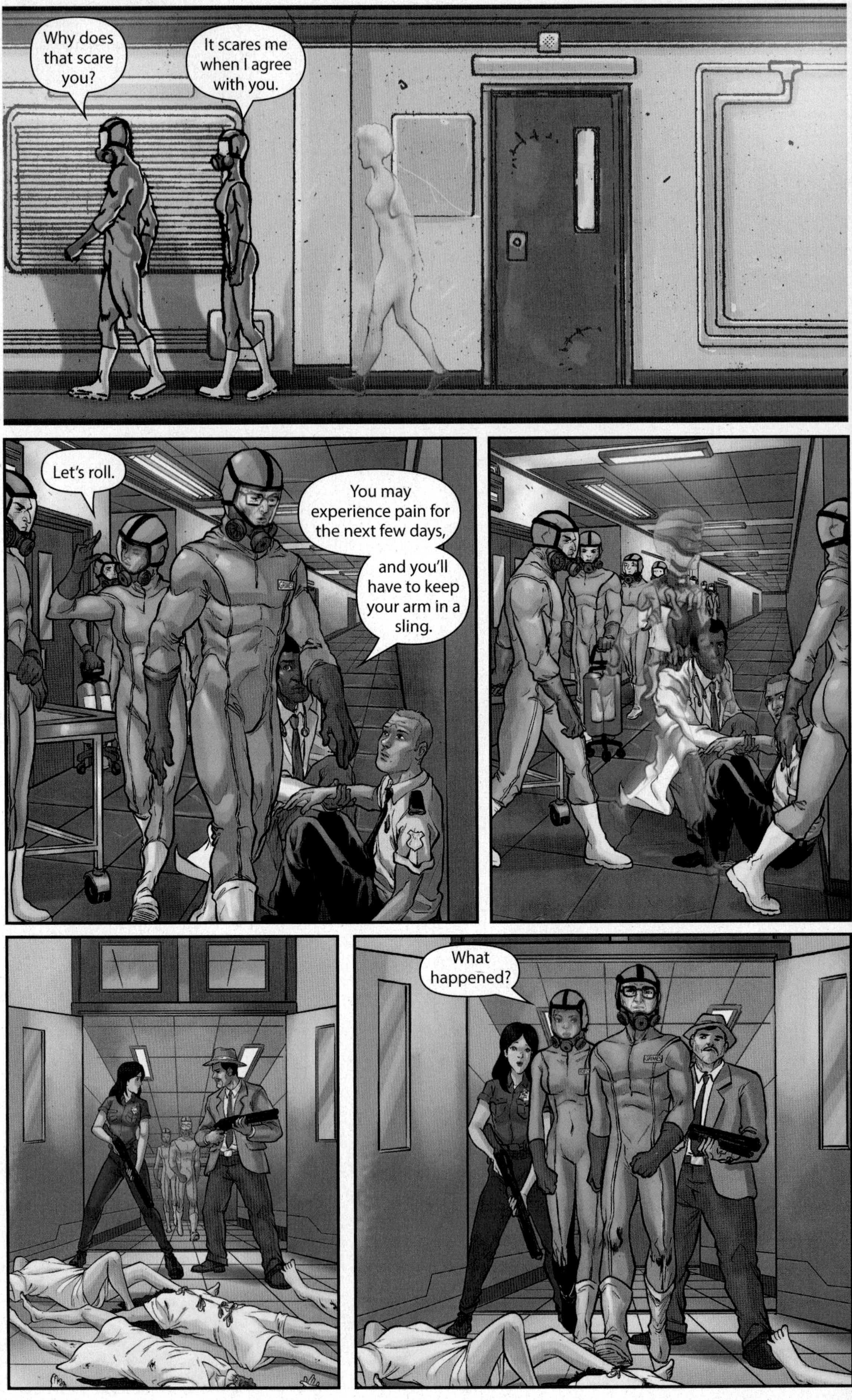
Why does that scare you?
It scares me when I agree with you.
Let's roll.
You may experience pain for the next few days,
and you'll have to keep your arm in a sling.
What happened?

Five minutes earlier...

Animals.

A$$holes.

Wing 'em if you can, but do what you gotta do, Long.

Freeze! Hands in the air!

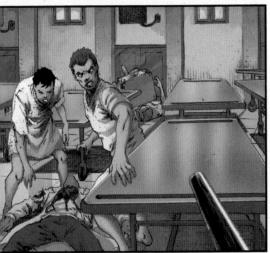

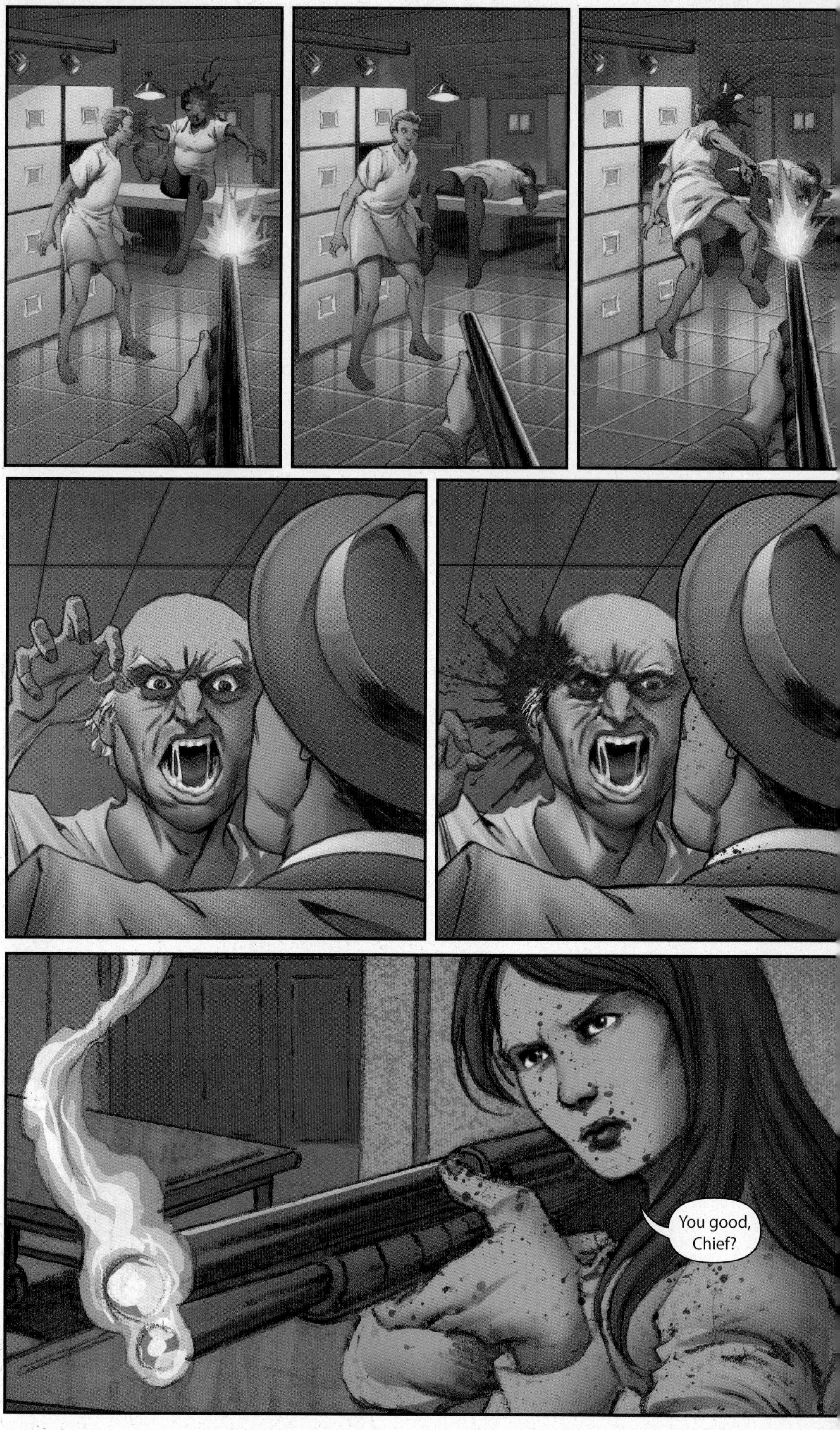
You good,
Chief?

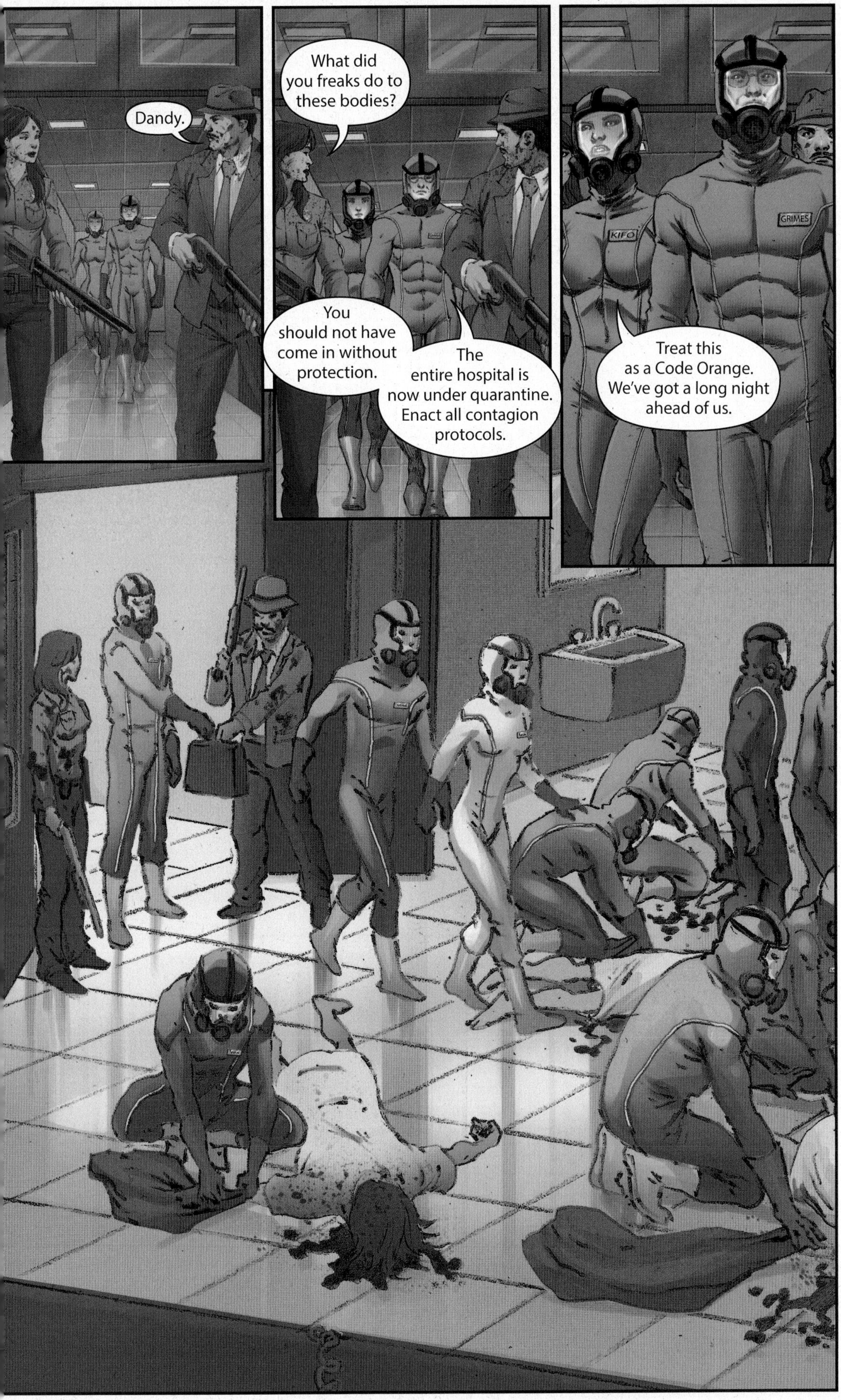
Dandy.
What did you freaks do to these bodies?
You should not have come in without protection.
The entire hospital is now under quarantine. Enact all contagion protocols.
KIFO
GRIMES
Treat this as a Code Orange. We've got a long night ahead of us.

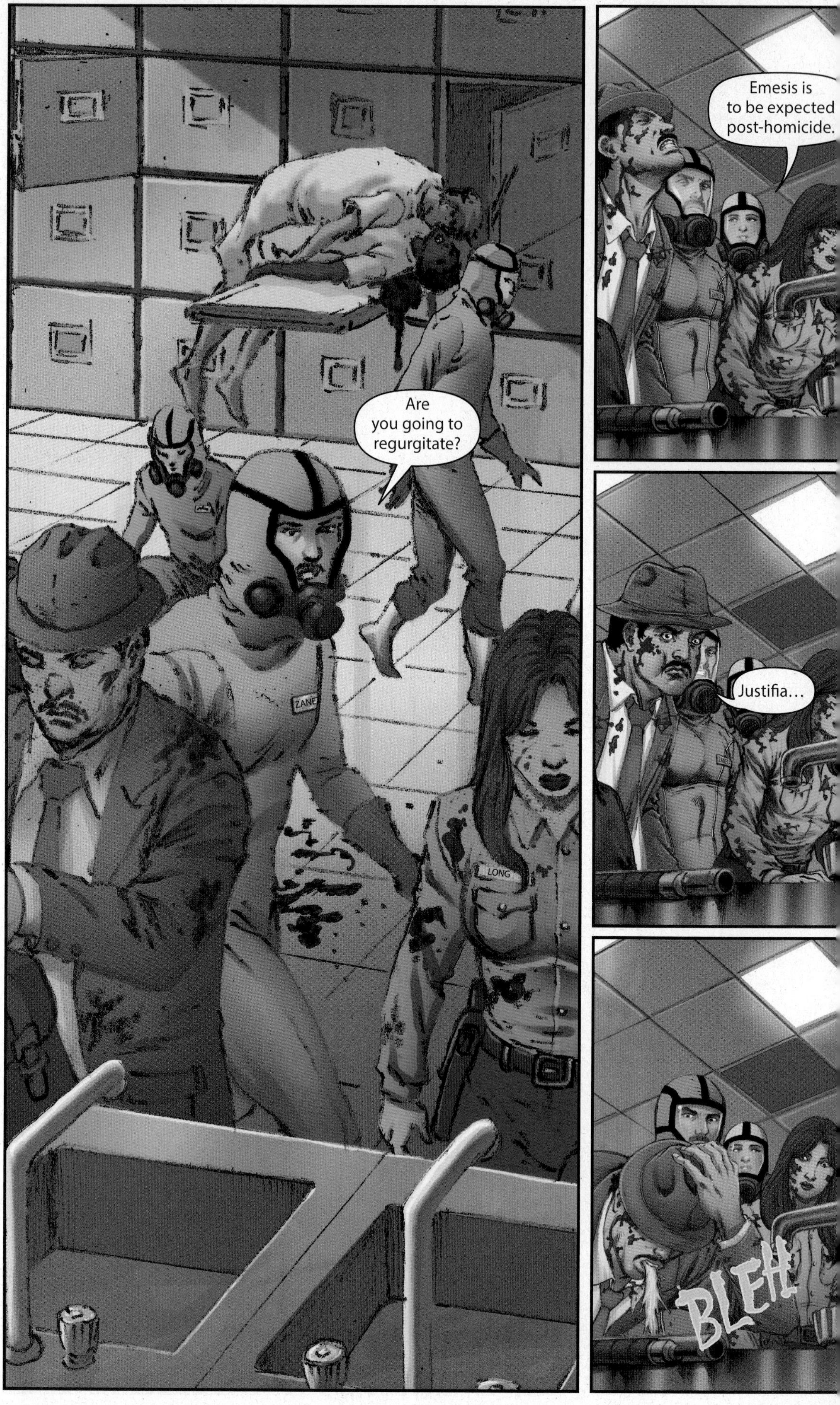
Are you going to regurgitate?
Emesis is to be expected post-homicide.
Justifia…
BLEH

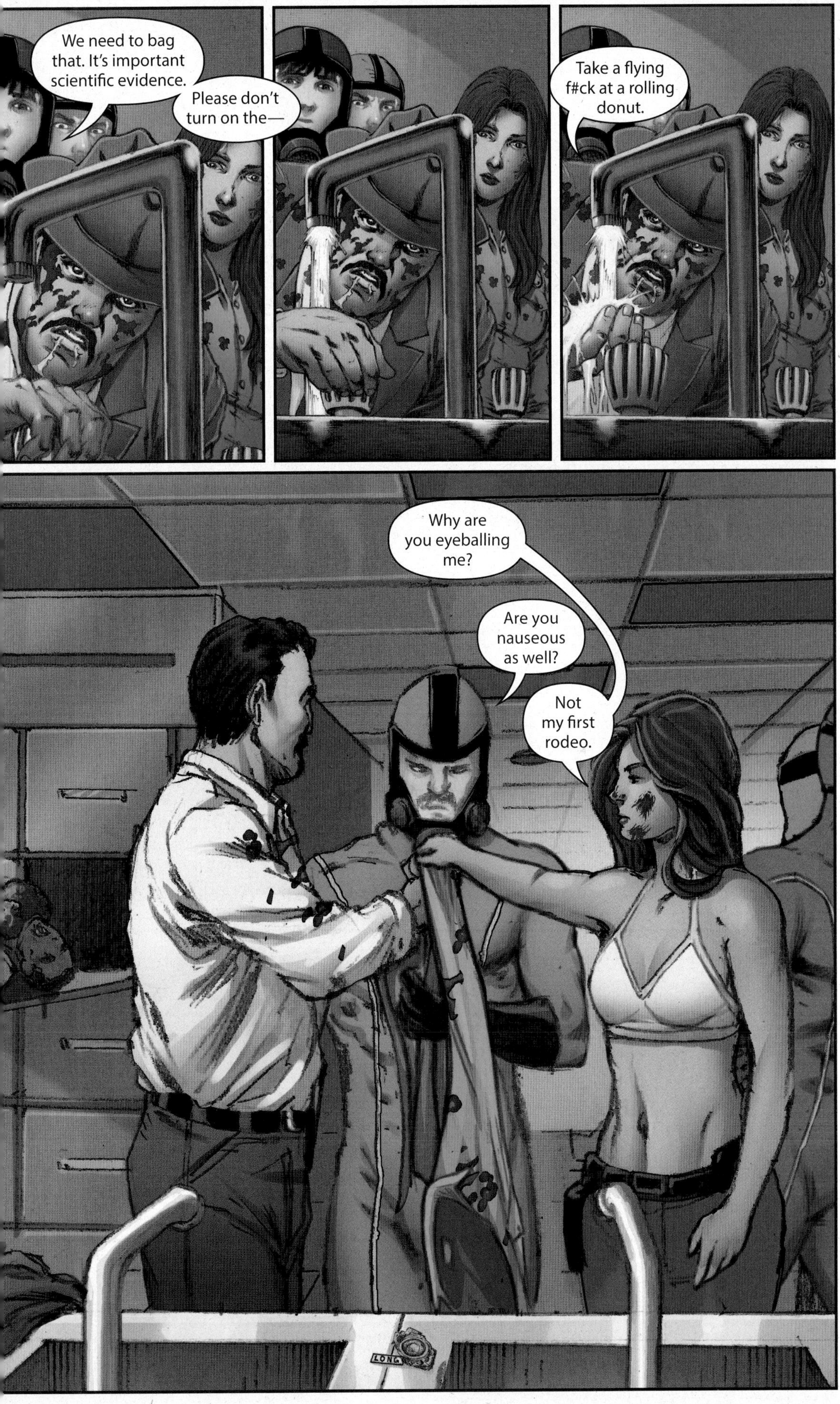
We need to bag that. It's important scientific evidence.
Please don't turn on the—
Take a flying f#ck at a rolling donut.
Why are you eyeballing me?
Are you nauseous as well?
Not my first rodeo.
LONG

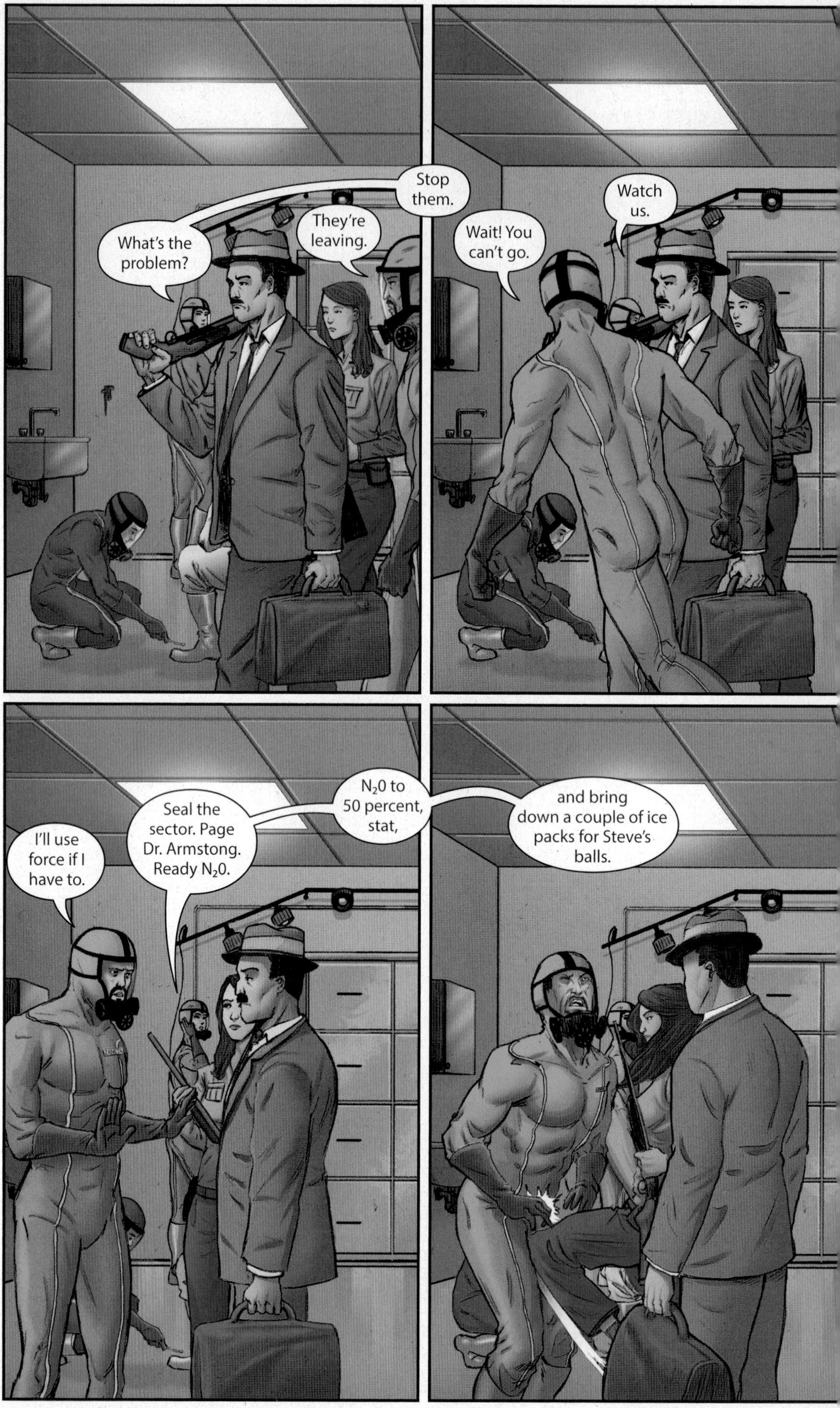
What's the problem?
Stop them.
They're leaving.
Wait! You can't go.
Watch us.
I'll use force if I have to.
Seal the sector. Page Dr. Armstong. Ready N_2O.
N_2O to 50 percent, stat,
and bring down a couple of ice packs for Steve's balls.

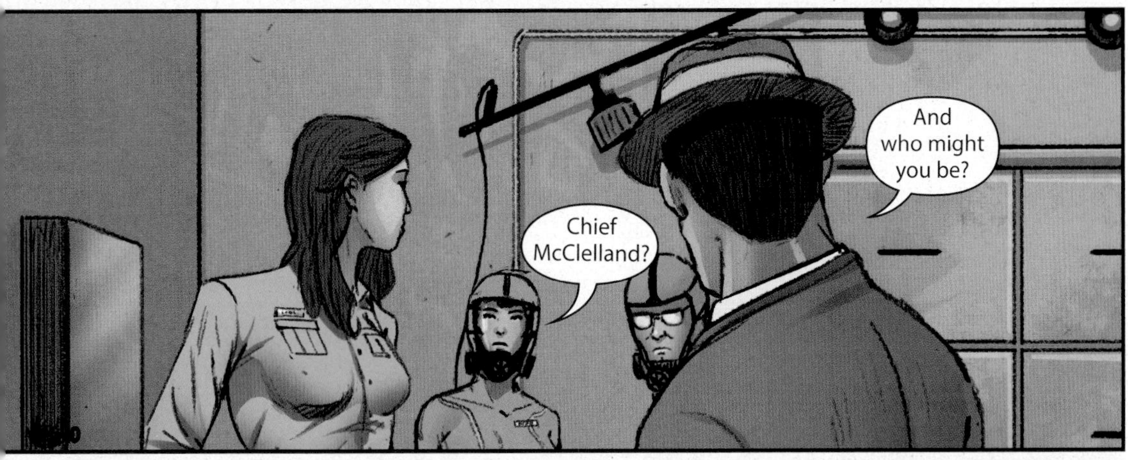
Chief McClelland?
And who might you be?
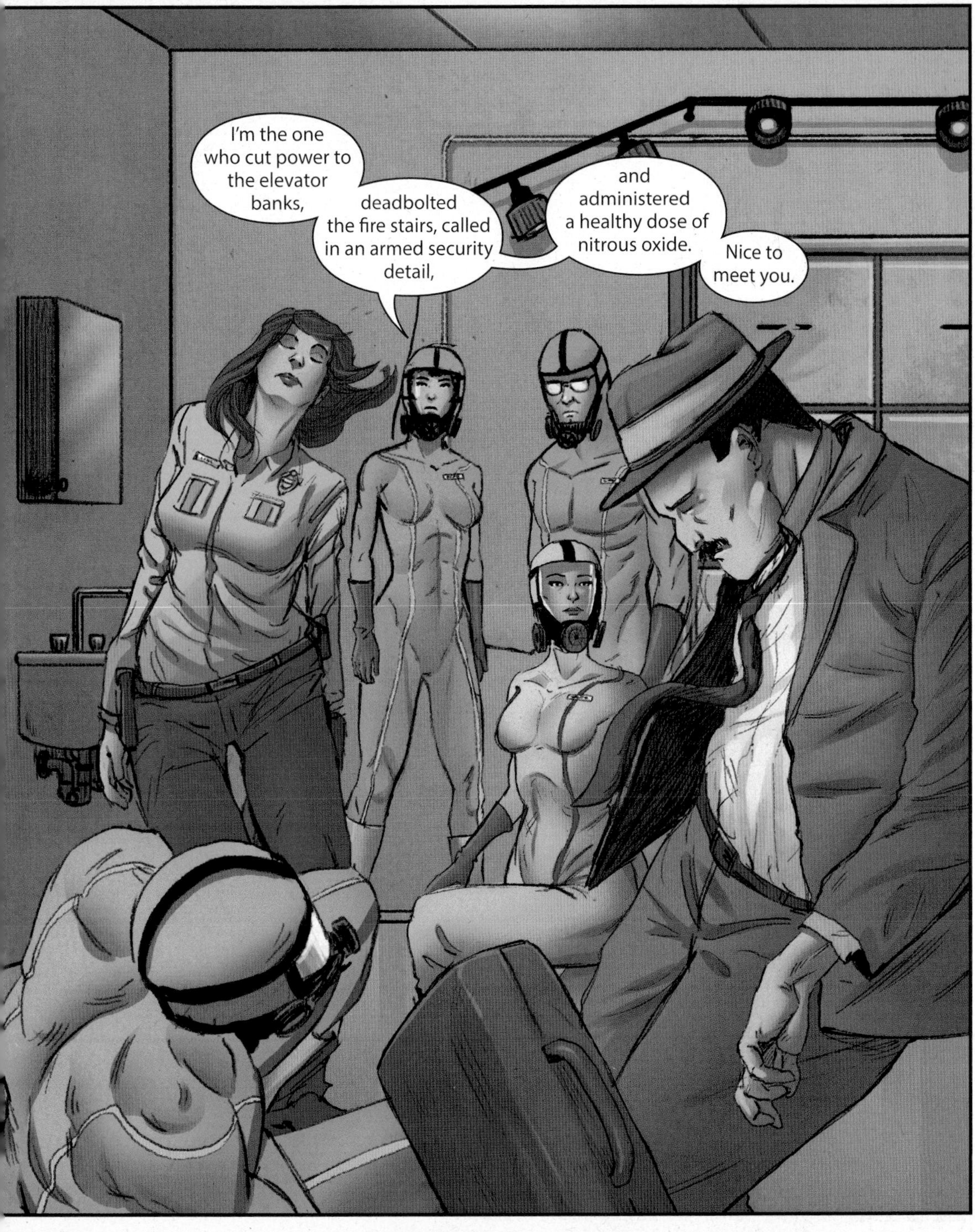
I'm the one who cut power to the elevator banks,
deadbolted the fire stairs, called in an armed security detail,
and administered a healthy dose of nitrous oxide.
Nice to meet you.

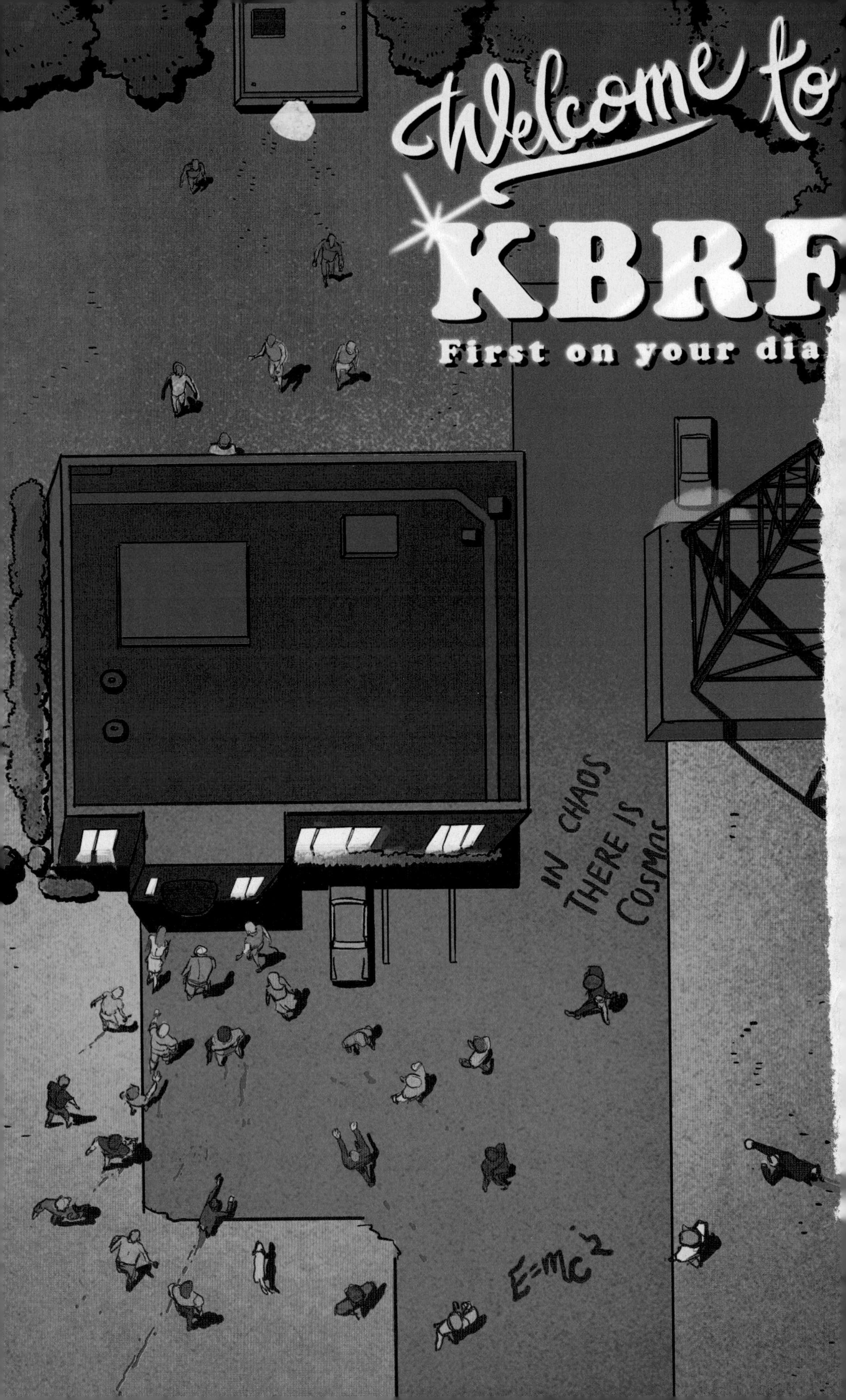
Welcome to
KBRF
First on your dia
IN CHAOS THERE IS COSMOS
E=mc2

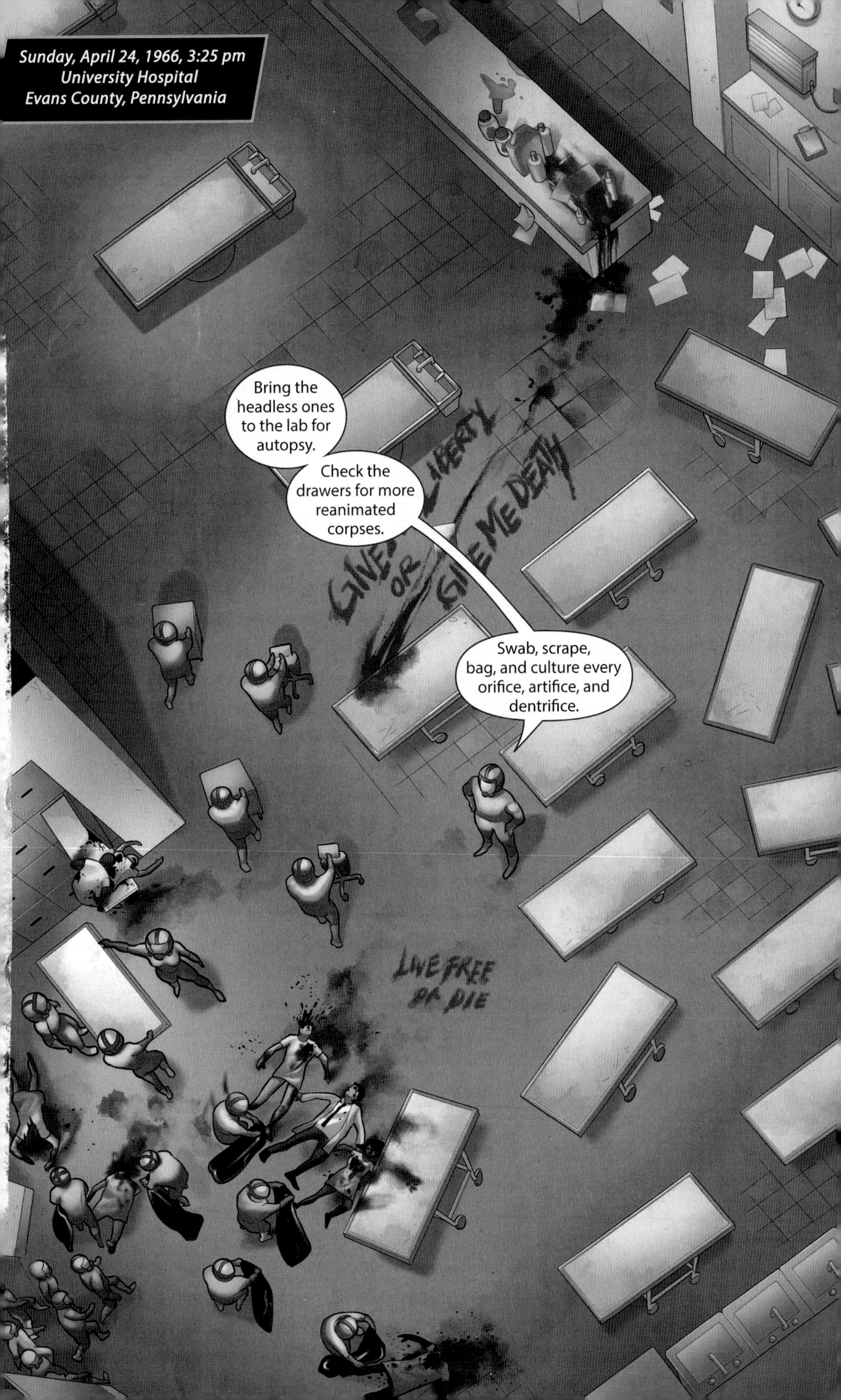
Sunday, April 24, 1966, 3:25 pm
University Hospital
Evans County, Pennsylvania
Bring the headless ones to the lab for autopsy.
Check the drawers for more reanimated corpses.
Swab, scrape, bag, and culture every orifice, artifice, and dentrifice.
LIVE FREE OR DIE

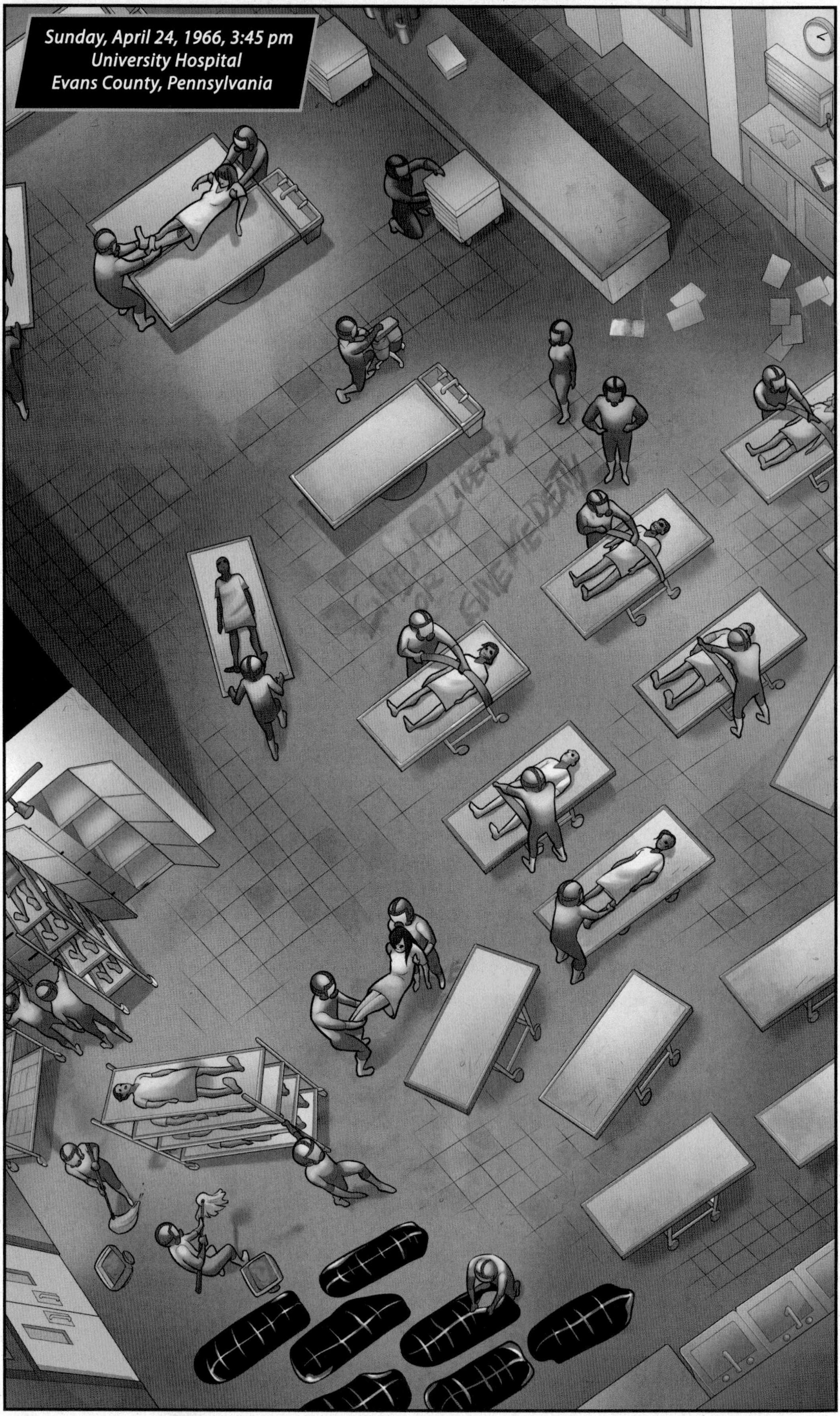
Sunday, April 24, 1966, 3:45 pm
University Hospital
Evans County, Pennsylvania

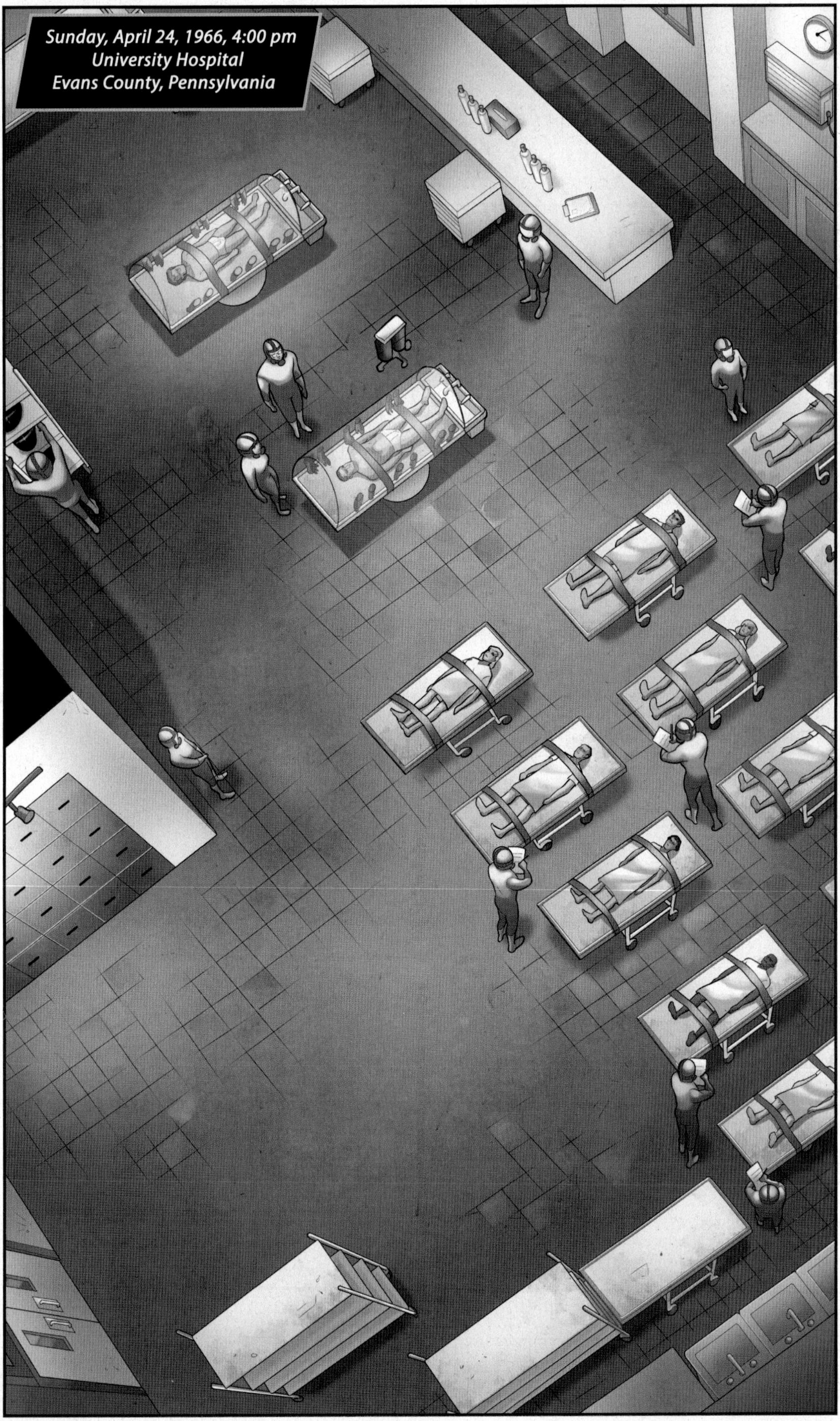
Sunday, April 24, 1966, 4:00 pm
University Hospital
Evans County, Pennsylvania

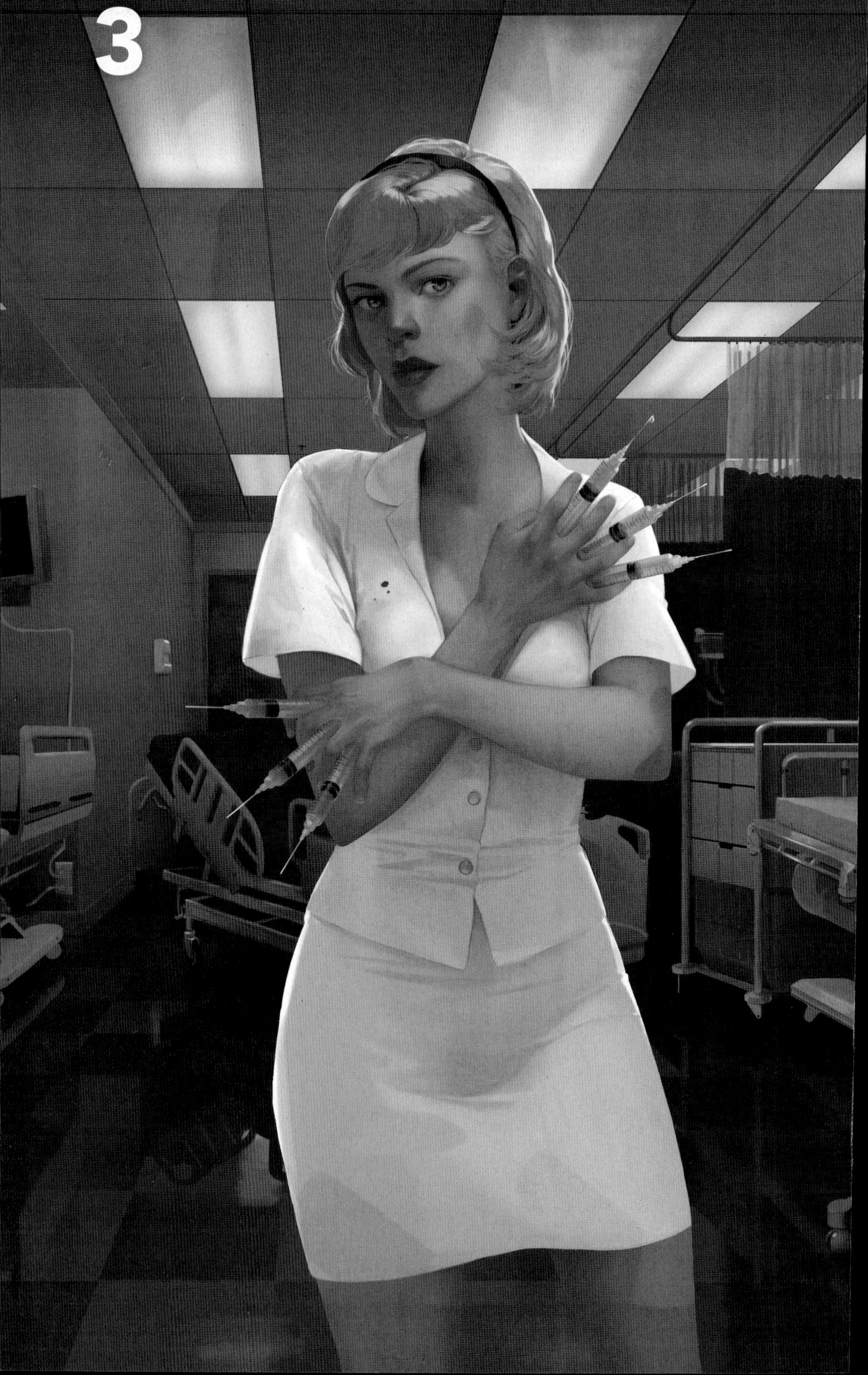
3

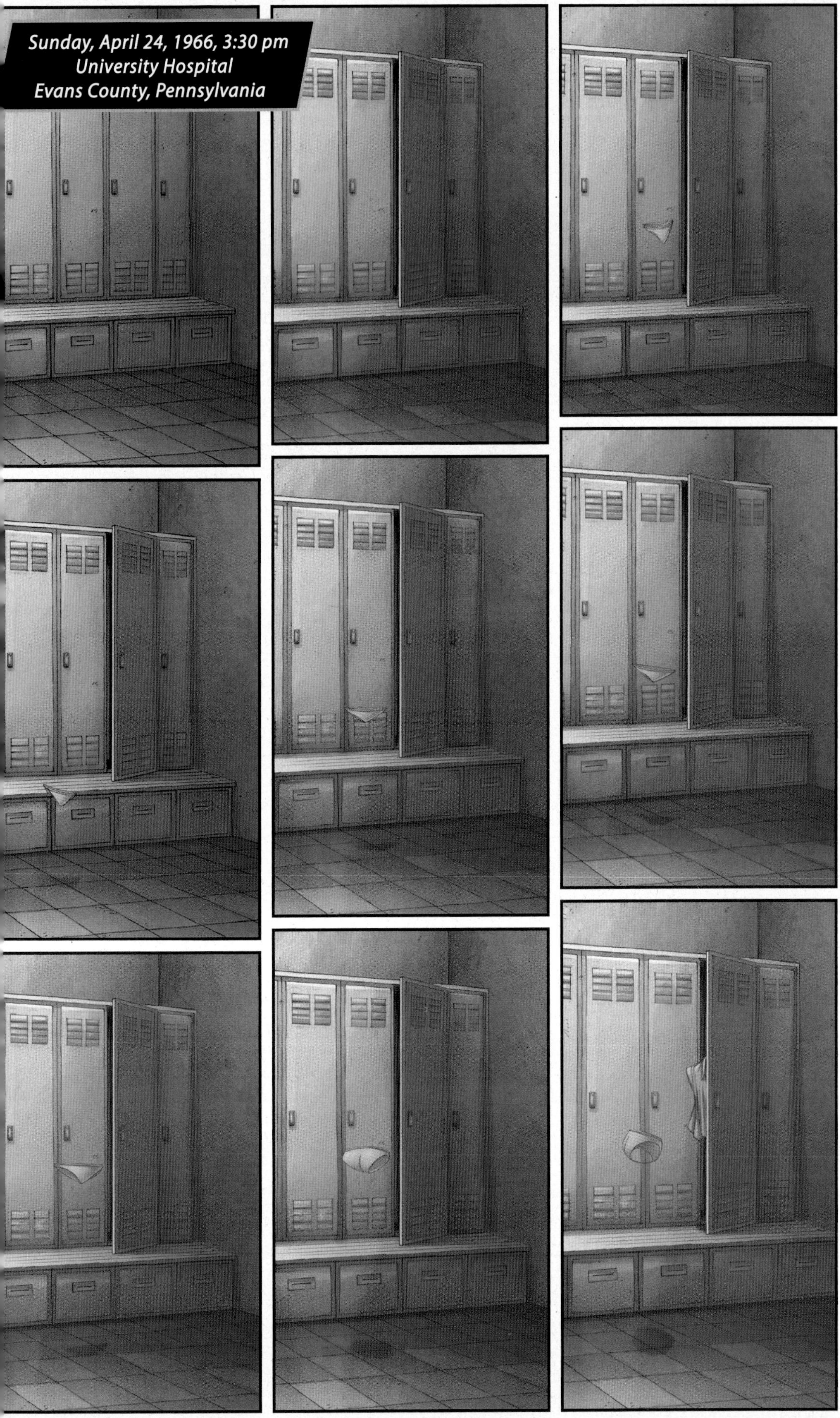
Sunday, April 24, 1966, 3:30 pm
University Hospital
Evans County, Pennsylvania

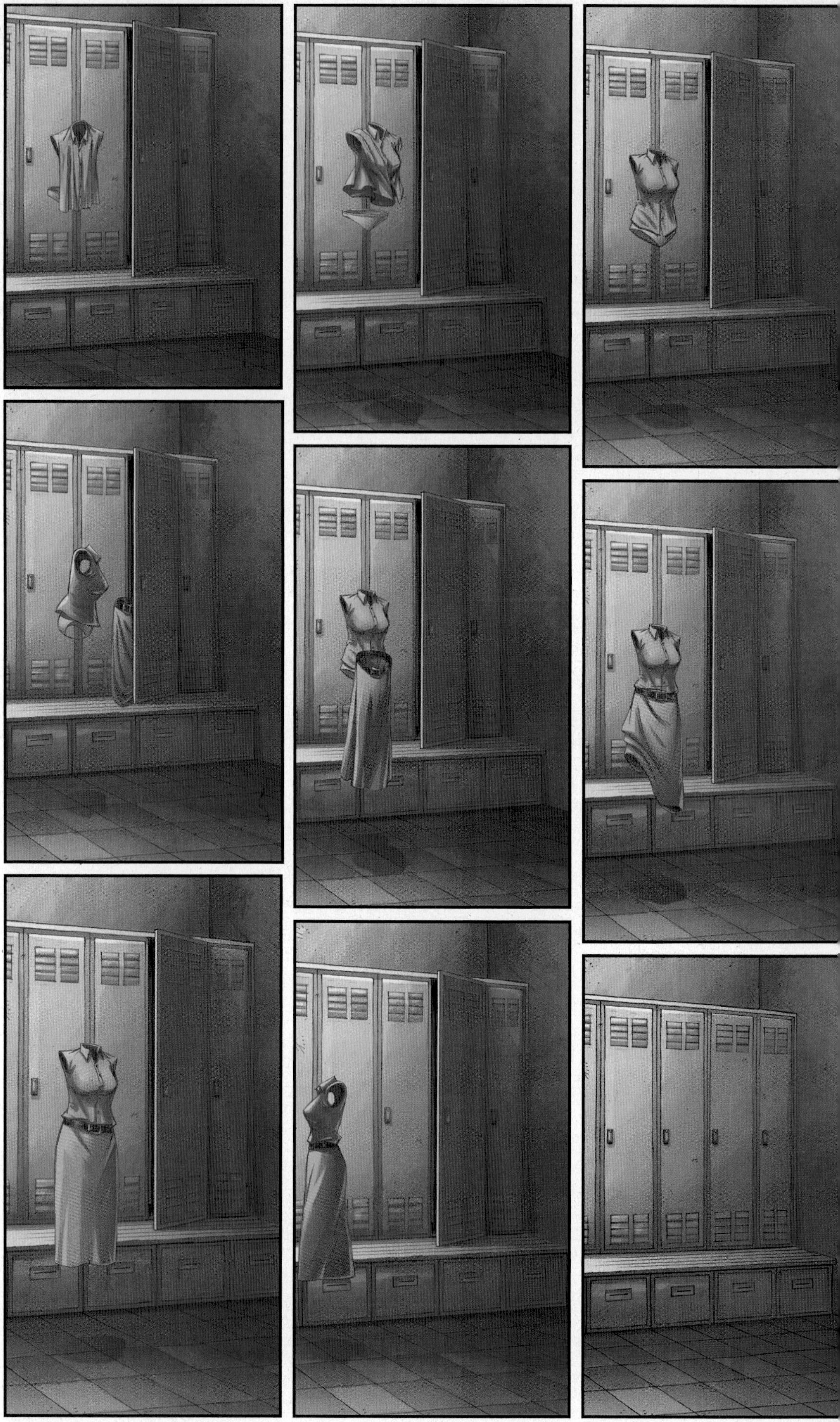

DOUBLE TAKE MANUAL OF STYLE

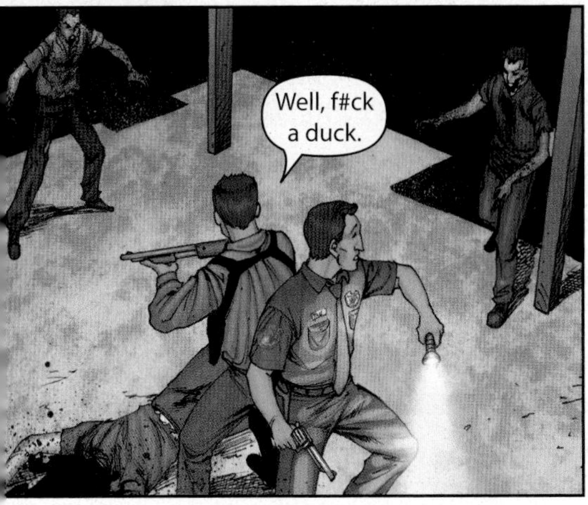
Well, f#ck a duck.

F#ck a Duck

First use: In Henry Miller's *Tropic of Cancer* (1934): the narrator saw another author's title that he wished he'd come up with and exclaimed, "Well, f#ck a duck! I congratulate him just the same."

Etymology: The original inspiration may have been "duckf#cker," which refers to a person aboard a transatlantic ship who is responsible for keeping the domestic animals alive (and not pleasuring them in exotic ways).

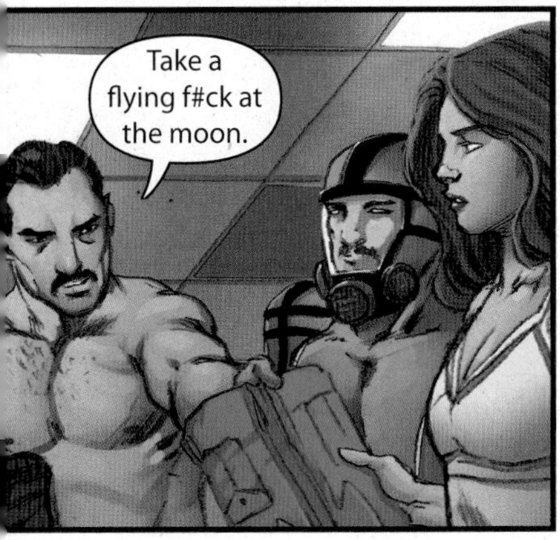
Take a flying f#ck at the moon.

Take a flying f#ck at a rolling donut

First use: Kurt Vonnegut used the phrase verbatim in *Slaughterhouse-Five* (1969) and again in *Slapstick* (1976): "Go take a flying f#ck at a rolling doughnut.... Go take a flying f#ck at the moon."

Etymology: Variations of the phrase date back to 1926: American author and US Army Colonel L.H. Nason used the phrase in *Chevrons*, a novel about life in the Field Artillery during WWI ("Me, I'd tell'em to take a flyin' fling at the moon."). "Flying f#ck" originally meant "sex had on horseback." The phrase appeared in 1800 in a oadside ballad called "New Feats of Horsemanship":

Well mounted on a mettled steed
Famed for his strength as well as speed
Corinna and her favorite buck
Are pleas'd to have a flying f#ck.

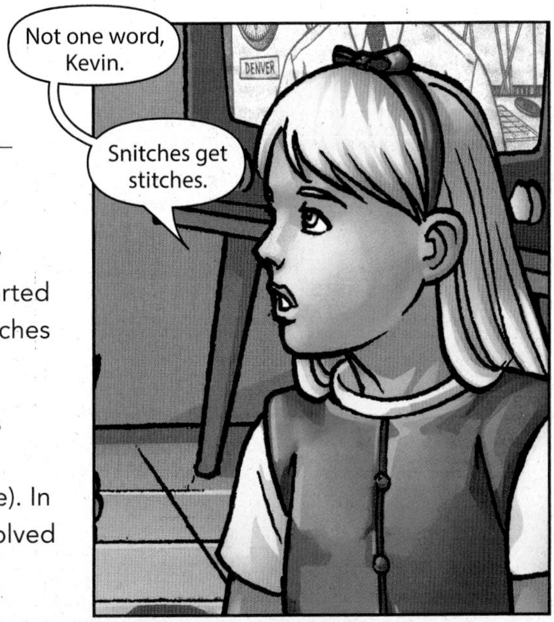
Not one word, Kevin.
Snitches get stitches.
DENVER

nitches get stitches

rst use: Possibly in the streets of late 1980s New rk City; around this time, newspapers in NYC started ing this phrase in articles. Other phrasings: "Snitches t stitches and end up in ditches."

ymology: "Snitch" as slang for "informer" dates ck to 1785. In the late 1600s, "snitch" originally eant a "fillip on the nose" (i.e., a flick on the nose). In e early 18th century, the meaning of "snitch" evolved mean "nose," a symbol of intrusion into others' siness ("nosy").

THEN NOW

USA

Health & Nutrition	1960s	2010s	Increase
Average female adult	140.2 lbs	166.3 lbs	18.6%
Average male adult	166.3 lbs	195.5 lbs	17.6%
Adult obesity	10.7%	35.9%	235.5%
Childhood obesity	9.0%	39.9%	333.3%
US population with diabetes	2,770,000	29,100,000	950.5%
Estimated daily caloric intake	2,200	3,300	50.0%
Pounds per person per year			
All sugars	114.0	152.0	33.3%
Corn sweeteners	15.0	85.0	467.0%
High fructose corn syrup	0.2	43.7	2175.0%
Meat	161.7	252.7	56.3%
Cheese	9.5	33.2	249.0%
Added fats	47.8	83.9	75.5%
Grains	142.5	175.2	23.0%
Soft drinks	18.3	46.5	154.0%

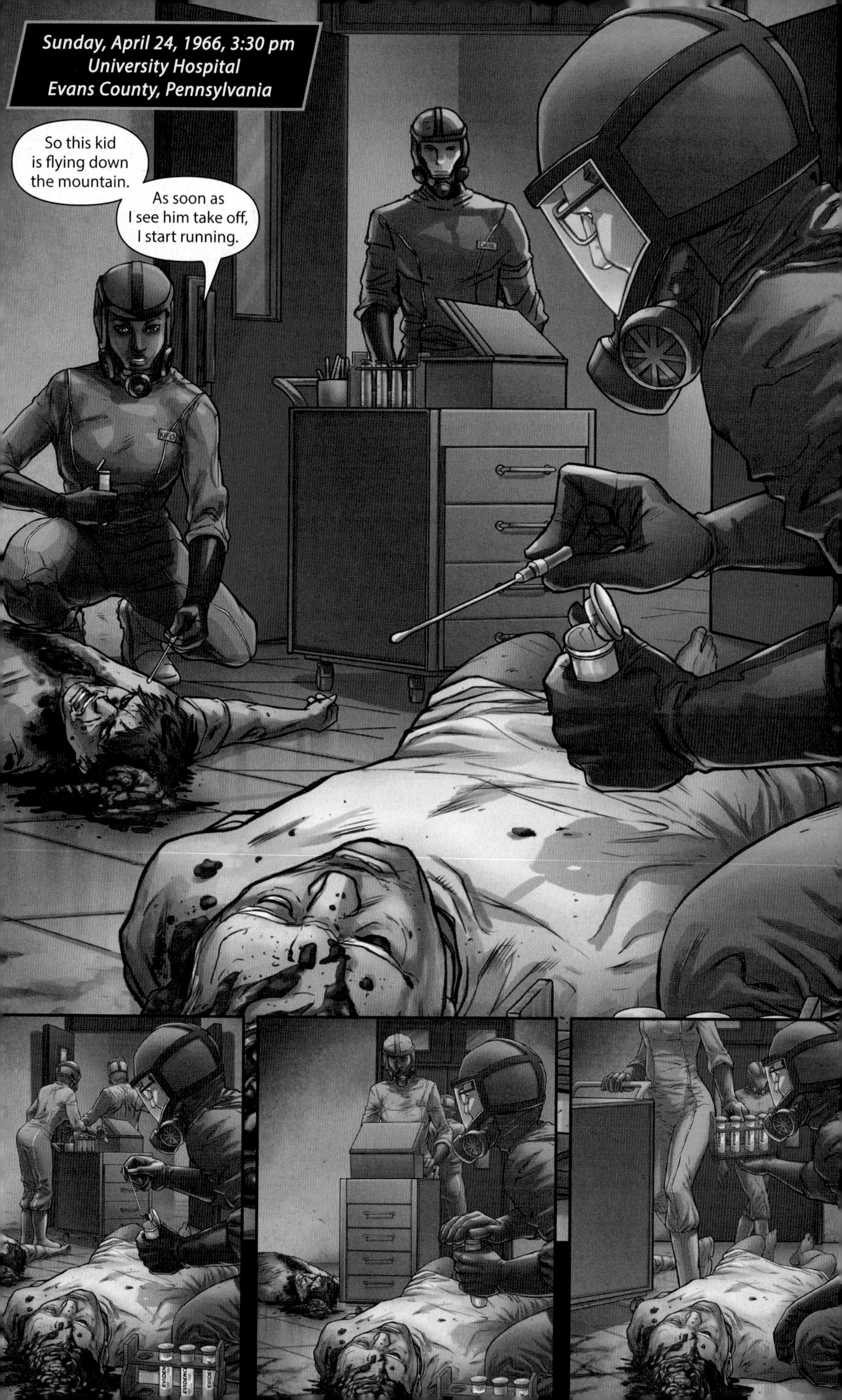
Sunday, April 24, 1966, 3:30 pm
University Hospital
Evans County, Pennsylvania
So this kid is flying down the mountain.
As soon as I see him take off, I start running.

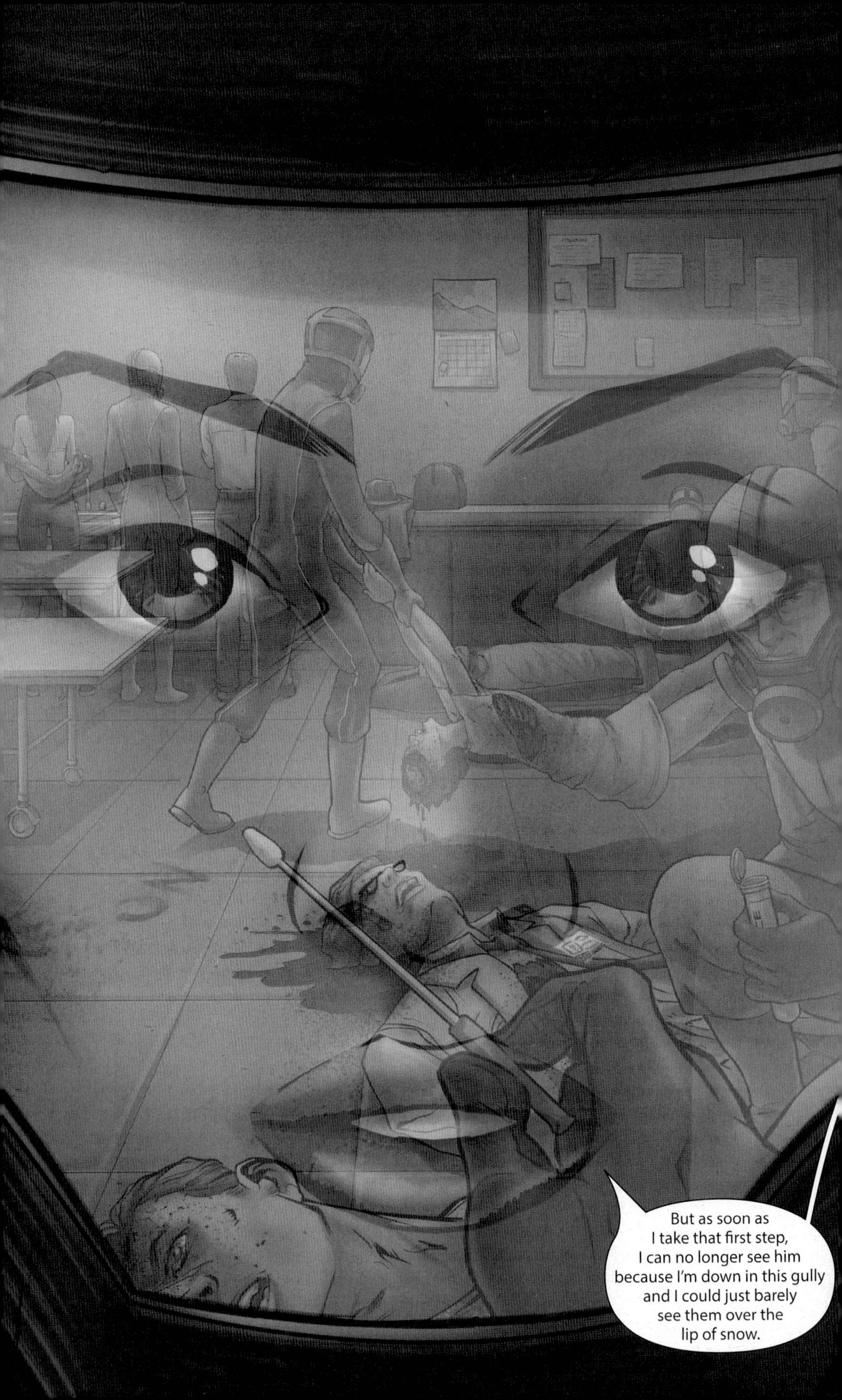
But as soon as I take that first step, I can no longer see him because I'm down in this gully and I could just barely see them over the lip of snow.

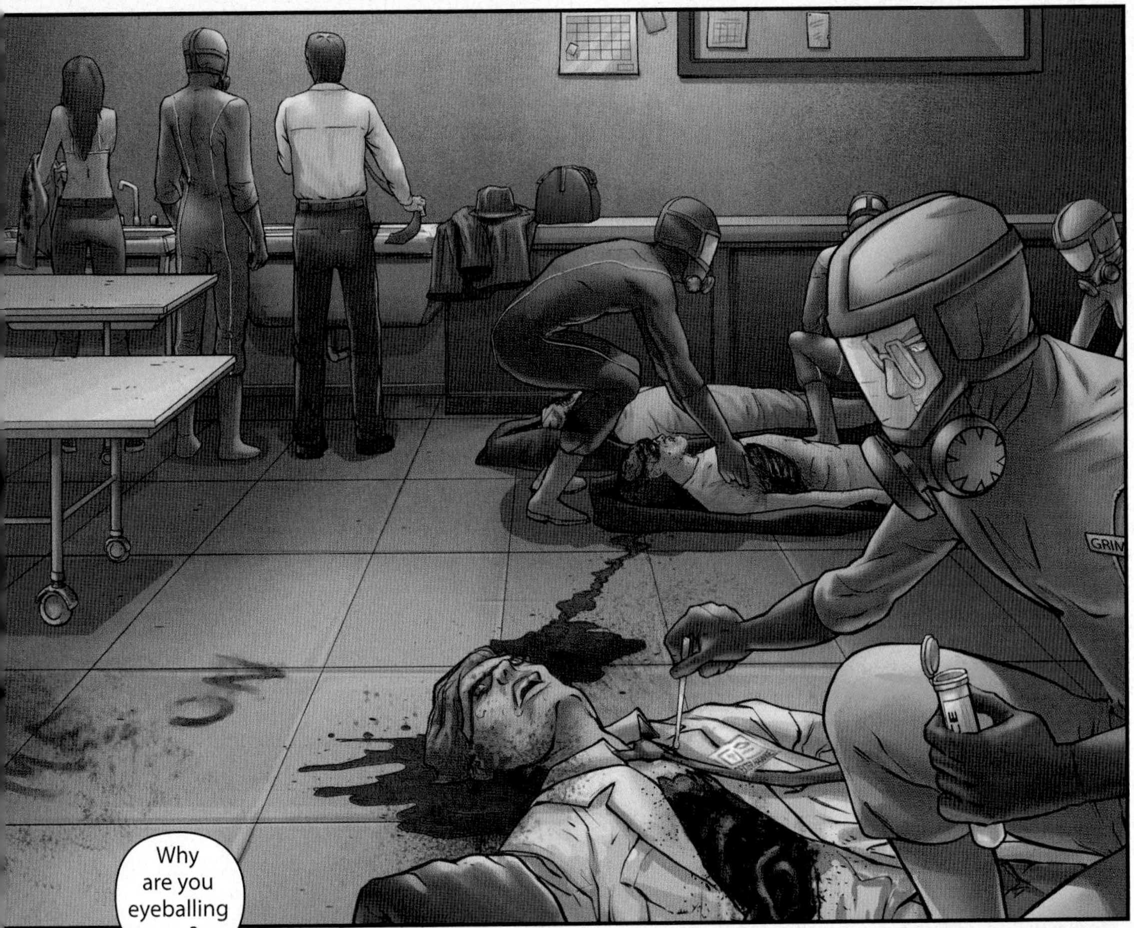
Why are you eyeballing me?

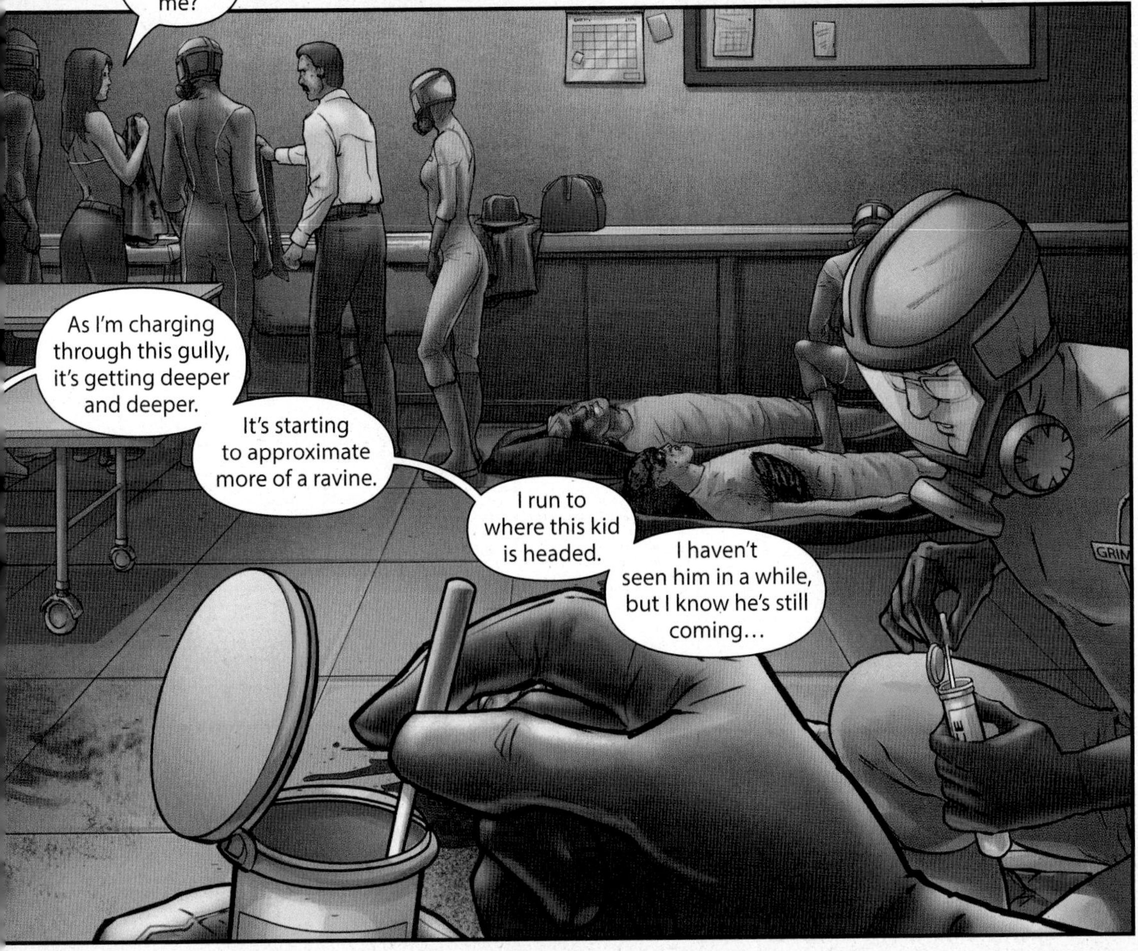
As I'm charging through this gully, it's getting deeper and deeper.
It's starting to approximate more of a ravine.
I run to where this kid is headed.
I haven't seen him in a while, but I know he's still coming…

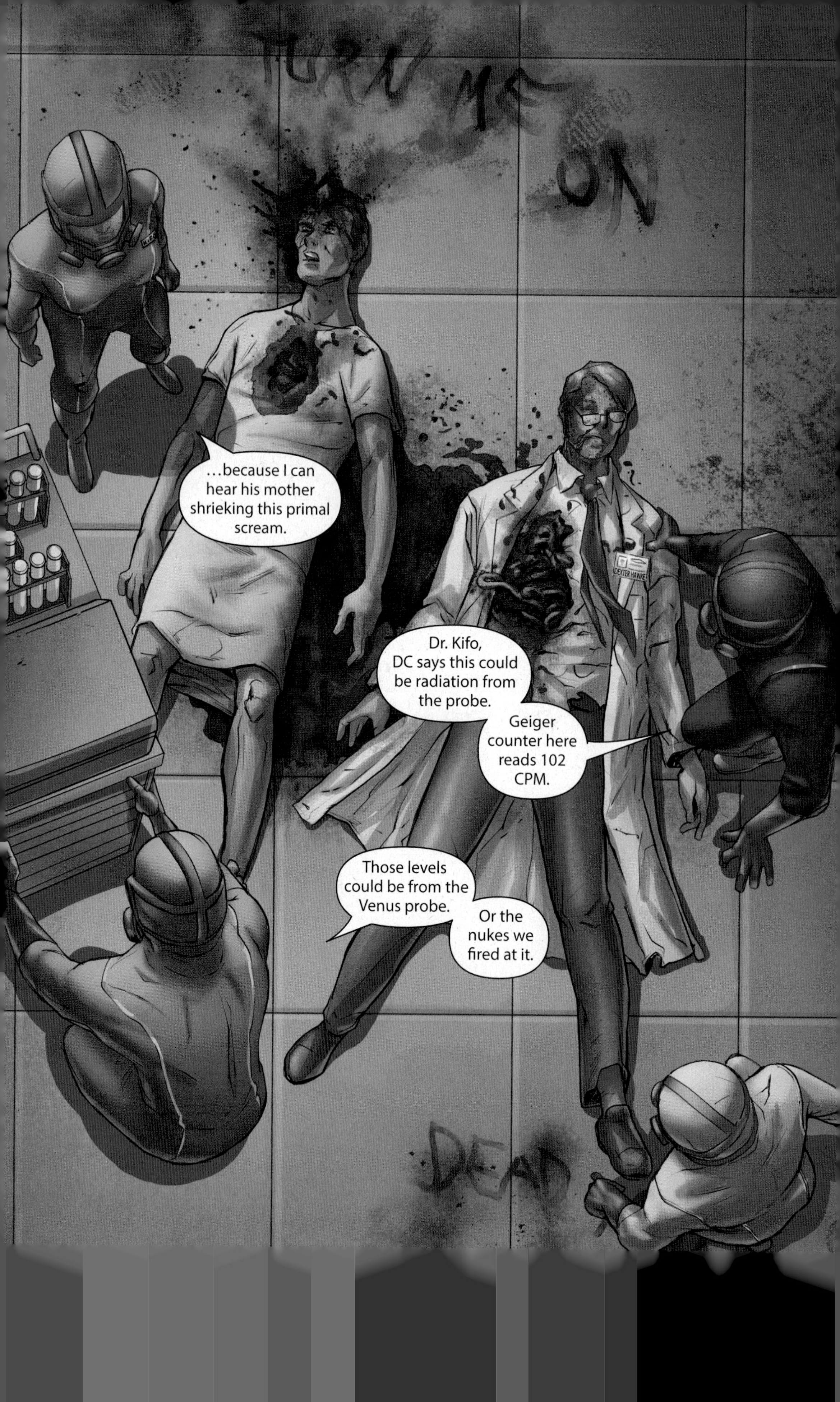
TURN ME ON
…because I can hear his mother shrieking this primal scream.
DEXTER HAWKE
Dr. Kifo, DC says this could be radiation from the probe.
Geiger counter here reads 102 CPM.
Those levels could be from the Venus probe.
Or the nukes we fired at it.
DEAD

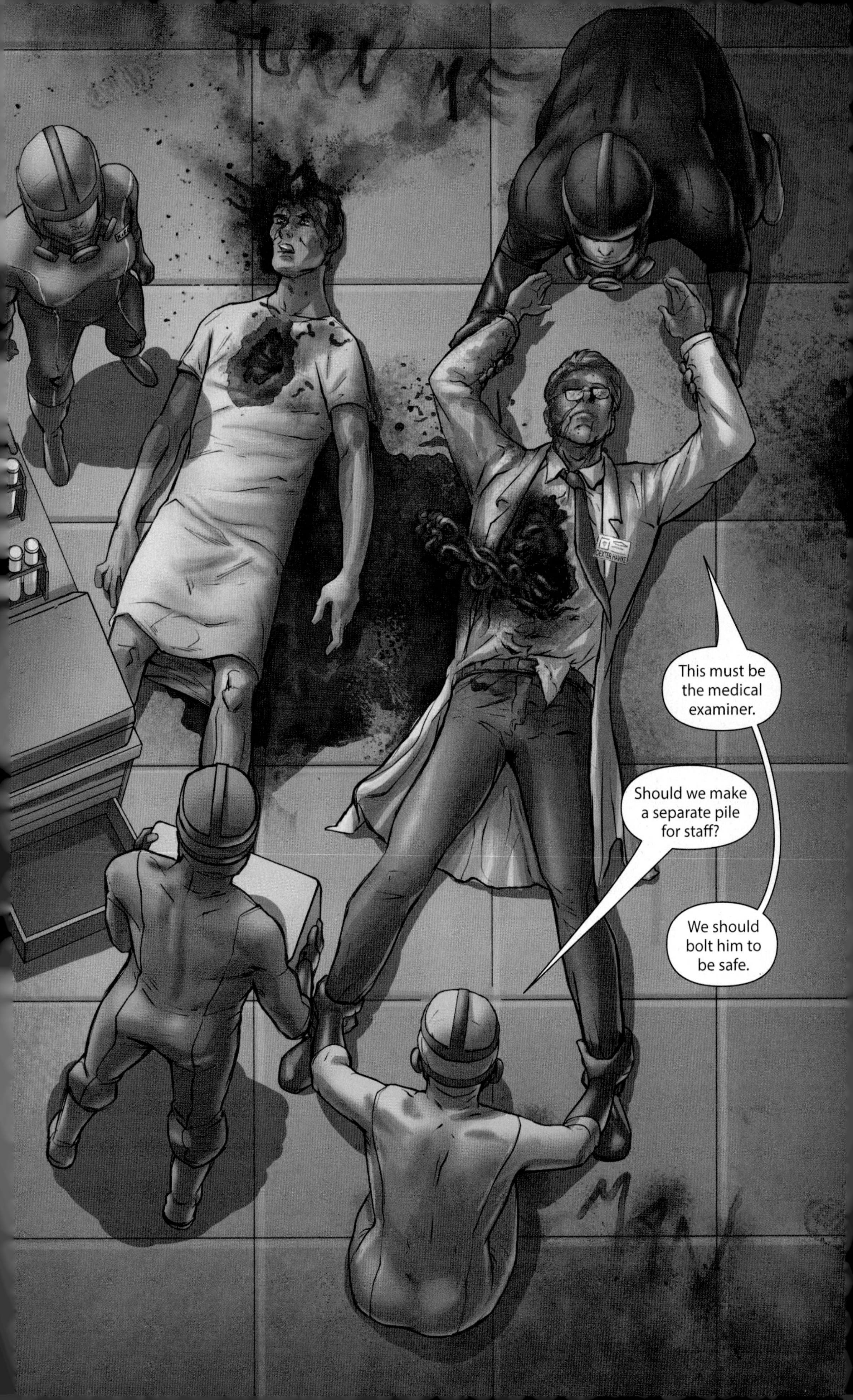
DEXTER HAWKE
This must be the medical examiner.
Should we make a separate pile for staff?
We should bolt him to be safe.

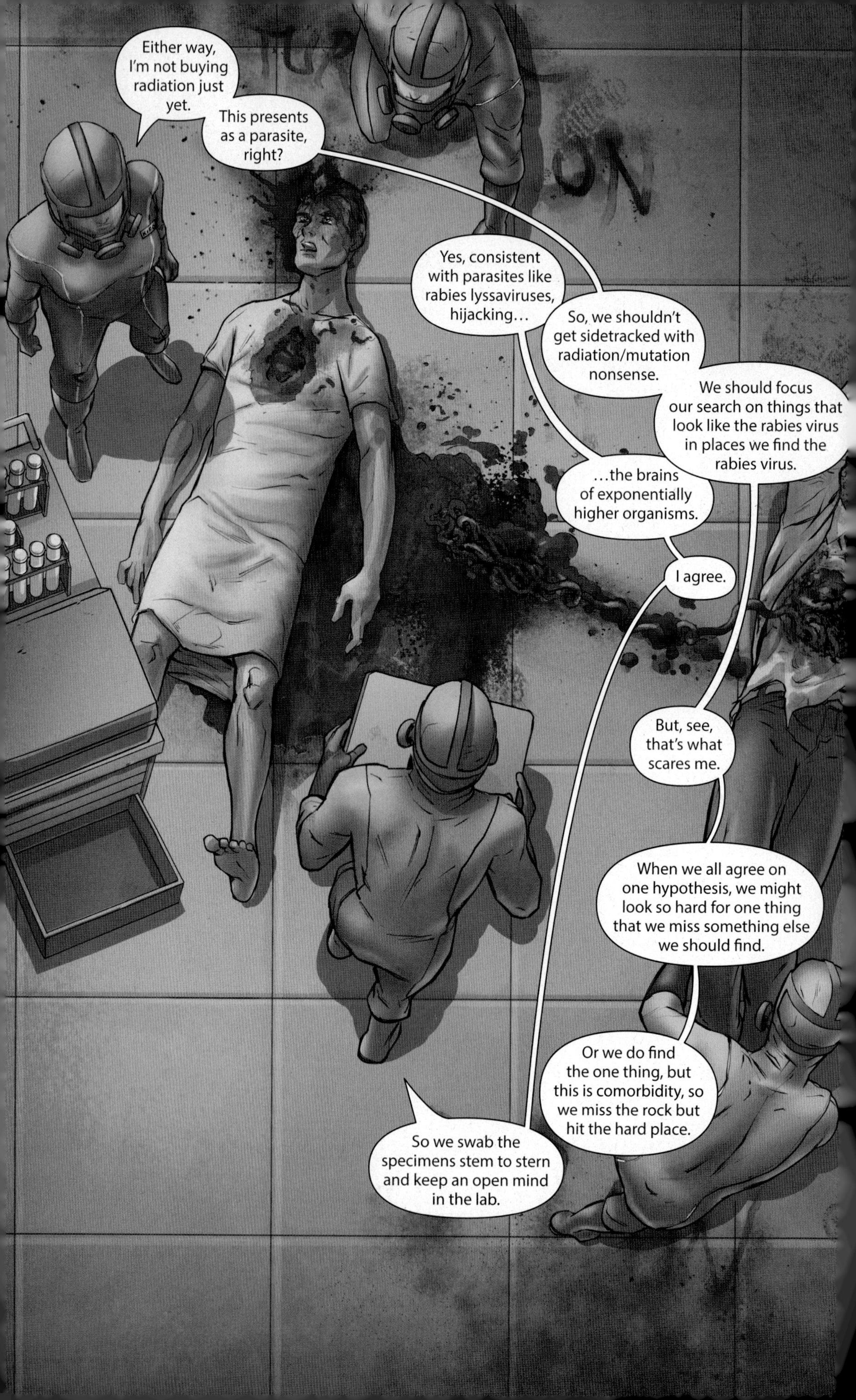
Either way, I'm not buying radiation just yet.
This presents as a parasite, right?
Yes, consistent with parasites like rabies lyssaviruses, hijacking…
So, we shouldn't get sidetracked with radiation/mutation nonsense.
We should focus our search on things that look like the rabies virus in places we find the rabies virus.
…the brains of exponentially higher organisms.
I agree.
But, see, that's what scares me.
When we all agree on one hypothesis, we might look so hard for one thing that we miss something else we should find.
Or we do find the one thing, but this is comorbidity, so we miss the rock but hit the hard place.
So we swab the specimens stem to stern and keep an open mind in the lab.

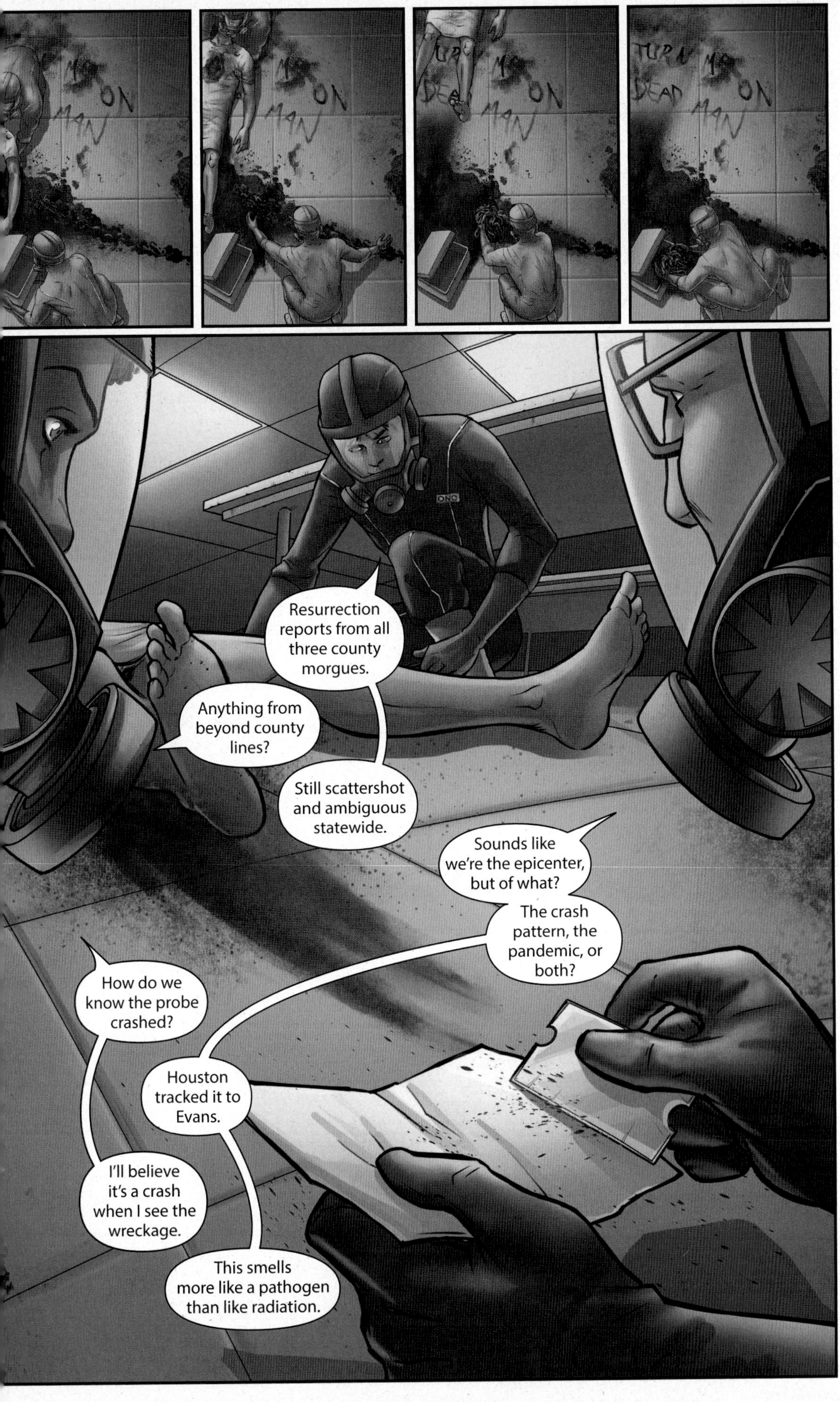

TURN ME ON DEAD MAN
Resurrection reports from all three county morgues.
Anything from beyond county lines?
Still scattershot and ambiguous statewide.
Sounds like we're the epicenter, but of what?
The crash pattern, the pandemic, or both?
How do we know the probe crashed?
Houston tracked it to Evans.
I'll believe it's a crash when I see the wreckage.
This smells more like a pathogen than like radiation.

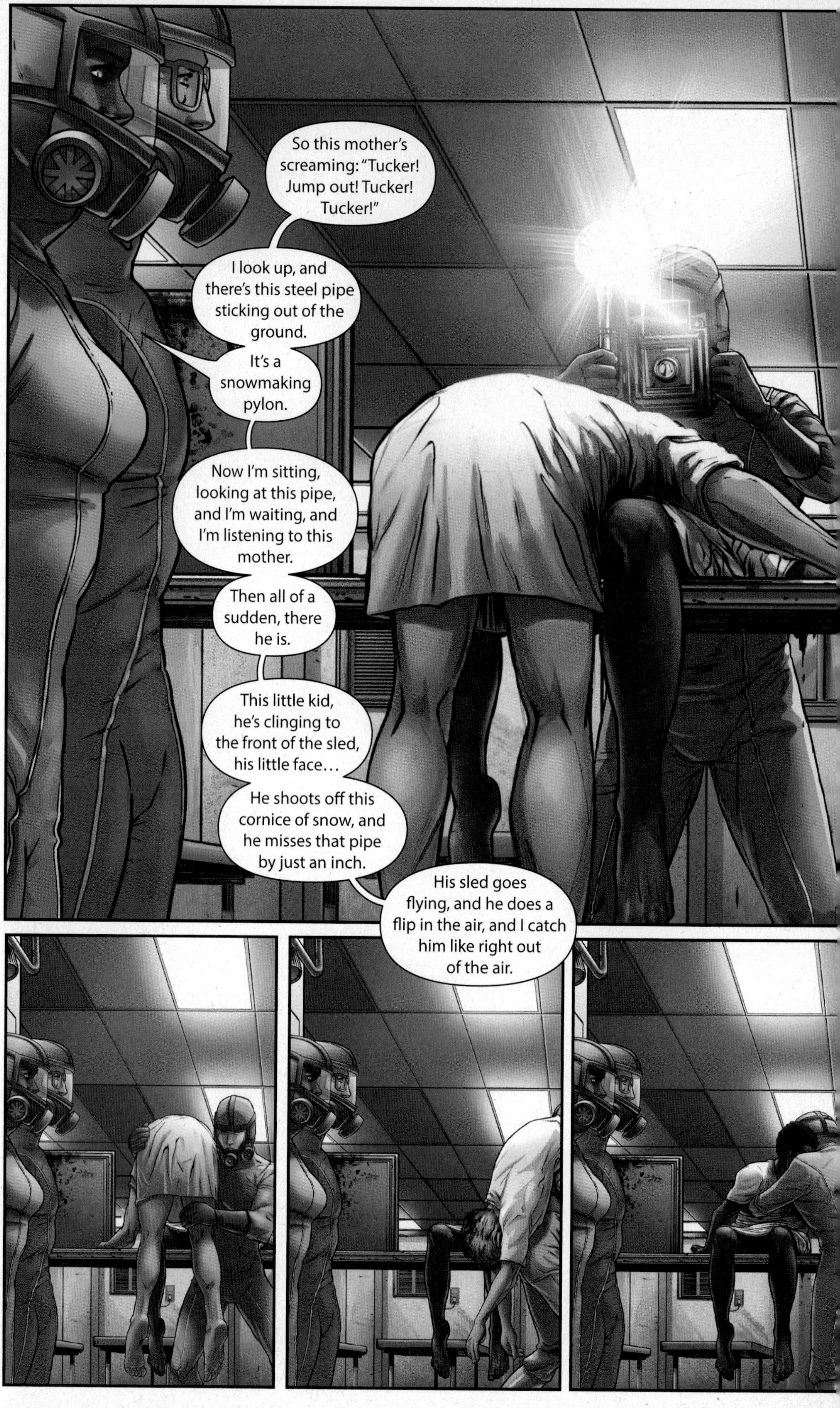
So this mother's screaming: "Tucker! Jump out! Tucker! Tucker!"
I look up, and there's this steel pipe sticking out of the ground.
It's a snowmaking pylon.
Now I'm sitting, looking at this pipe, and I'm waiting, and I'm listening to this mother.
Then all of a sudden, there he is.
This little kid, he's clinging to the front of the sled, his little face…
He shoots off this cornice of snow, and he misses that pipe by just an inch.
His sled goes flying, and he does a flip in the air, and I catch him like right out of the air.

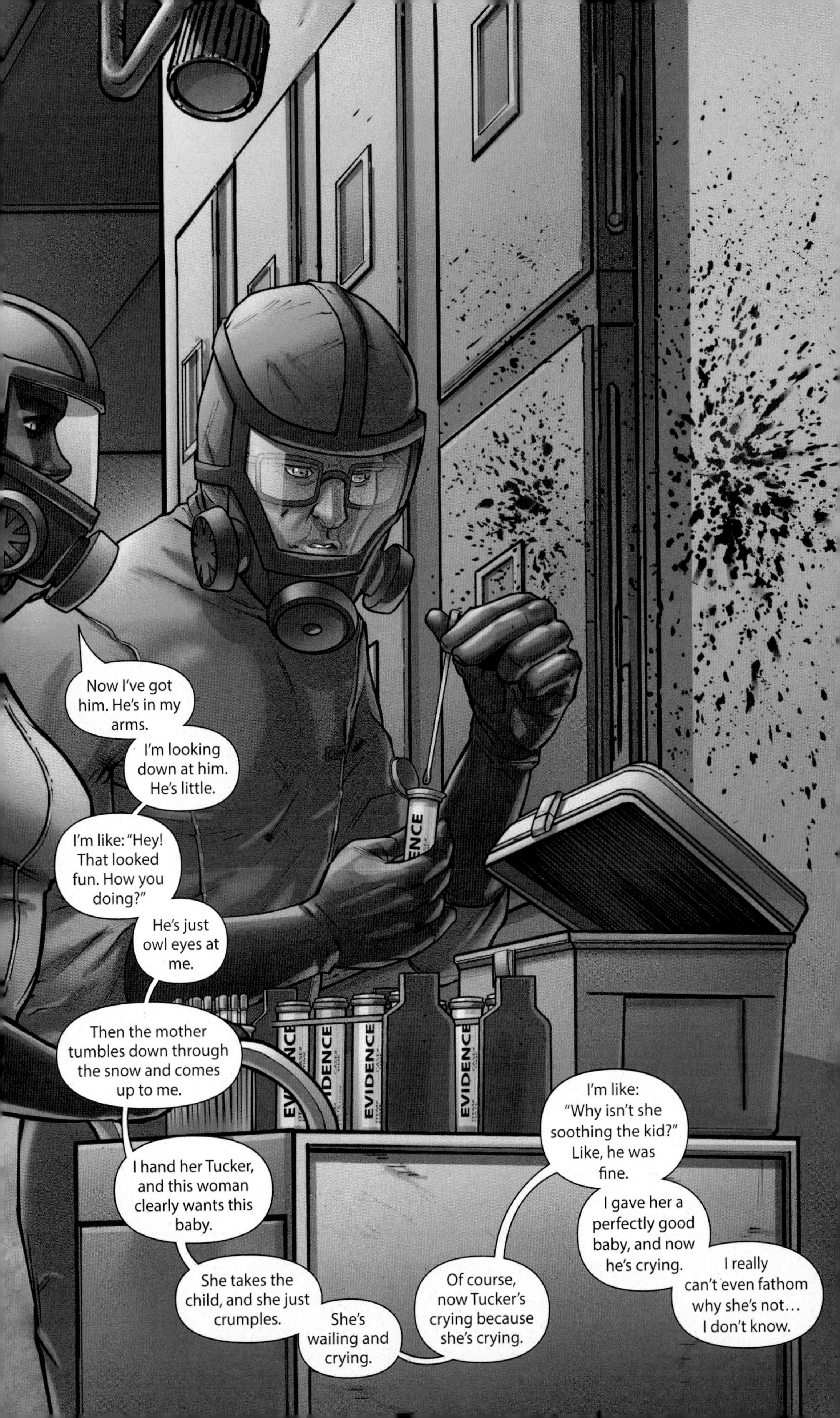
Now I've got him. He's in my arms.
I'm looking down at him. He's little.
I'm like: "Hey! That looked fun. How you doing?"
He's just owl eyes at me.
Then the mother tumbles down through the snow and comes up to me.
I hand her Tucker, and this woman clearly wants this baby.
She takes the child, and she just crumples.
She's wailing and crying.
Of course, now Tucker's crying because she's crying.
I'm like: "Why isn't she soothing the kid?" Like, he was fine.
I gave her a perfectly good baby, and now he's crying.
I really can't even fathom why she's not… I don't know.
EVIDENCE
EVIDENCE
EVIDENCE
EVIDENCE

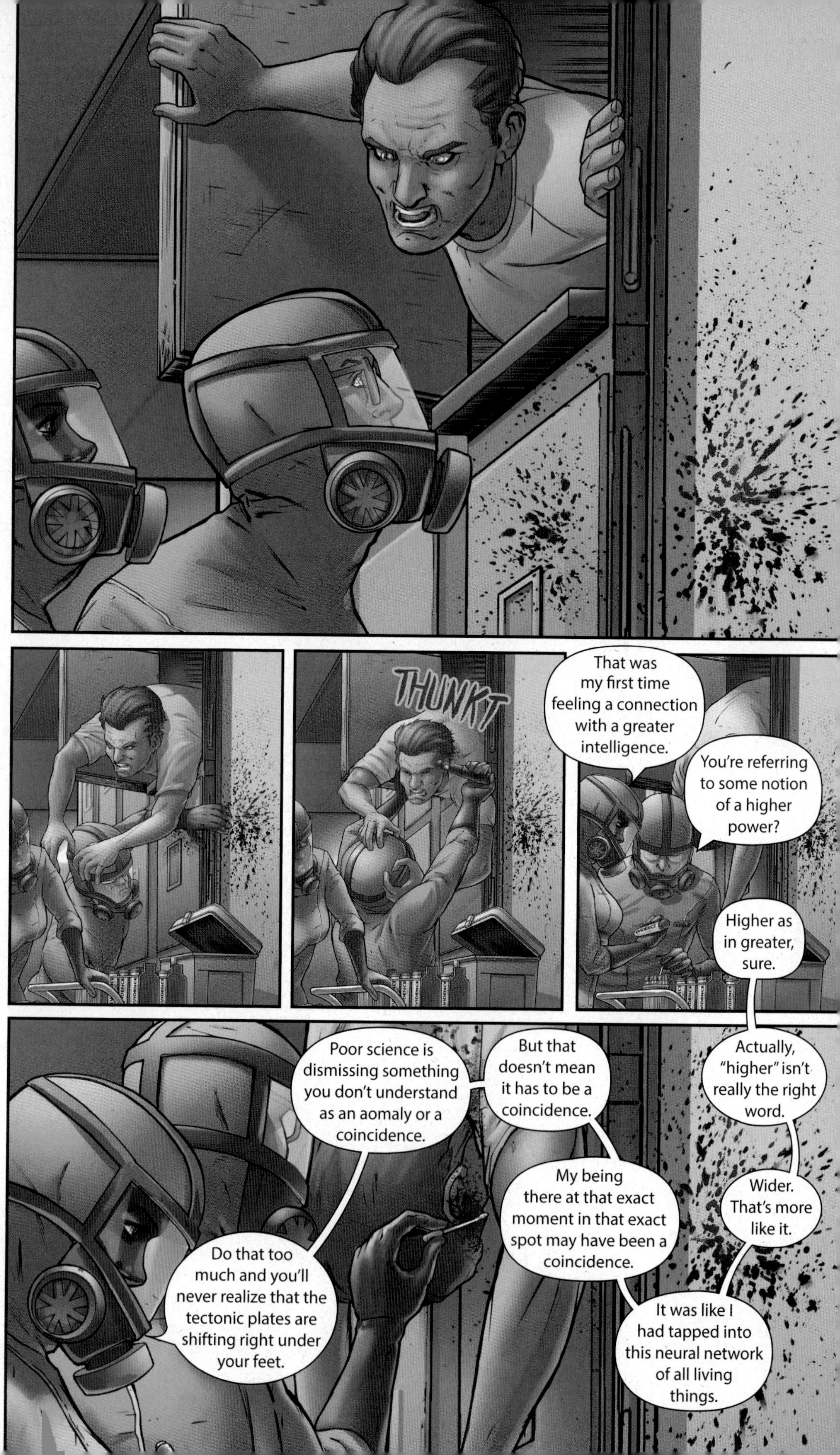

THUNKT
That was my first time feeling a connection with a greater intelligence.
You're referring to some notion of a higher power?
Higher as in greater, sure.
Actually, "higher" isn't really the right word.
Wider. That's more like it.
It was like I had tapped into this neural network of all living things.
My being there at that exact moment in that exact spot may have been a coincidence.
But that doesn't mean it has to be a coincidence.
Poor science is dismissing something you don't understand as an aomaly or a coincidence.
Do that too much and you'll never realize that the tectonic plates are shifting right under your feet.

1960s Movements

IVIL RIGHTS

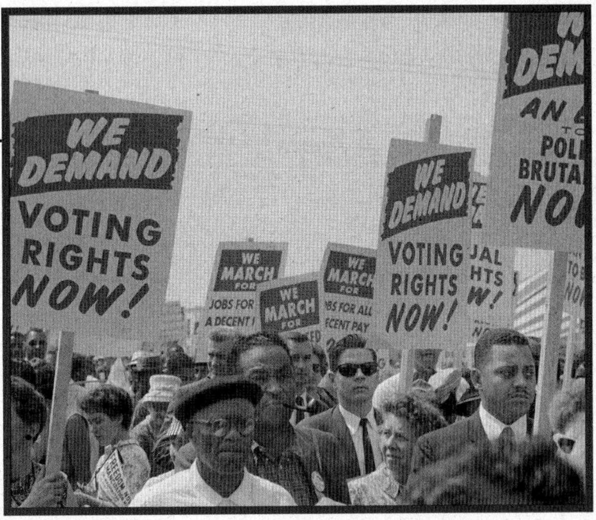
WE DEMAND
VOTING RIGHTS NOW!
WE MARCH FOR
JOBS FOR A DECENT
WE MARCH FOR
WE DEMAND
VOTING RIGHTS NOW!

OPULAR SLOGANS

'e shall overcome"

eep your eyes on the prize and hold on"

ay it loud: I'm Black and proud"

n't going to let nobody turn me round"

lack is beautiful"

lack power"

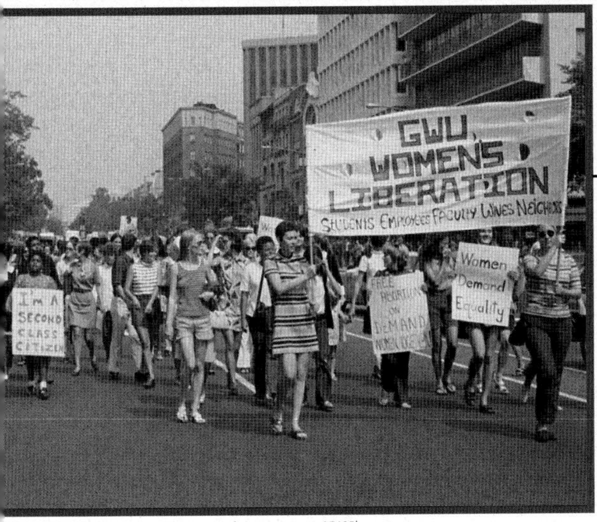
GWU WOMENS LIBERATION
STUDENTS EMPLOYEES FACULTY WIVES NEIGHBORS
Women Demand Equality
I'M A SECOND CLASS CITIZEN

lit: Warren K. Leffler, Library of Congress (LC-DIG-ppmsca-03425)

WOMEN'S LIBERATION

POPULAR SLOGANS

"The Personal is Political"

"Sisterhood is Powerful"

"Equal Pay for Equal Work"

"Women Demand Equality"

"We're not beautiful. We're not ugly. We're angry."

NTI WAR

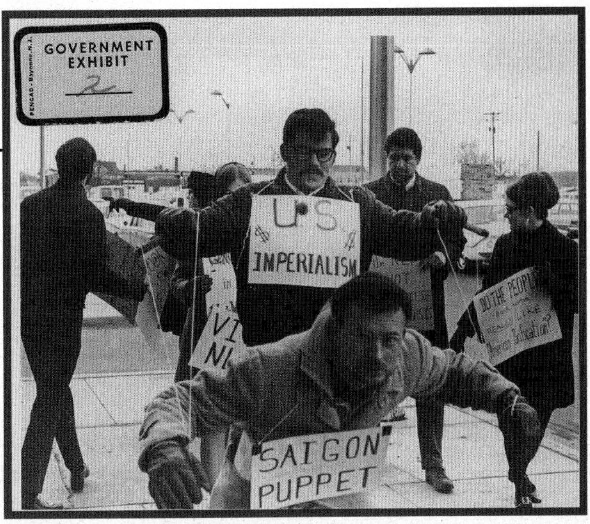
GOVERNMENT EXHIBIT
US
IMPERIALISM
SAIGON PUPPET

OPULAR SLOGANS

ey, hey, LBJ,
ow many kids did you kill today?"

raft beer, not boys"

ell no, we won't go"

lake love, not war"

ighteen today, dead tomorrow"

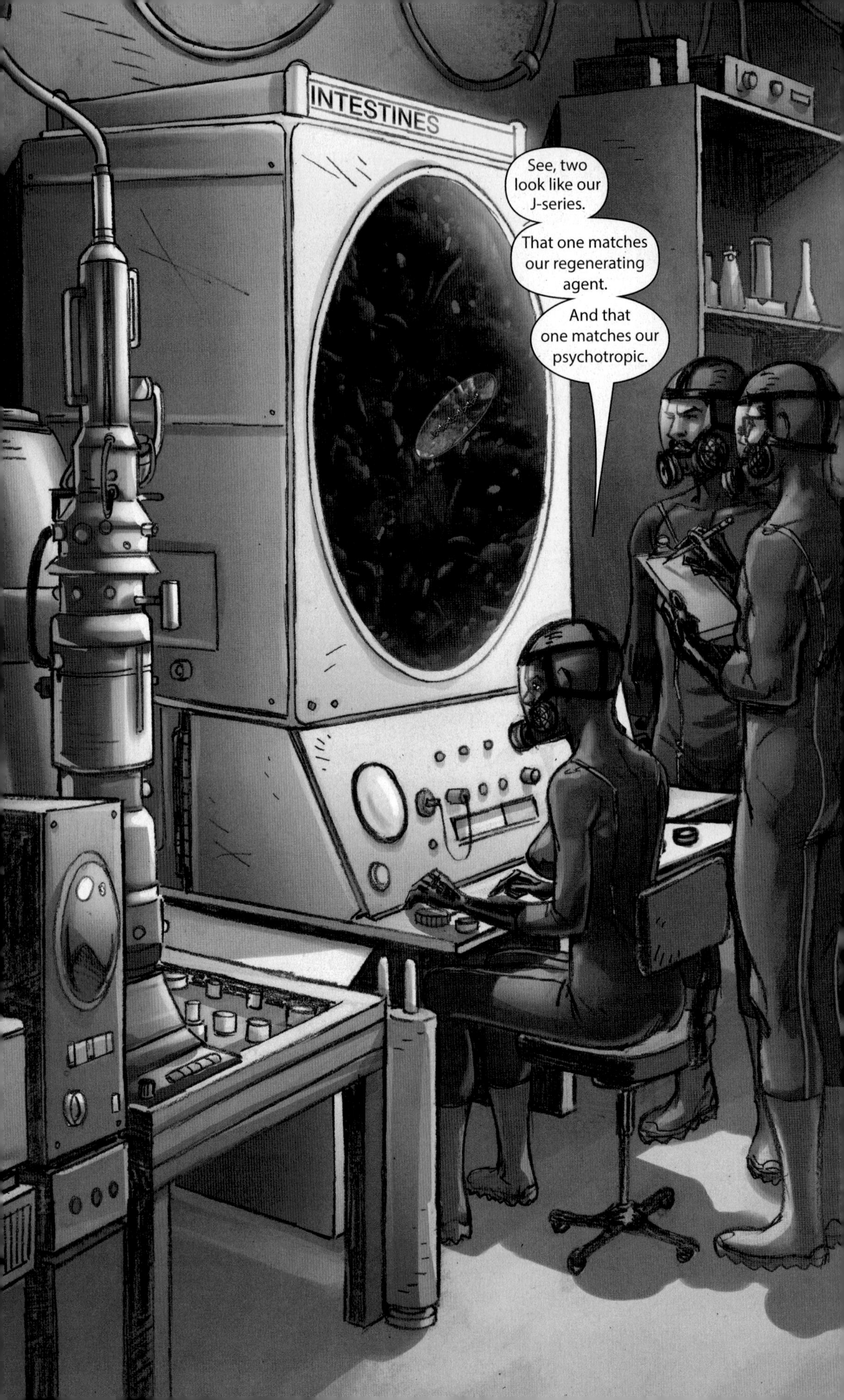
INTESTINES
See, two look like our J-series.
That one matches our regenerating agent.
And that one matches our psychotropic.

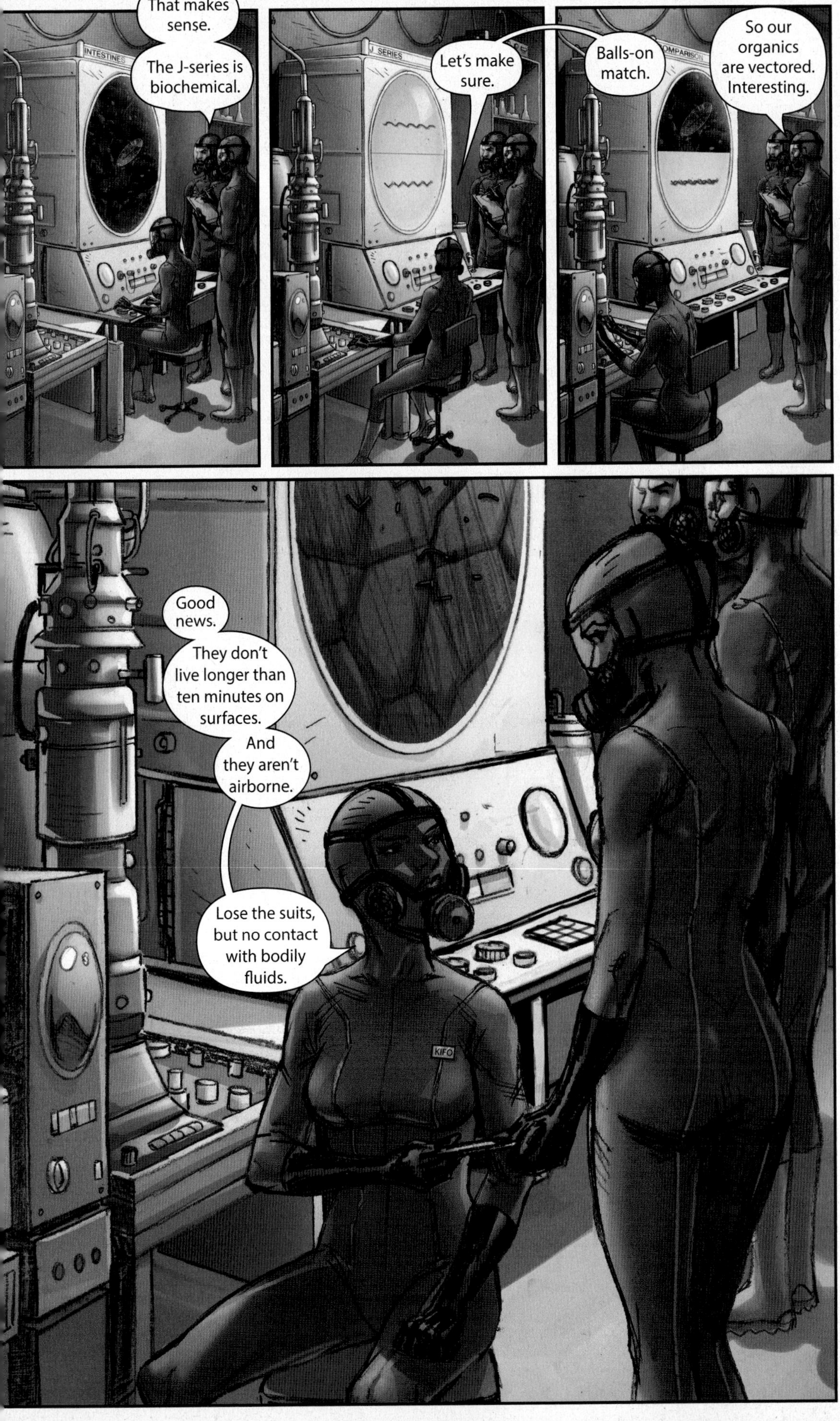
That makes sense.
The J-series is biochemical.
INTESTINES
Let's make sure.
J SERIES
Balls-on match.
So our organics are vectored. Interesting.
Good news.
They don't live longer than ten minutes on surfaces.
And they aren't airborne.
Lose the suits, but no contact with bodily fluids.
KIFO

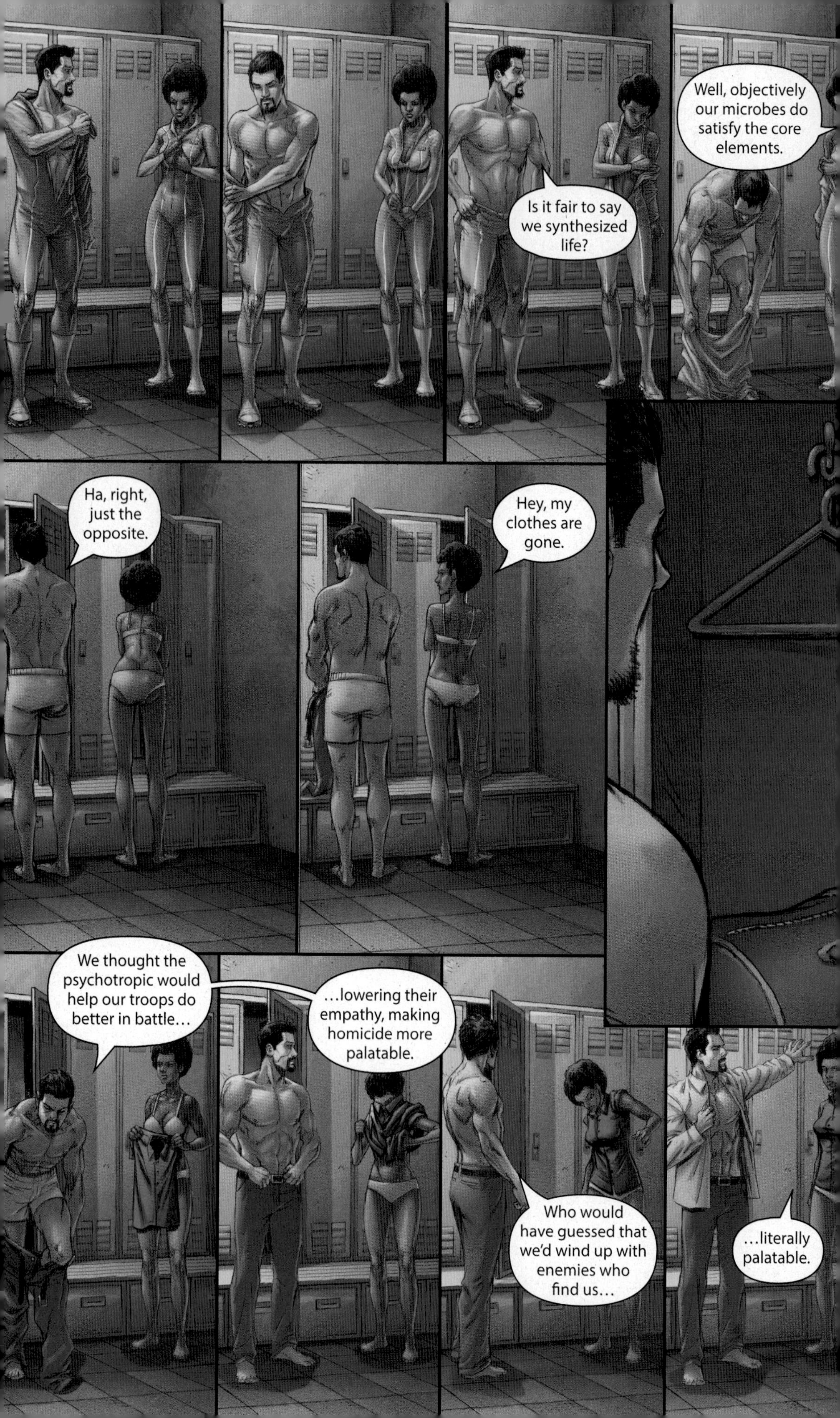
Is it fair to say we synthesized life?
Well, objectively our microbes do satisfy the core elements.
Ha, right, just the opposite.
Hey, my clothes are gone.
We thought the psychotropic would help our troops do better in battle…
…lowering their empathy, making homicide more palatable.
Who would have guessed that we'd wind up with enemies who find us…
…literally palatable.

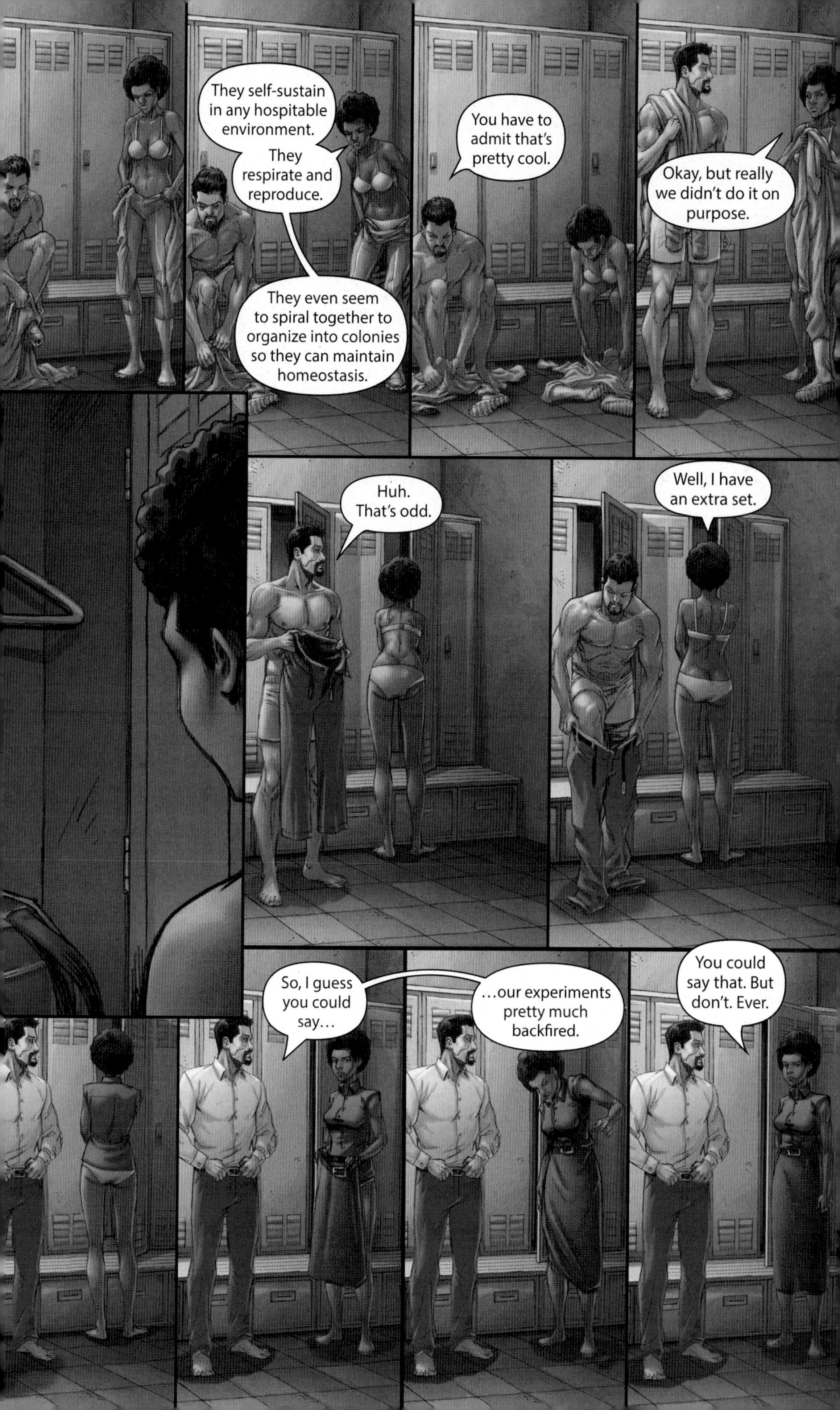
They self-sustain in any hospitable environment.
They respirate and reproduce.
They even seem to spiral together to organize into colonies so they can maintain homeostasis.
You have to admit that's pretty cool.
Okay, but really we didn't do it on purpose.
Huh. That's odd.
Well, I have an extra set.
So, I guess you could say…
…our experiments pretty much backfired.
You could say that. But don't. Ever.

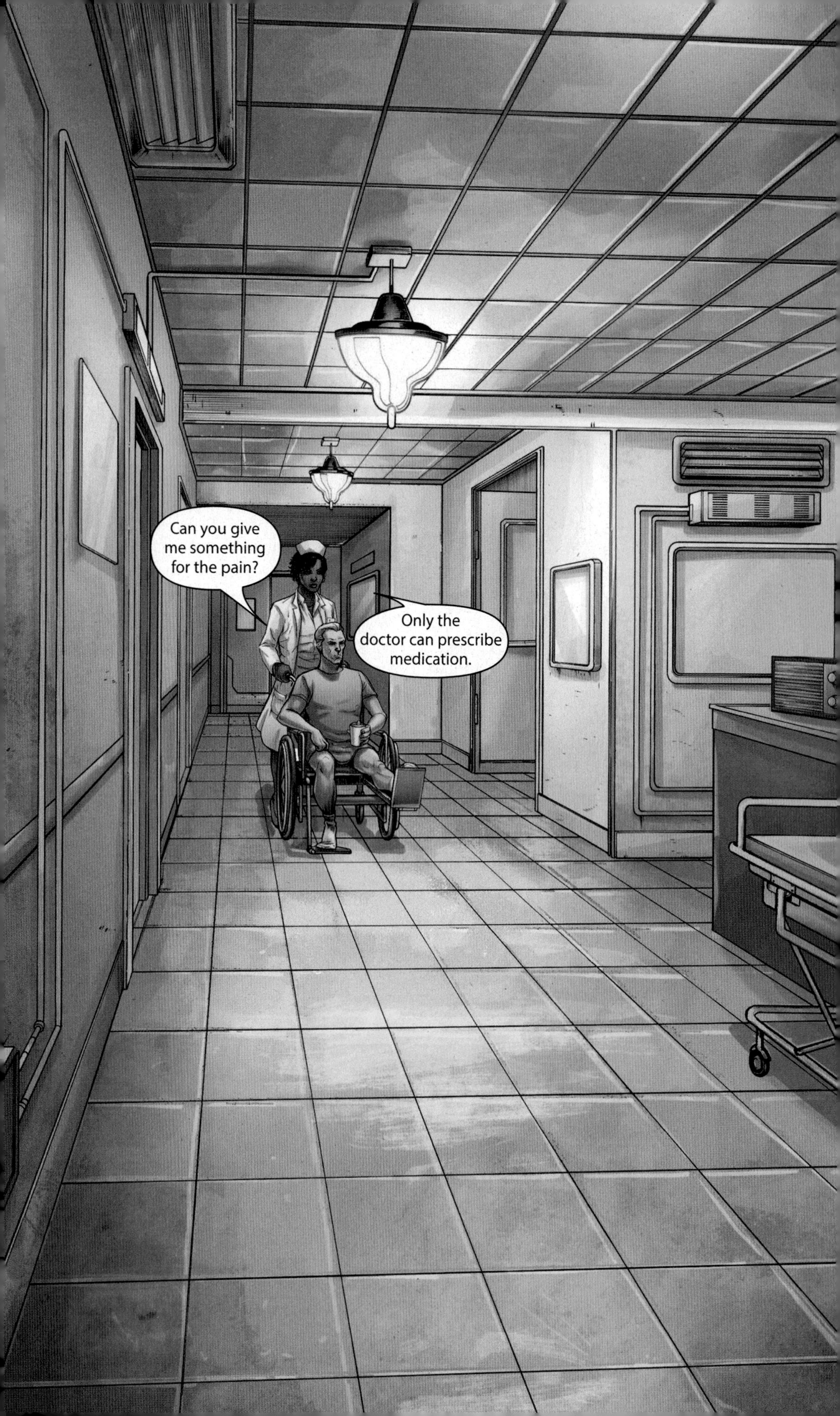
Can you give me something for the pain?
Only the doctor can prescribe medication.

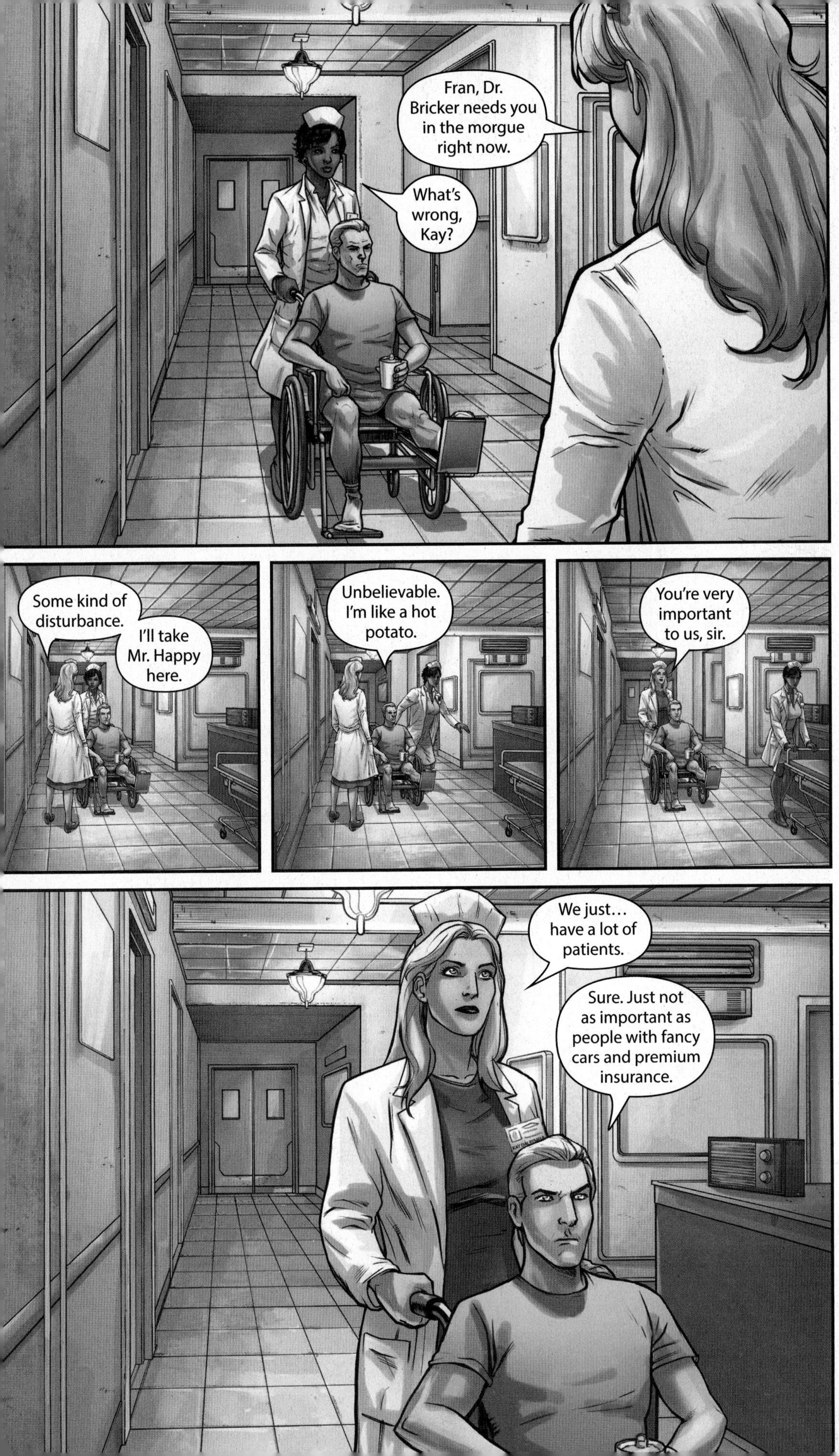
Fran, Dr. Bricker needs you in the morgue right now.
What's wrong, Kay?
Some kind of disturbance.
I'll take Mr. Happy here.
Unbelievable. I'm like a hot potato.
You're very important to us, sir.
We just… have a lot of patients.
Sure. Just not as important as people with fancy cars and premium insurance.

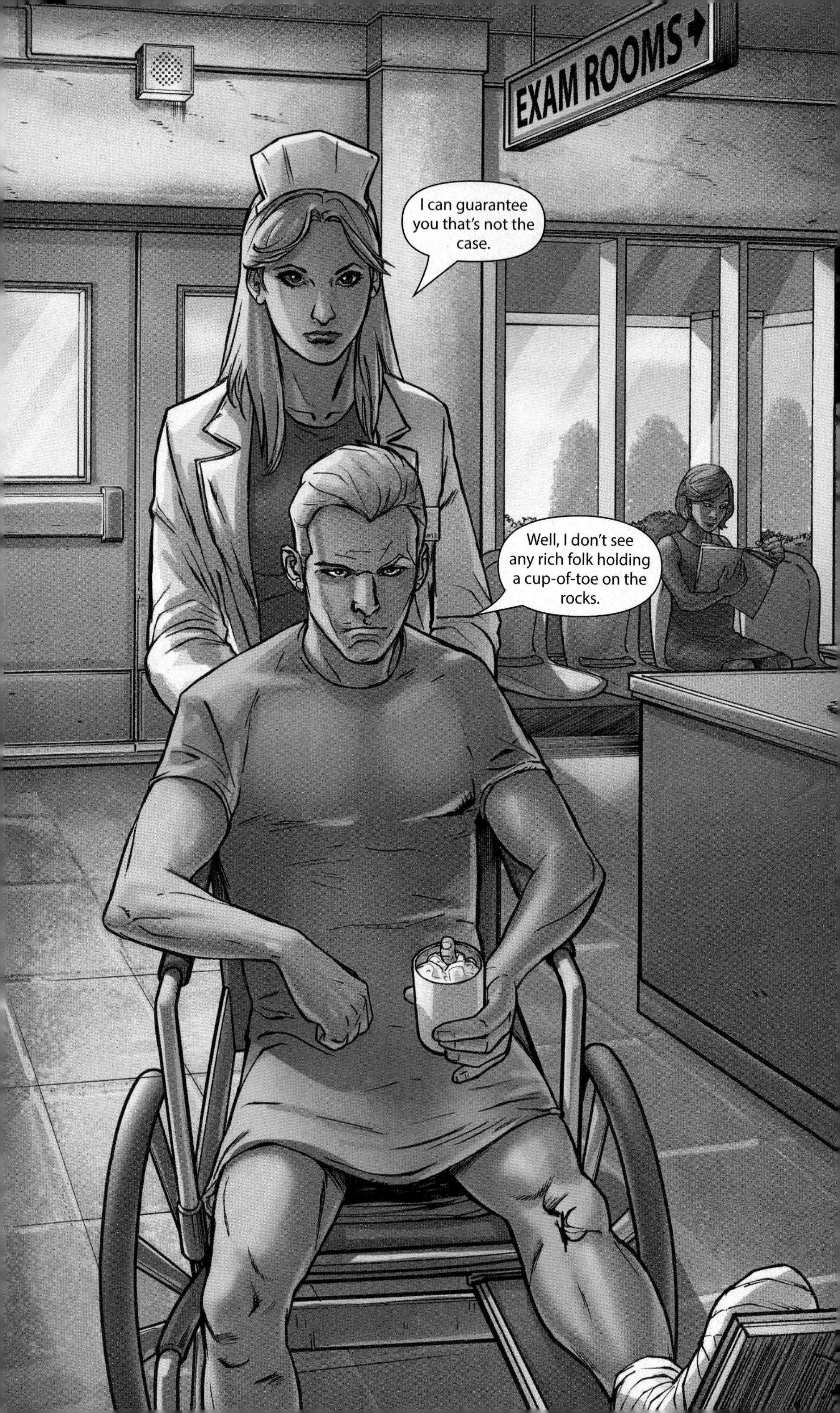
EXAM ROOMS
I can guarantee you that's not the case.
Well, I don't see any rich folk holding a cup-of-toe on the rocks.

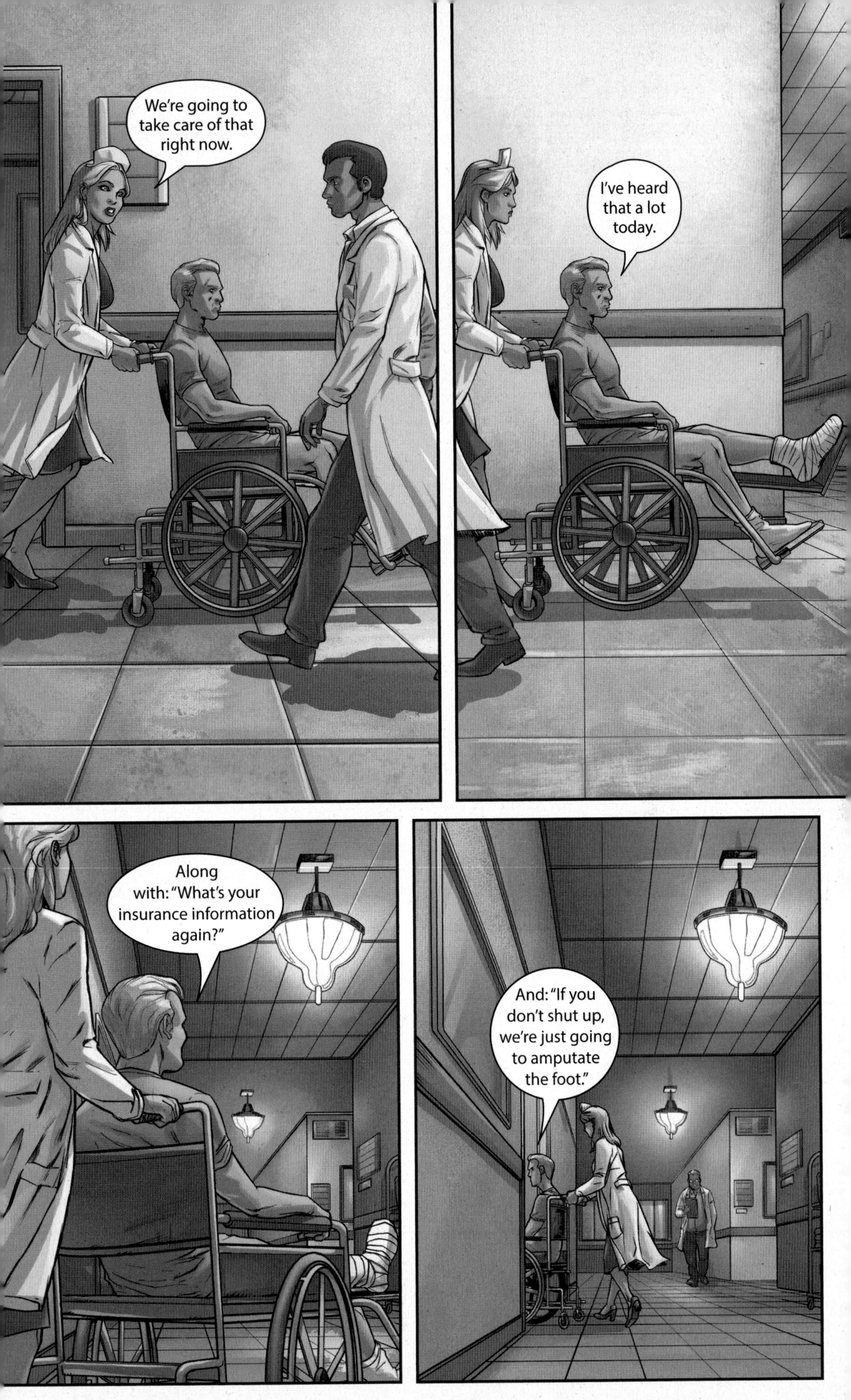
We're going to take care of that right now.
I've heard that a lot today.
Along with: "What's your insurance information again?"
And: "If you don't shut up, we're just going to amputate the foot."

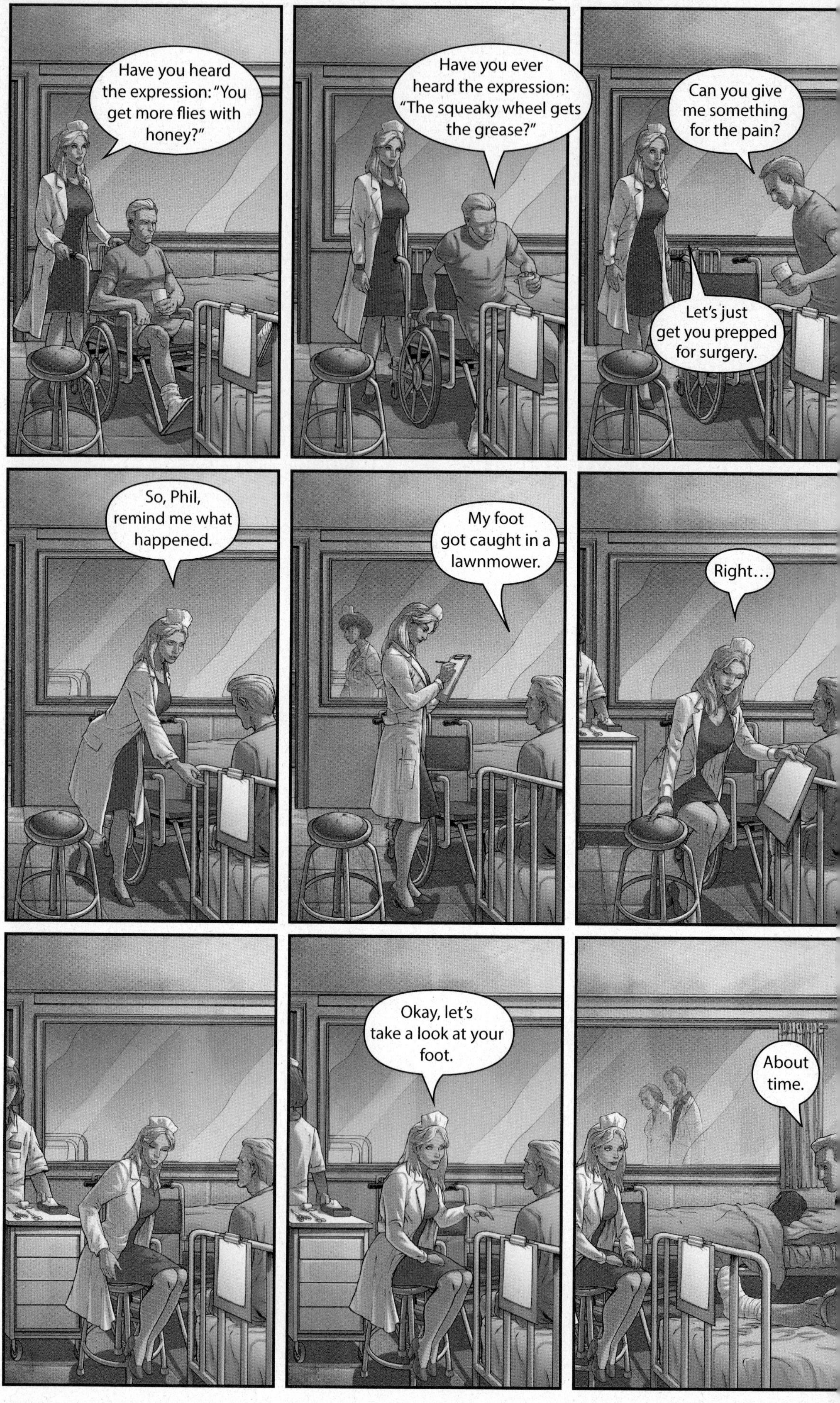
Have you heard the expression: "You get more flies with honey?"
Have you ever heard the expression: "The squeaky wheel gets the grease?"
Can you give me something for the pain?
Let's just get you prepped for surgery.
So, Phil, remind me what happened.
My foot got caught in a lawnmower.
Right…
Okay, let's take a look at your foot.
About time.

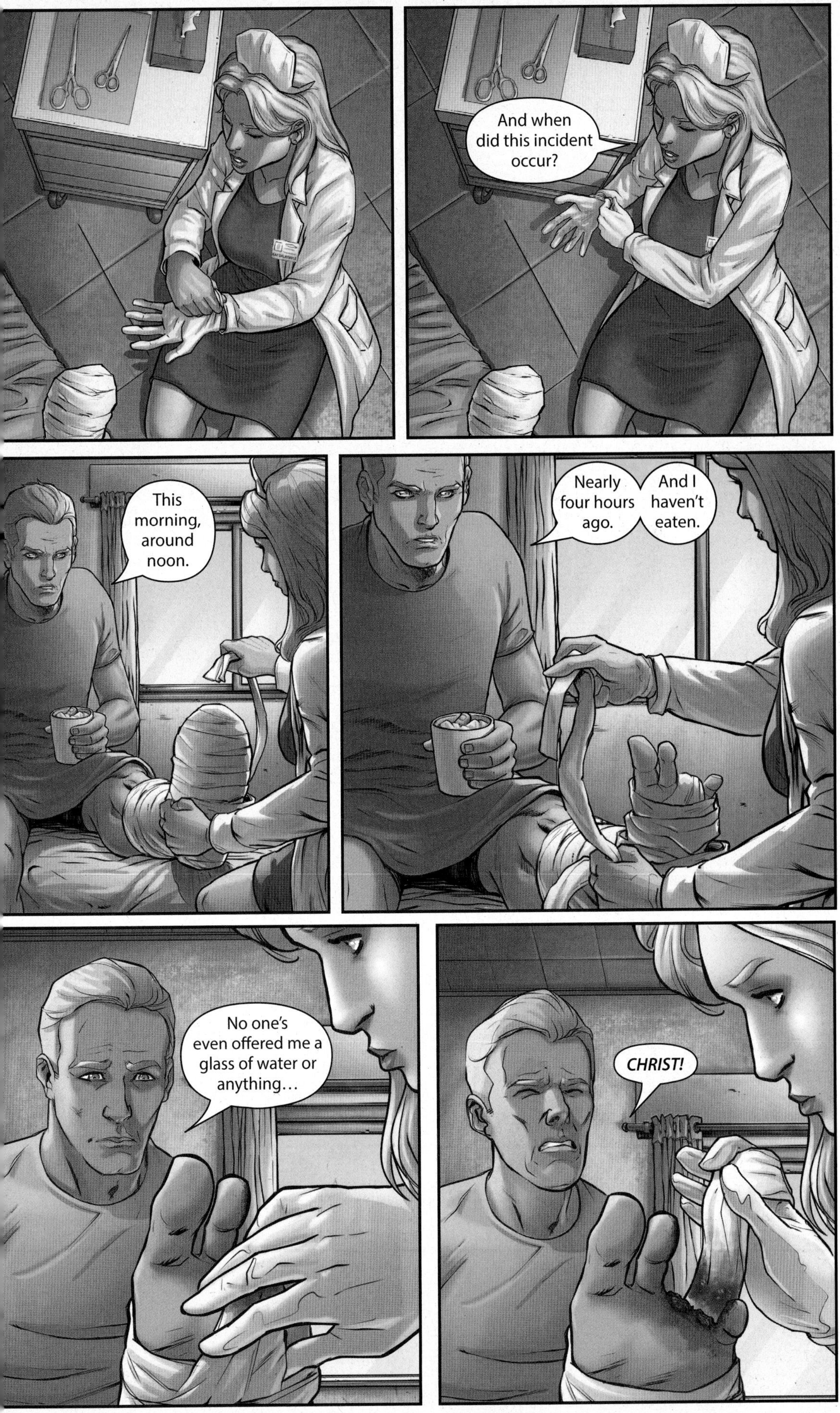
And when did this incident occur?
This morning, around noon.
Nearly four hours ago.
And I haven't eaten.
No one's even offered me a glass of water or anything…
CHRIST!

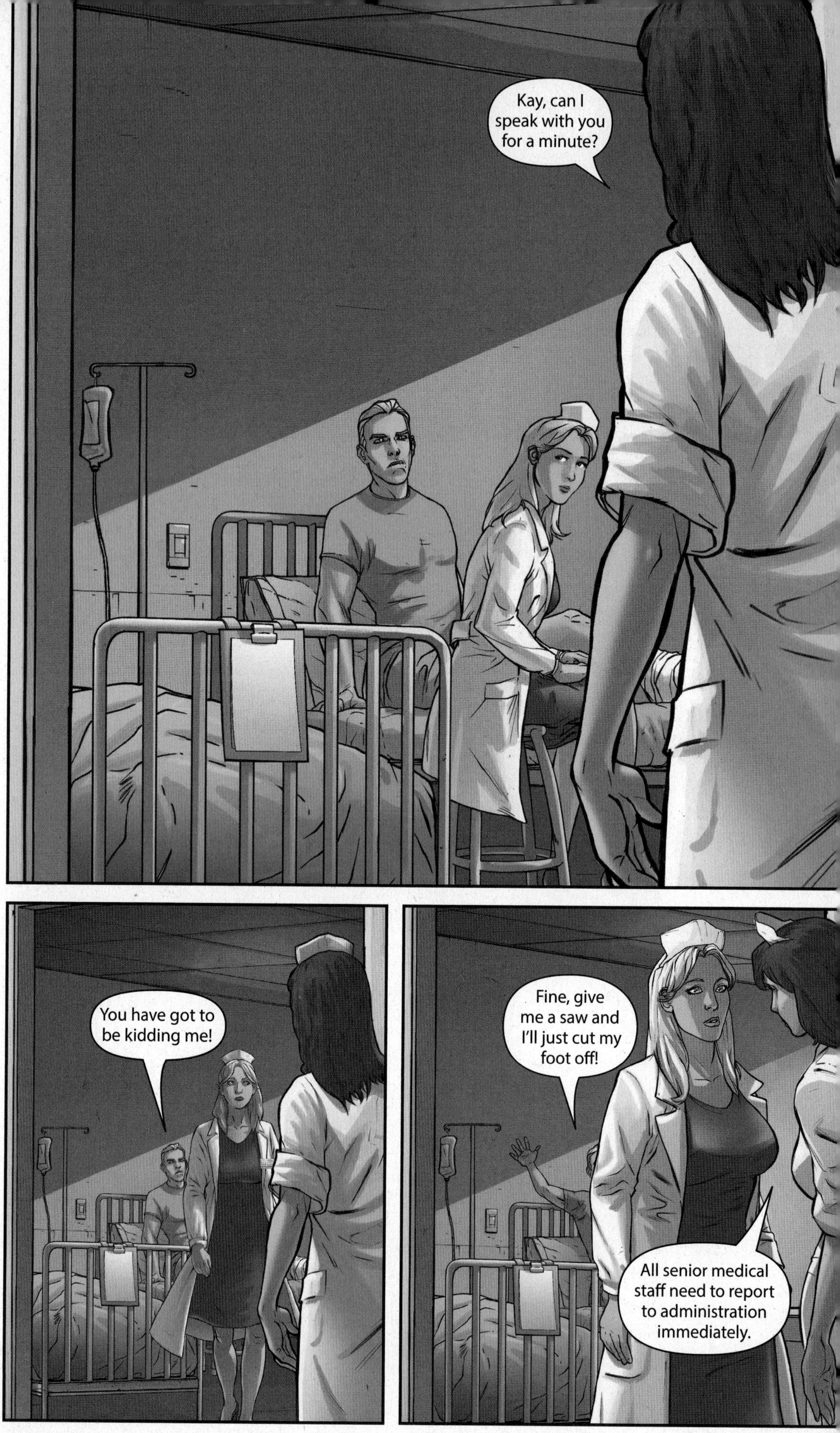
Kay, can I speak with you for a minute?
You have got to be kidding me!
Fine, give me a saw and I'll just cut my foot off!
All senior medical staff need to report to administration immediately.

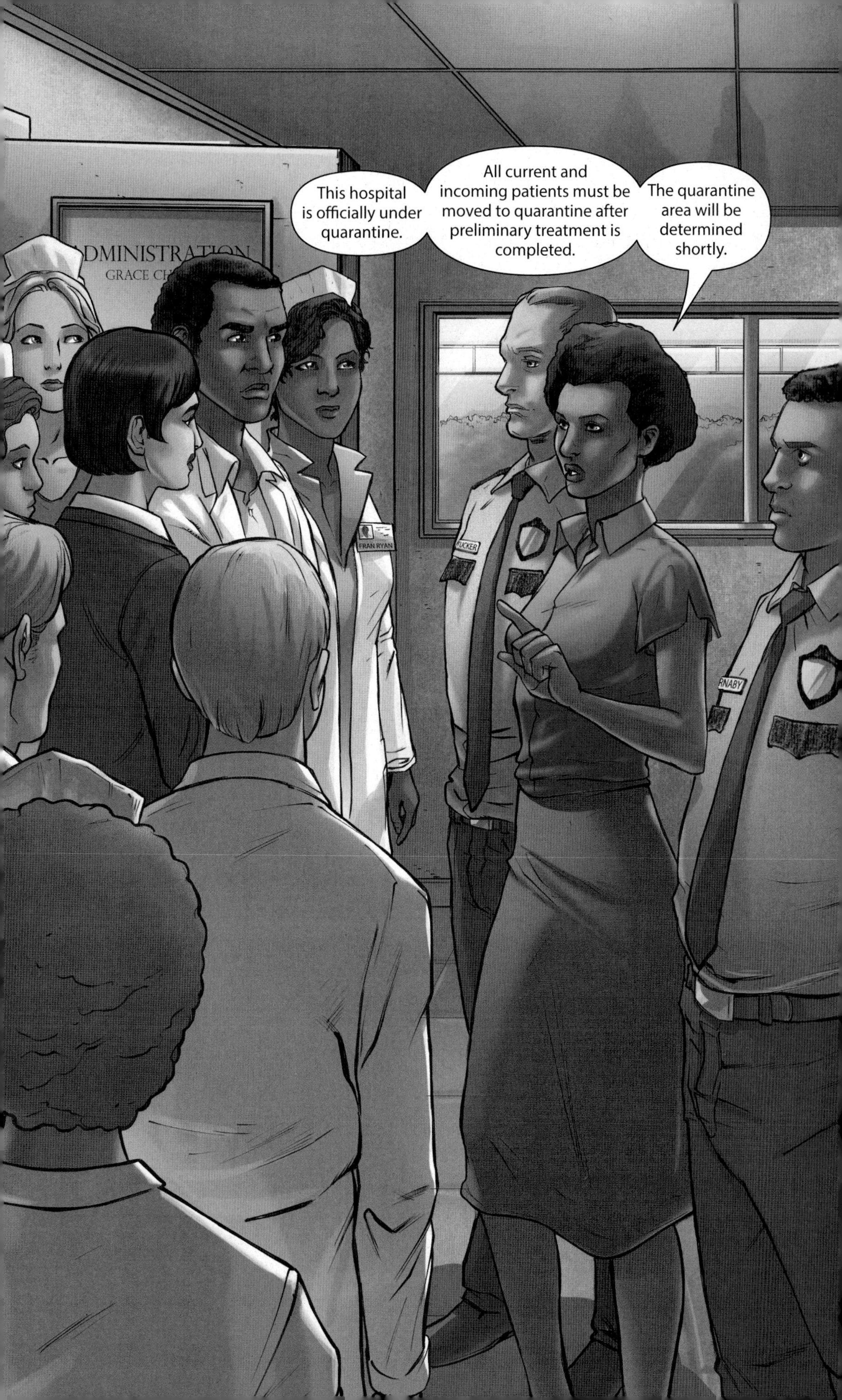
ADMINISTRATION
FRAN RYAN
This hospital is officially under quarantine.
All current and incoming patients must be moved to quarantine after preliminary treatment is completed.
The quarantine area will be determined shortly.

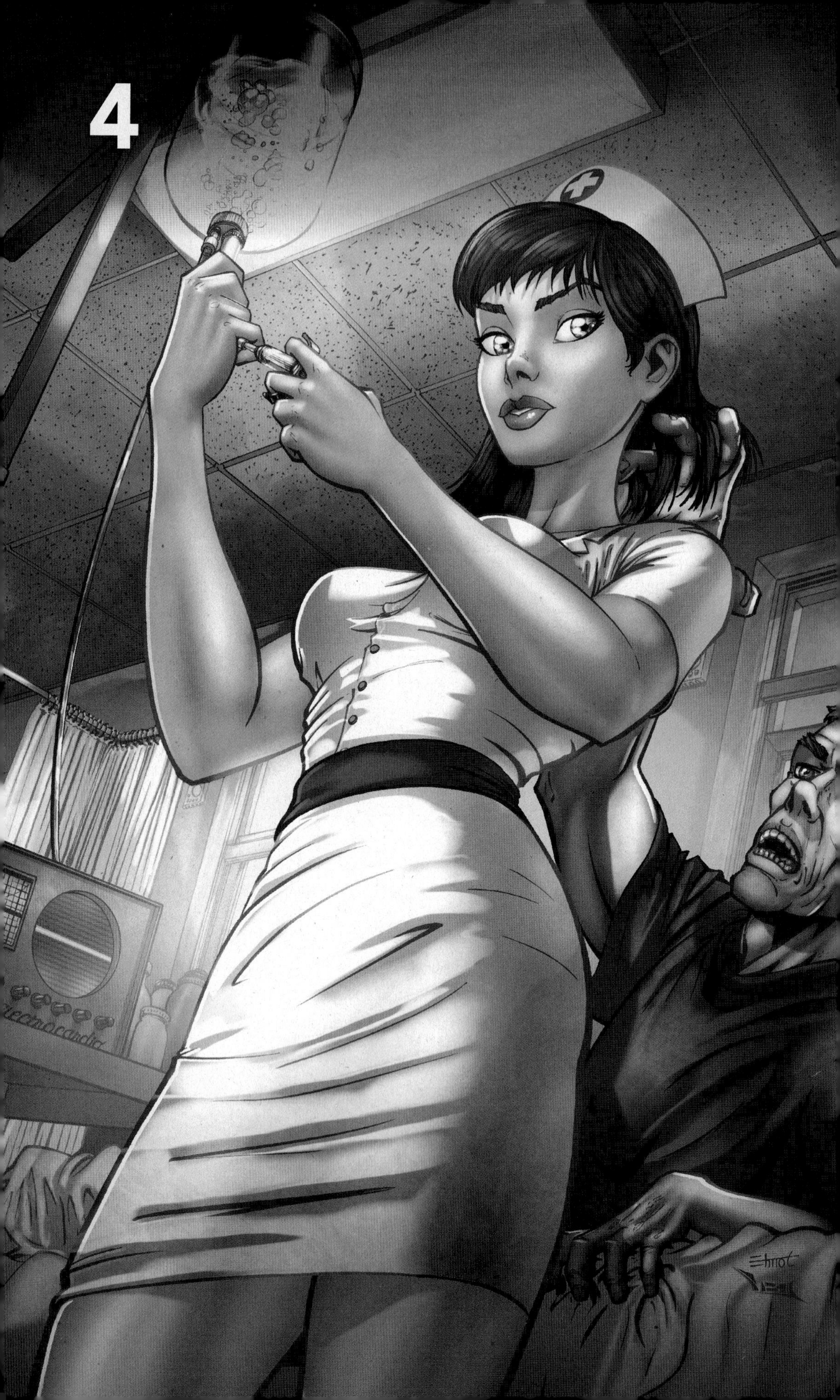
4

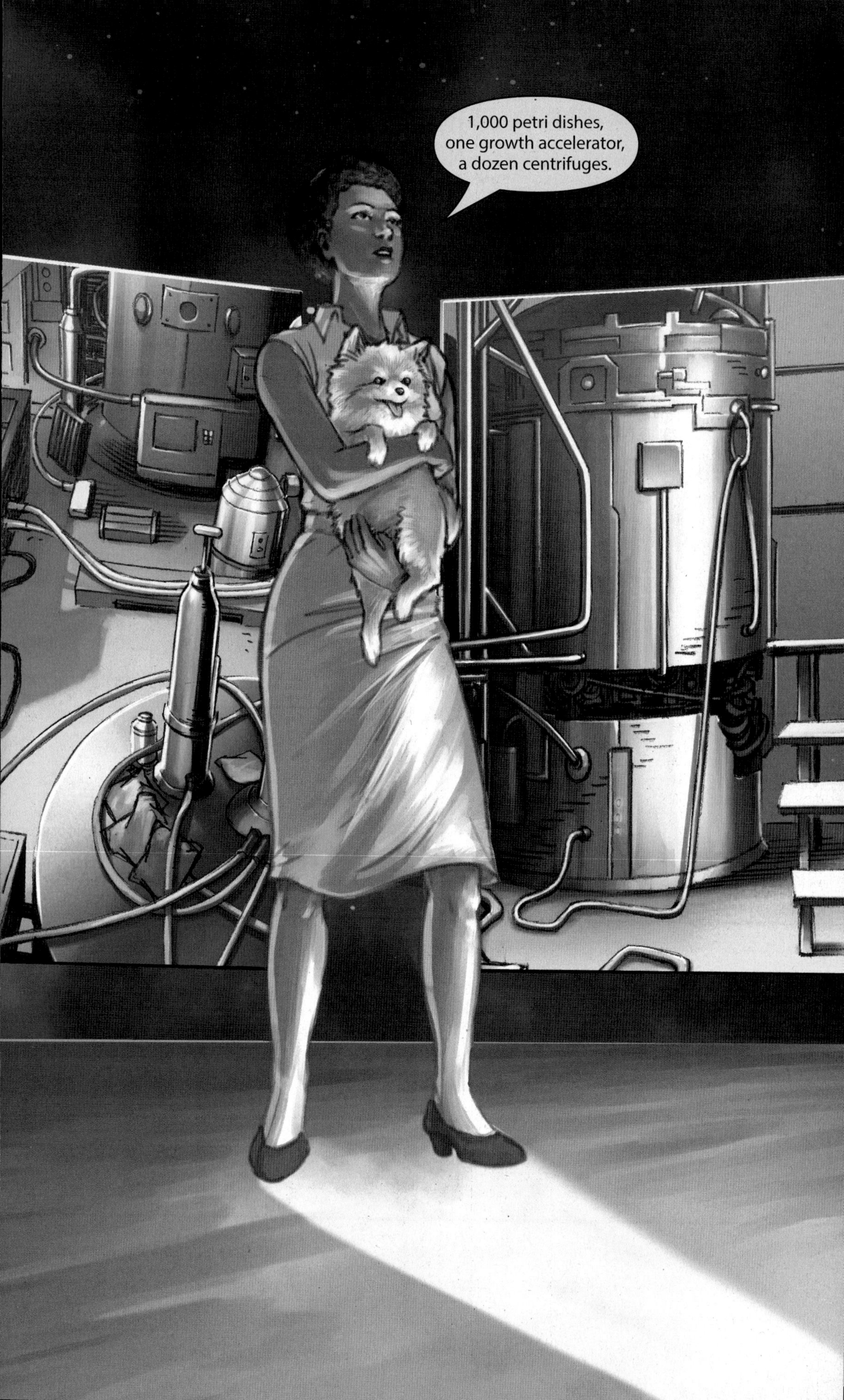
1,000 petri dishes, one growth accelerator, a dozen centrifuges.

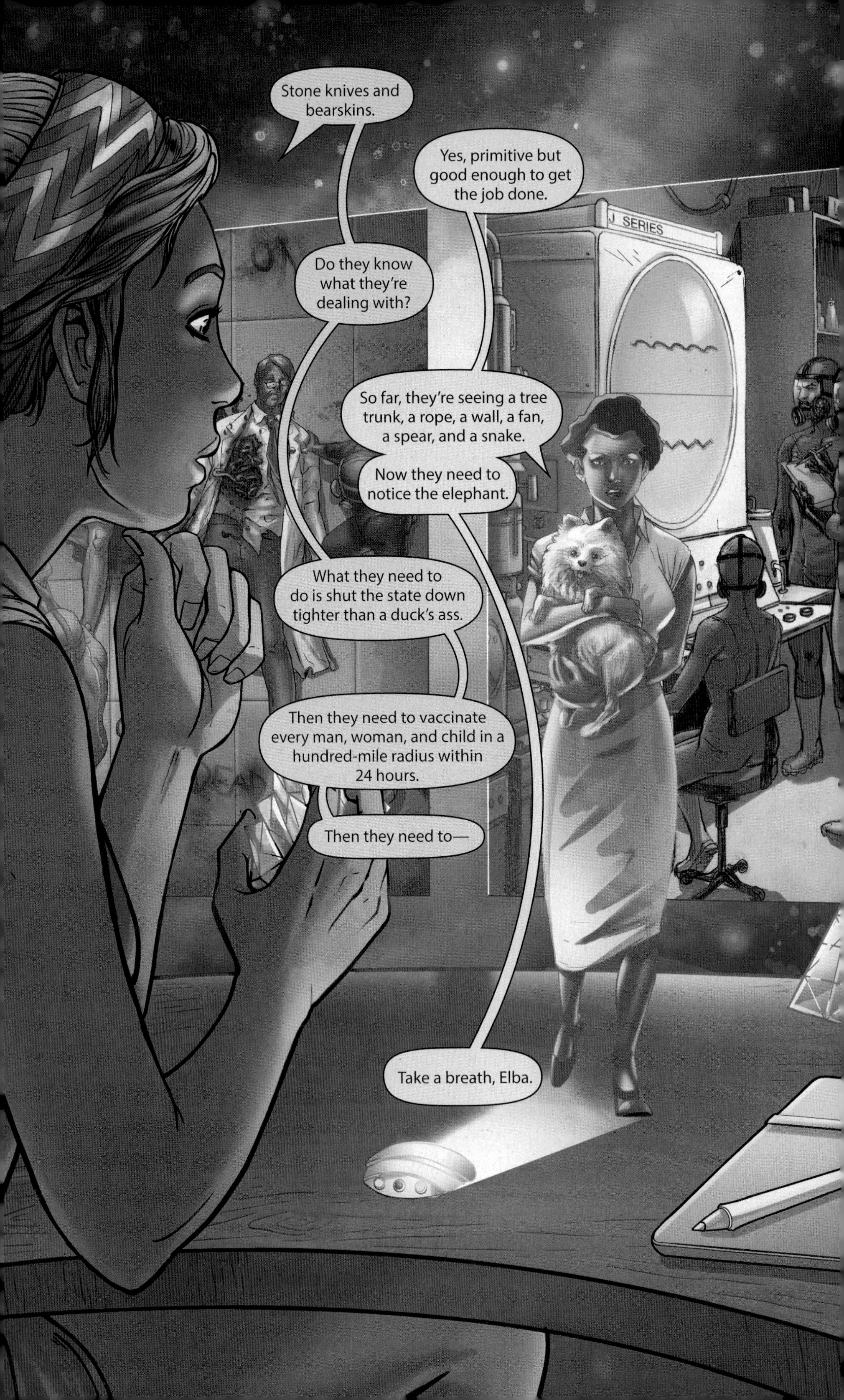

Stone knives and bearskins.
Yes, primitive but good enough to get the job done.
J SERIES
Do they know what they're dealing with?
So far, they're seeing a tree trunk, a rope, a wall, a fan, a spear, and a snake.
Now they need to notice the elephant.
What they need to do is shut the state down tighter than a duck's ass.
Then they need to vaccinate every man, woman, and child in a hundred-mile radius within 24 hours.
Then they need to—
Take a breath, Elba.

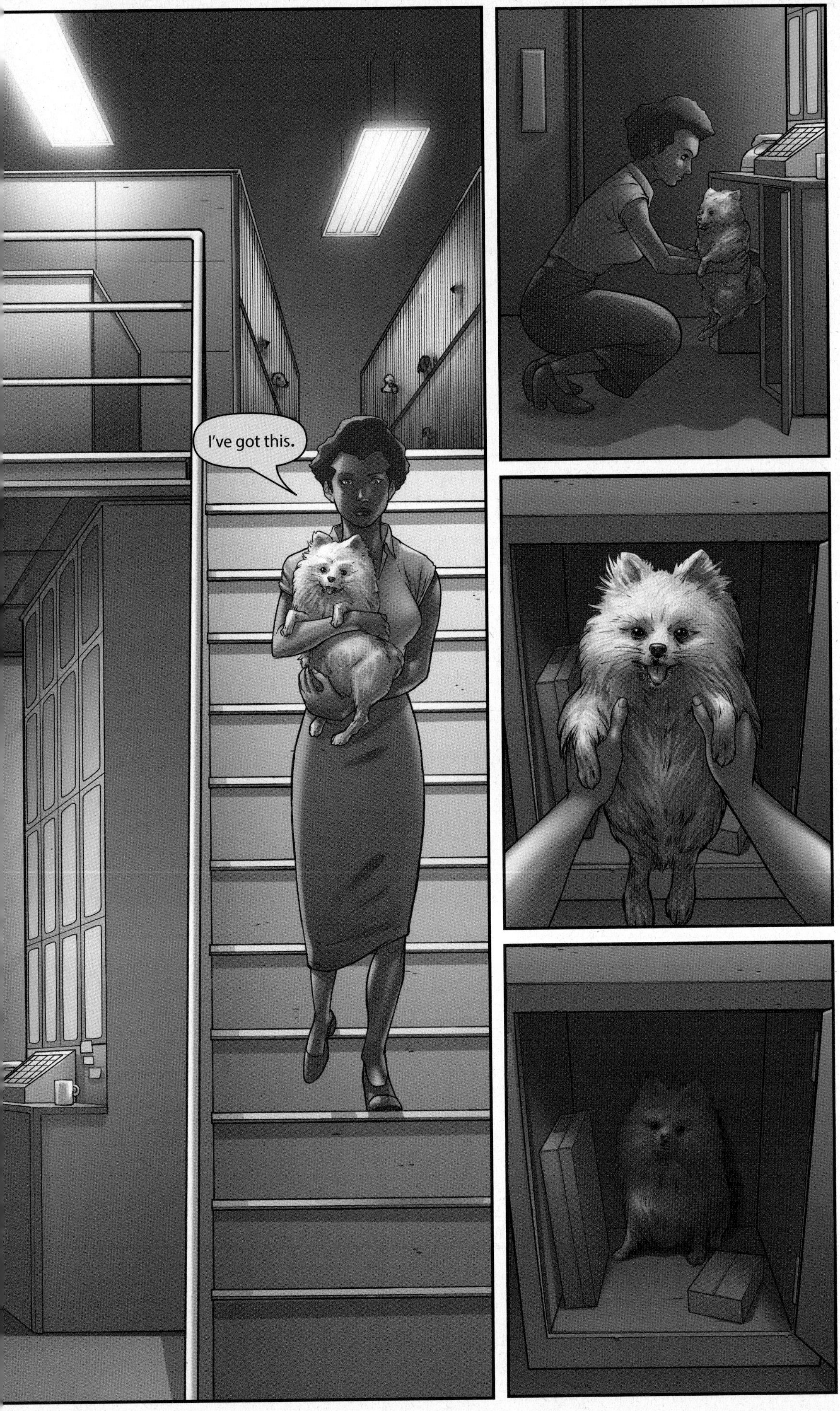
I've got this.

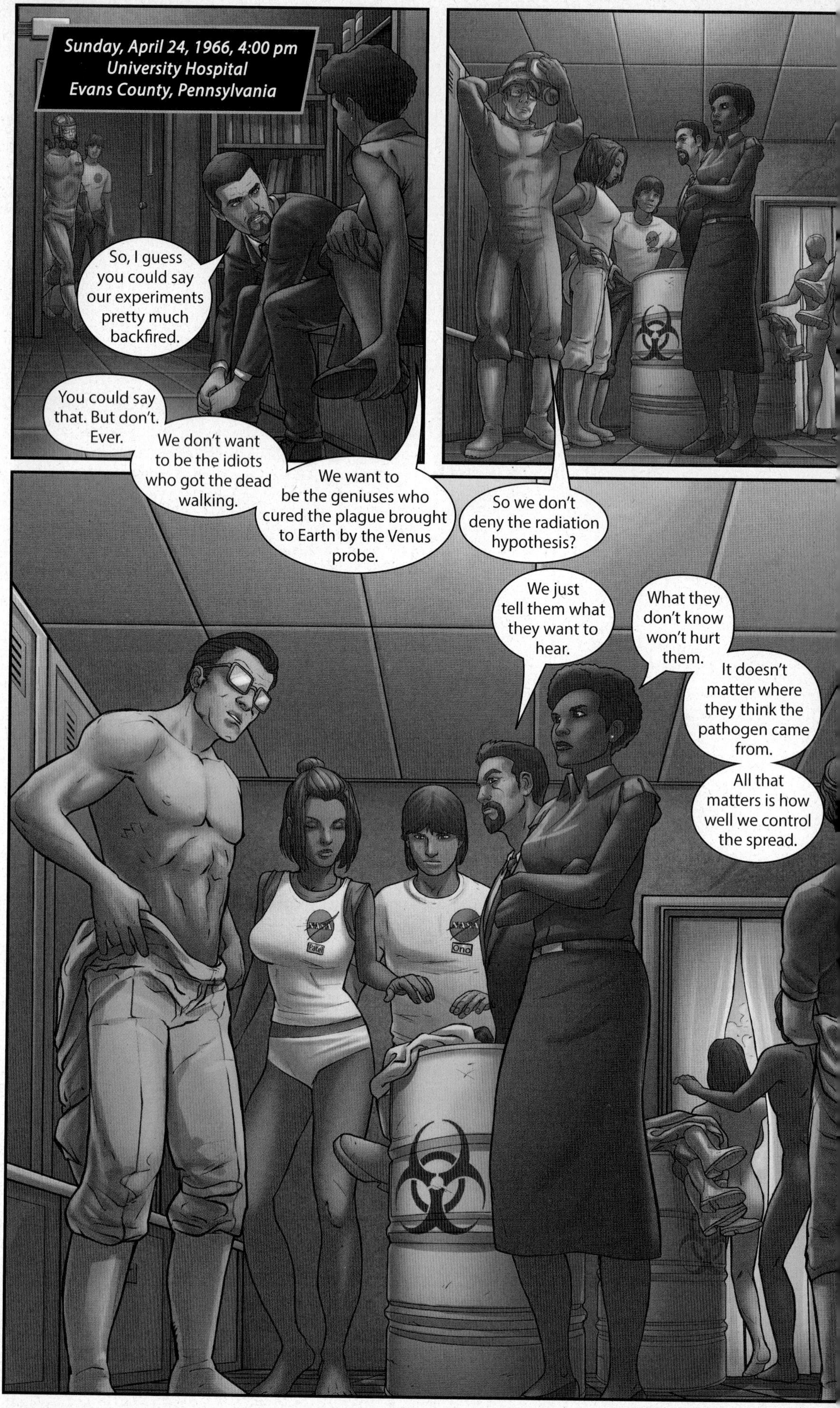
Sunday, April 24, 1966, 4:00 pm
University Hospital
Evans County, Pennsylvania
So, I guess you could say our experiments pretty much backfired.
You could say that. But don't. Ever.
We don't want to be the idiots who got the dead walking.
We want to be the geniuses who cured the plague brought to Earth by the Venus probe.
So we don't deny the radiation hypothesis?
We just tell them what they want to hear.
What they don't know won't hurt them.
It doesn't matter where they think the pathogen came from.
All that matters is how well we control the spread.
NASA
Patel
NASA
Ono

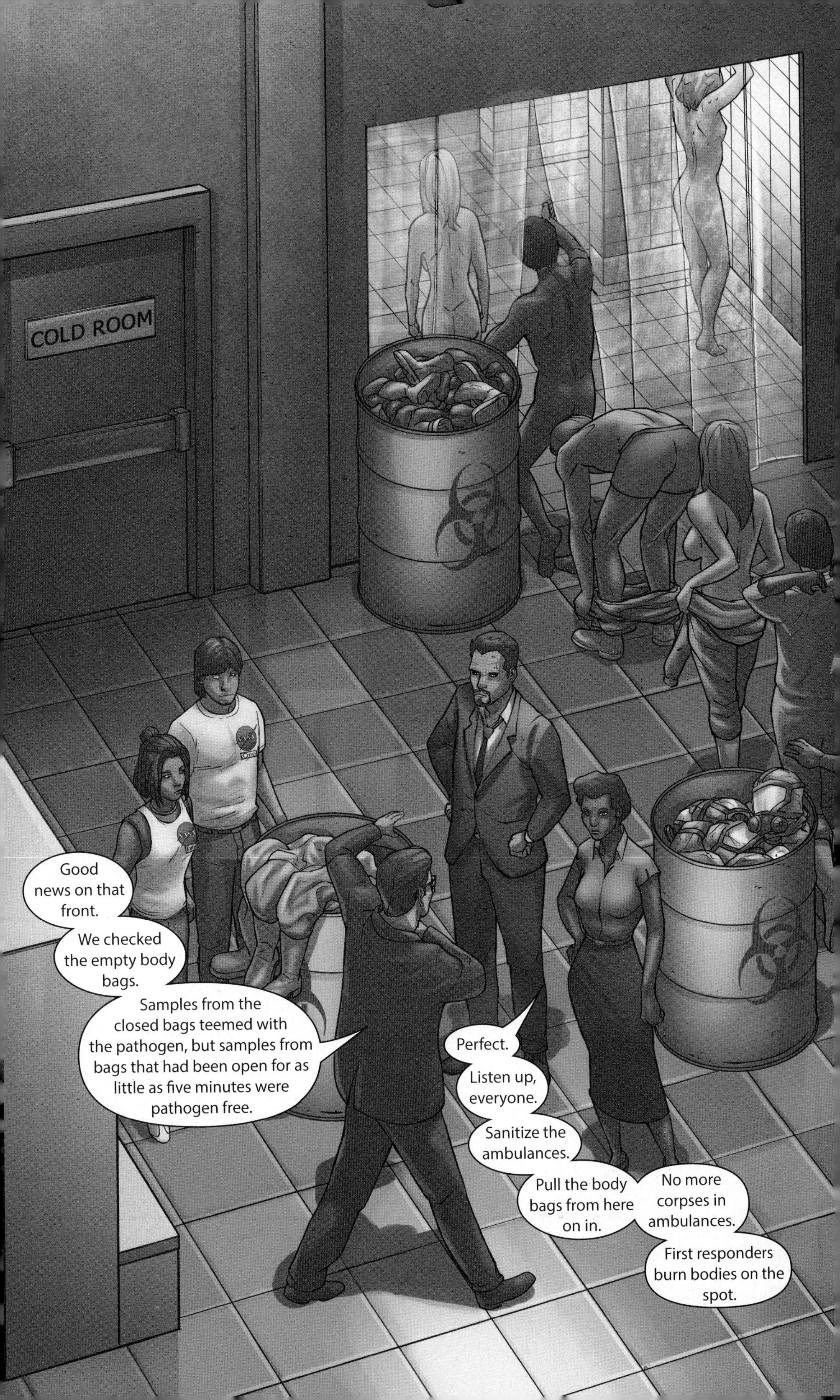
COLD ROOM
Good news on that front.
We checked the empty body bags.
Samples from the closed bags teemed with the pathogen, but samples from bags that had been open for as little as five minutes were pathogen free.
Perfect.
Listen up, everyone.
Sanitize the ambulances.
Pull the body bags from here on in.
No more corpses in ambulances.
First responders burn bodies on the spot.

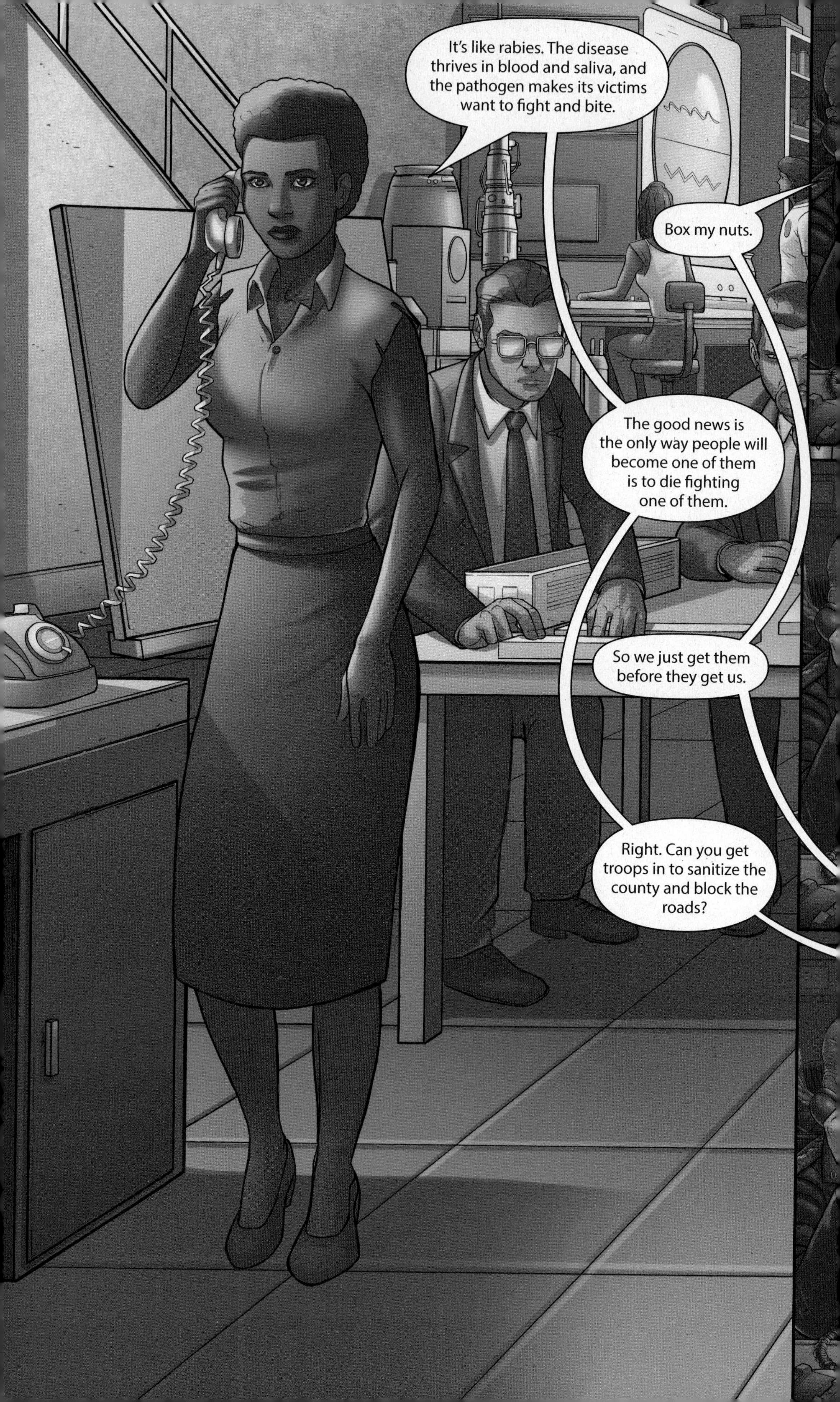
It's like rabies. The disease thrives in blood and saliva, and the pathogen makes its victims want to fight and bite.
Box my nuts.
The good news is the only way people will become one of them is to die fighting one of them.
So we just get them before they get us.
Right. Can you get troops in to sanitize the county and block the roads?

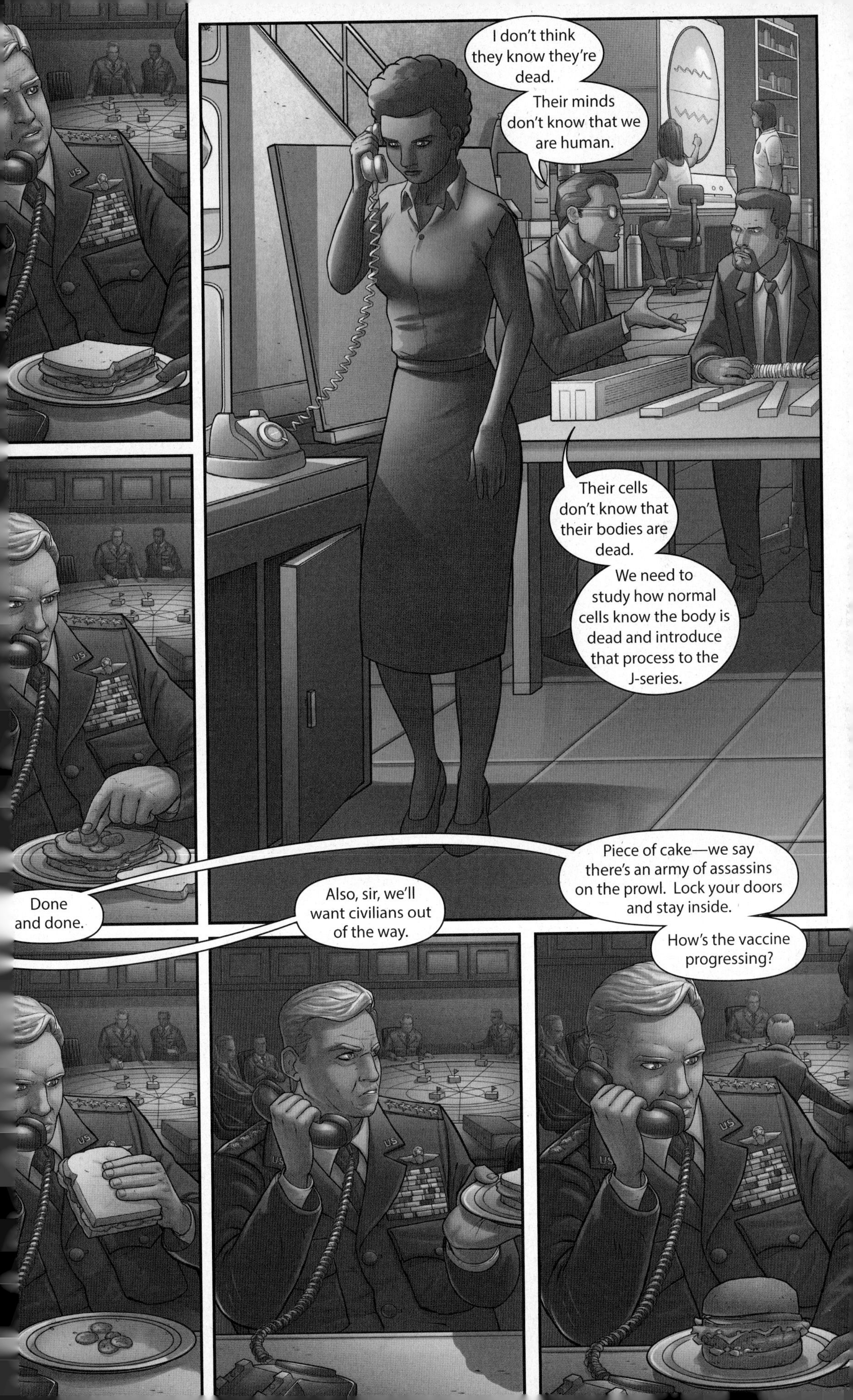

I don't think they know they're dead.
Their minds don't know that we are human.
Their cells don't know that their bodies are dead.
We need to study how normal cells know the body is dead and introduce that process to the J-series.
Piece of cake—we say there's an army of assassins on the prowl. Lock your doors and stay inside.
Done and done.
Also, sir, we'll want civilians out of the way.
How's the vaccine progressing?

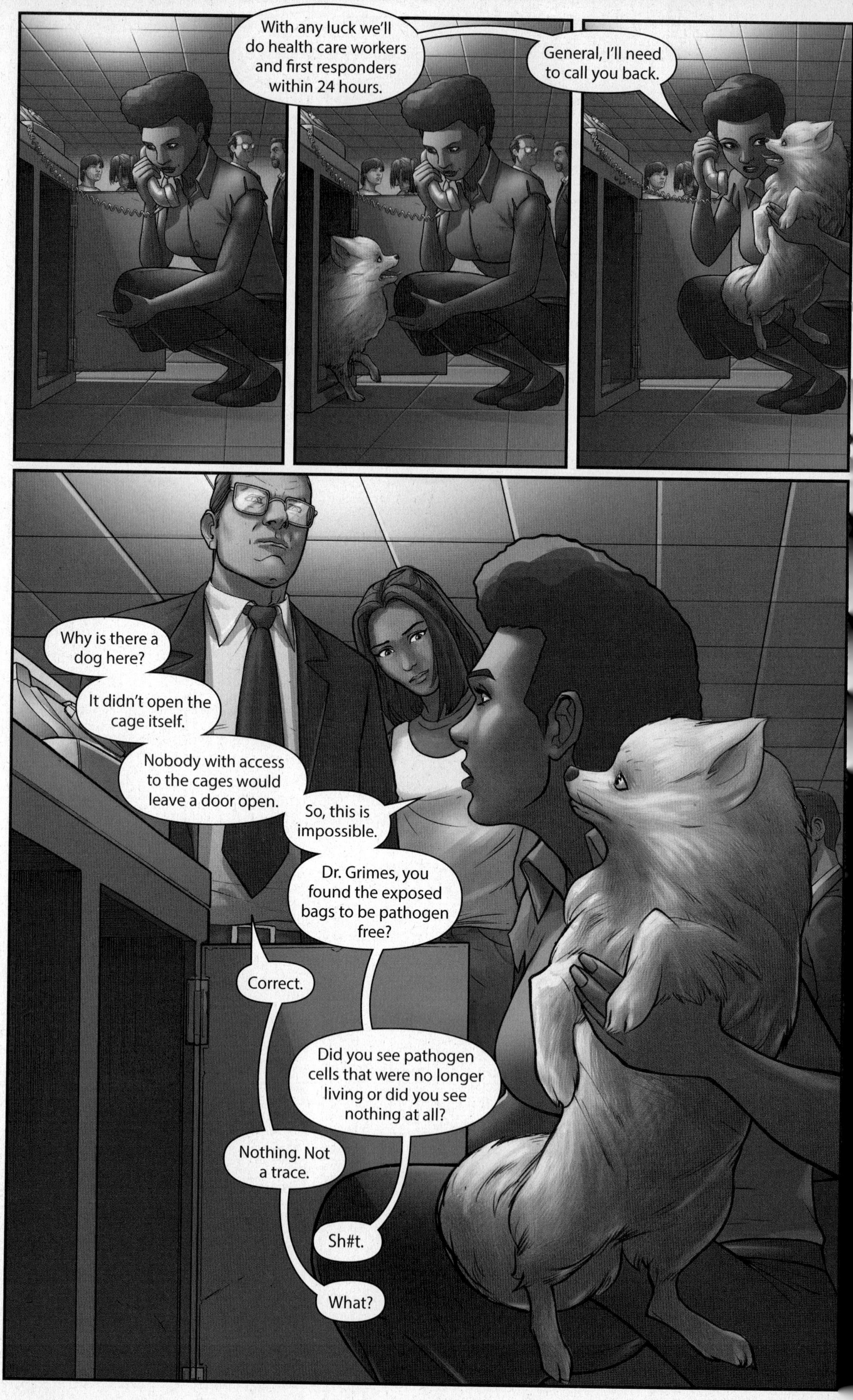
With any luck we'll do health care workers and first responders within 24 hours.
General, I'll need to call you back.
Why is there a dog here?
It didn't open the cage itself.
Nobody with access to the cages would leave a door open.
So, this is impossible.
Dr. Grimes, you found the exposed bags to be pathogen free?
Correct.
Did you see pathogen cells that were no longer living or did you see nothing at all?
Nothing. Not a trace.
Sh#t.
What?

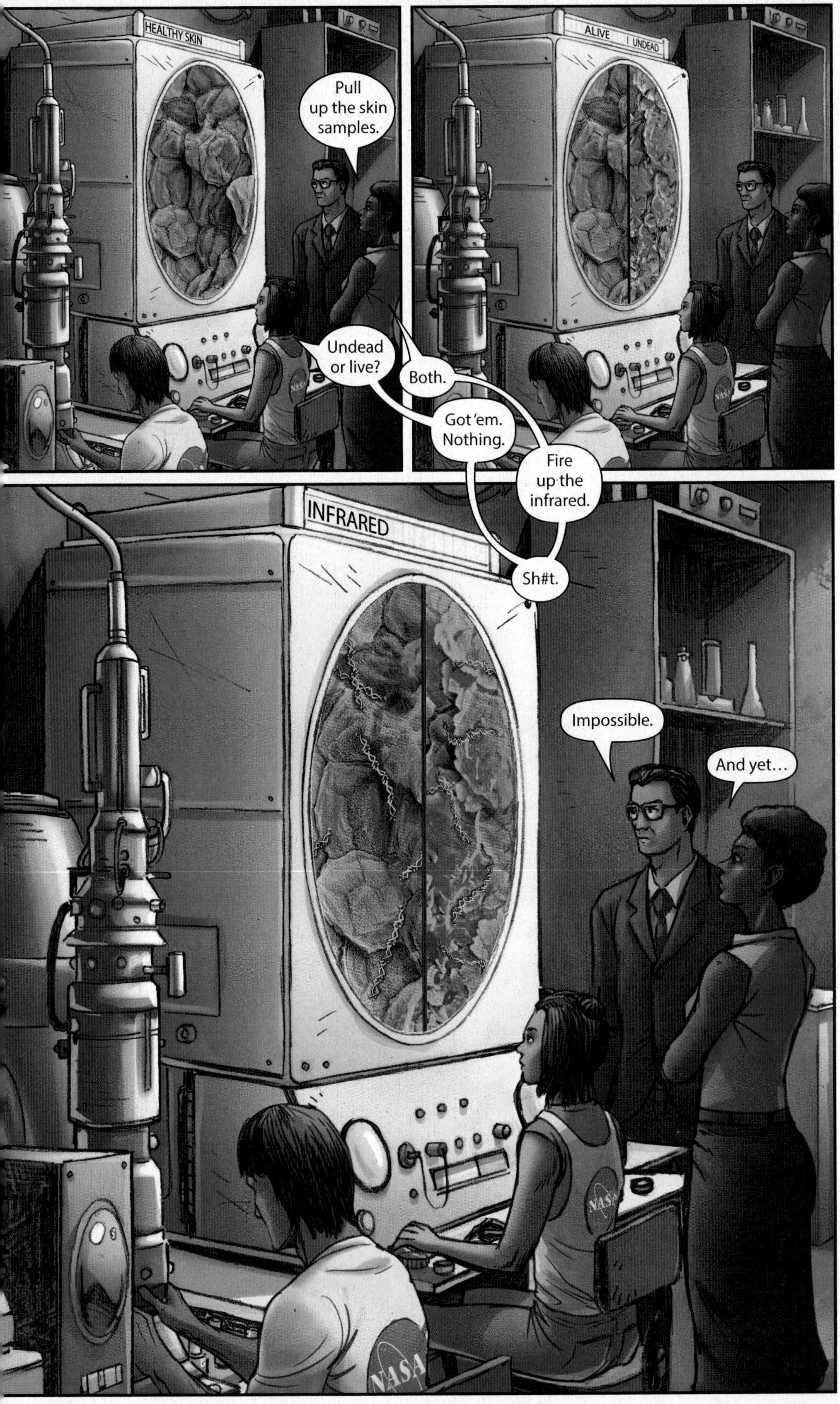
HEALTHY SKIN
Pull up the skin samples.
Undead or live?
Both.
ALIVE
UNDEAD
Got 'em. Nothing.
Fire up the infrared.
INFRARED
Sh#t.
Impossible.
And yet…
NASA

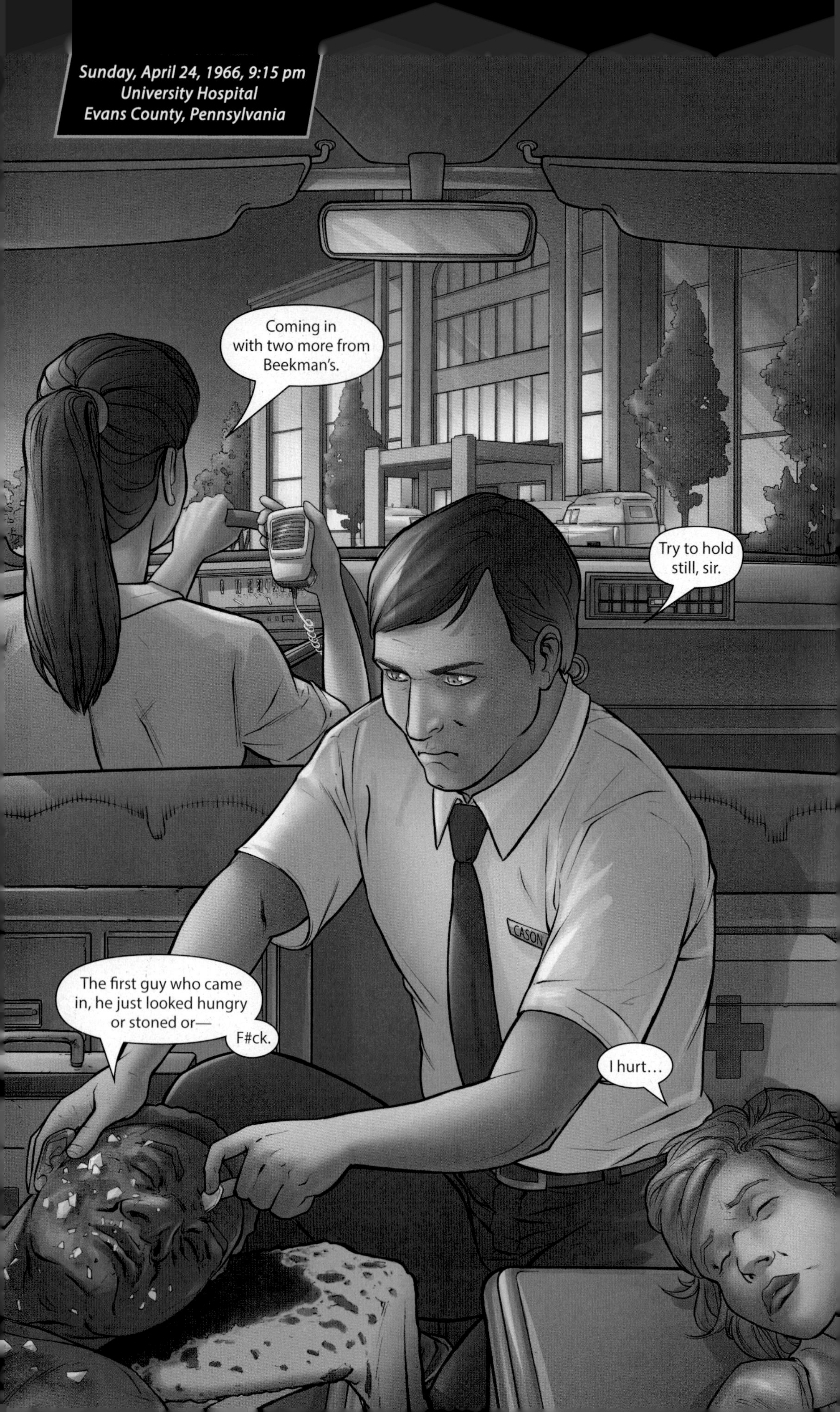
Sunday, April 24, 1966, 9:15 pm
University Hospital
Evans County, Pennsylvania
Coming in with two more from Beekman's.
Try to hold still, sir.
CASON
The first guy who came in, he just looked hungry or stoned or—
F#ck.
I hurt…

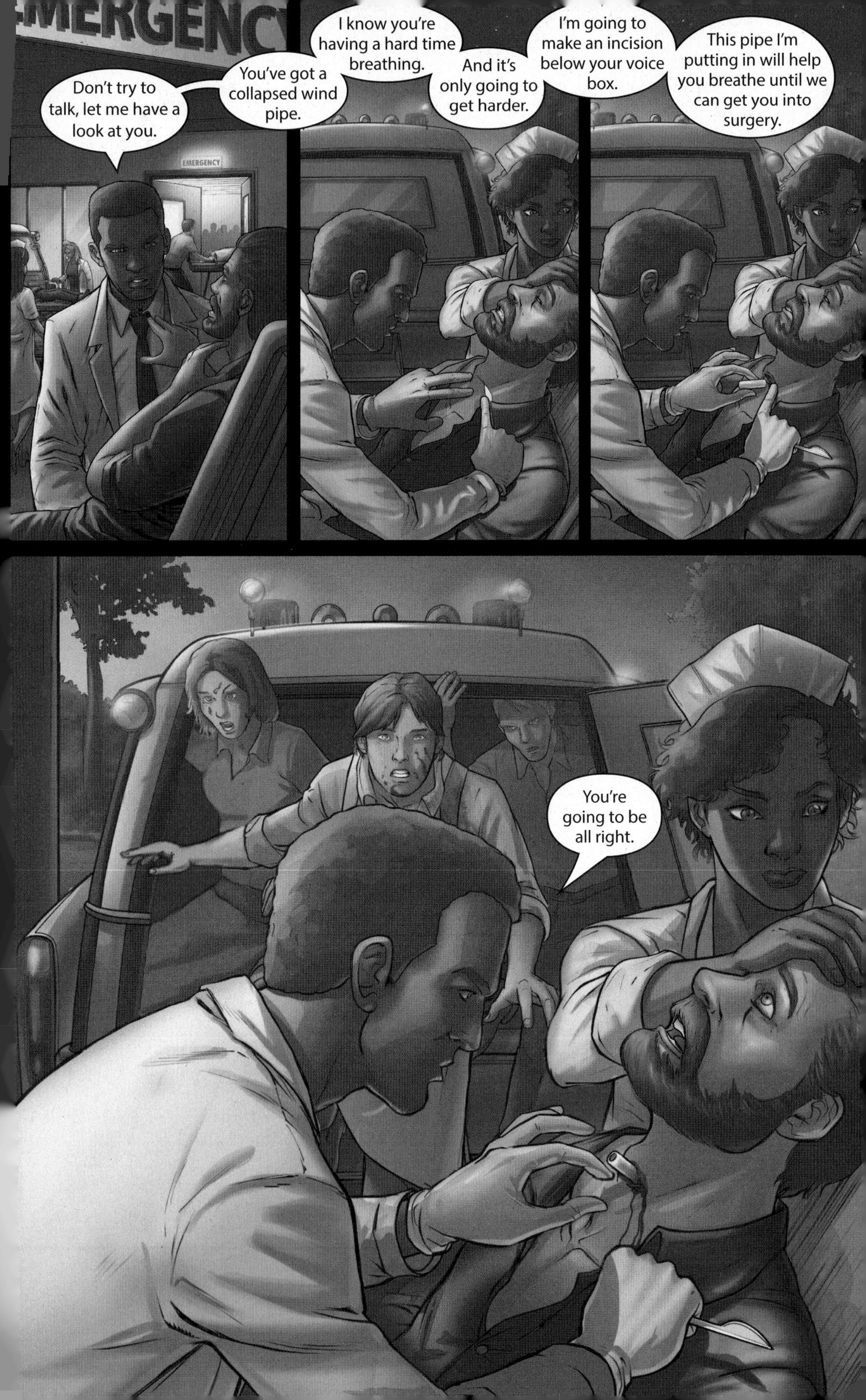
EMERGENCY
Don't try to talk, let me have a look at you.
EMERGENCY
You've got a collapsed wind pipe.
I know you're having a hard time breathing.
And it's only going to get harder.
I'm going to make an incision below your voice box.
This pipe I'm putting in will help you breathe until we can get you into surgery.
You're going to be all right.

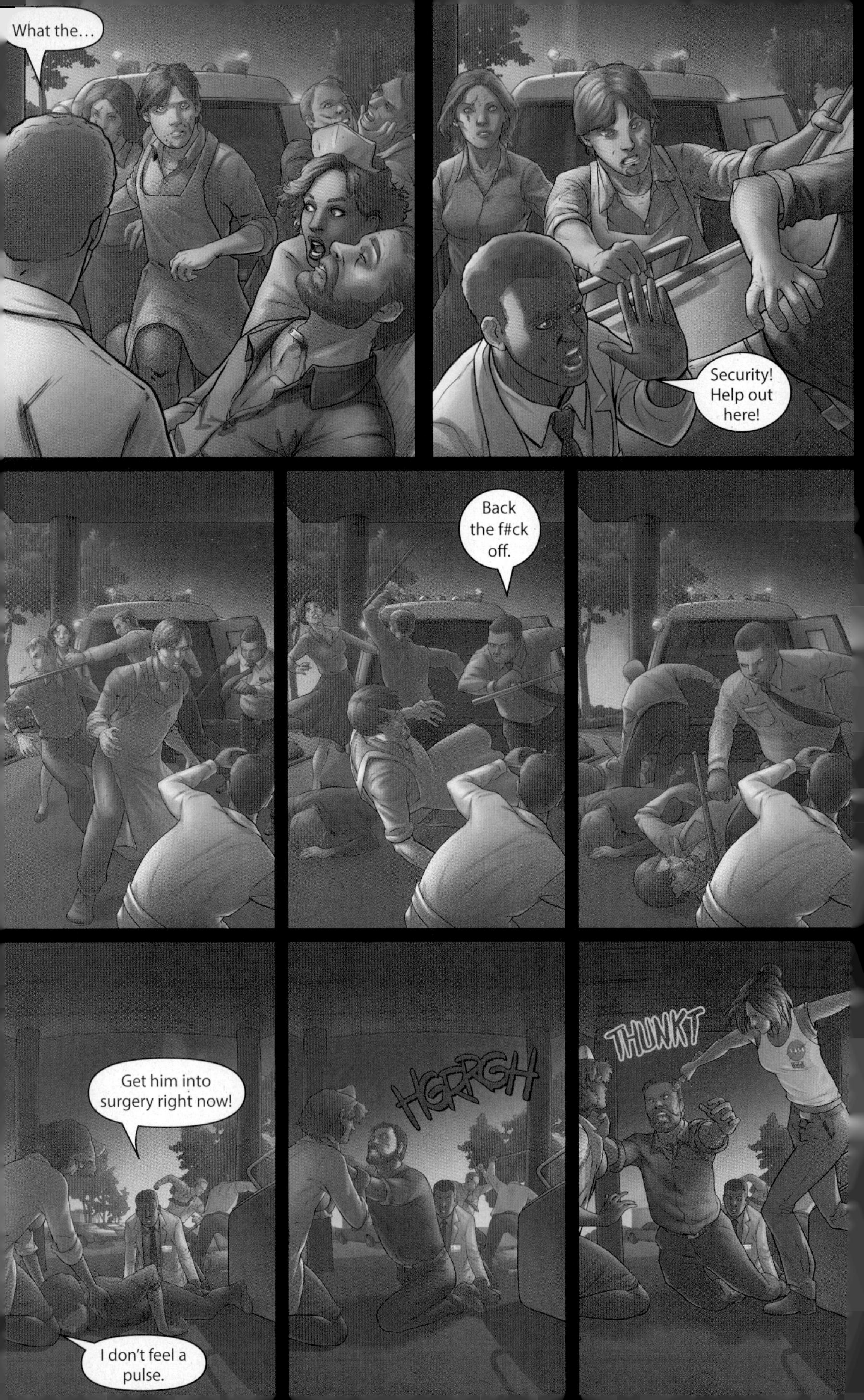
What the…
Security! Help out here!
Back the f#ck off.
Get him into surgery right now!
I don't feel a pulse.
HGRRGH
THUNKT

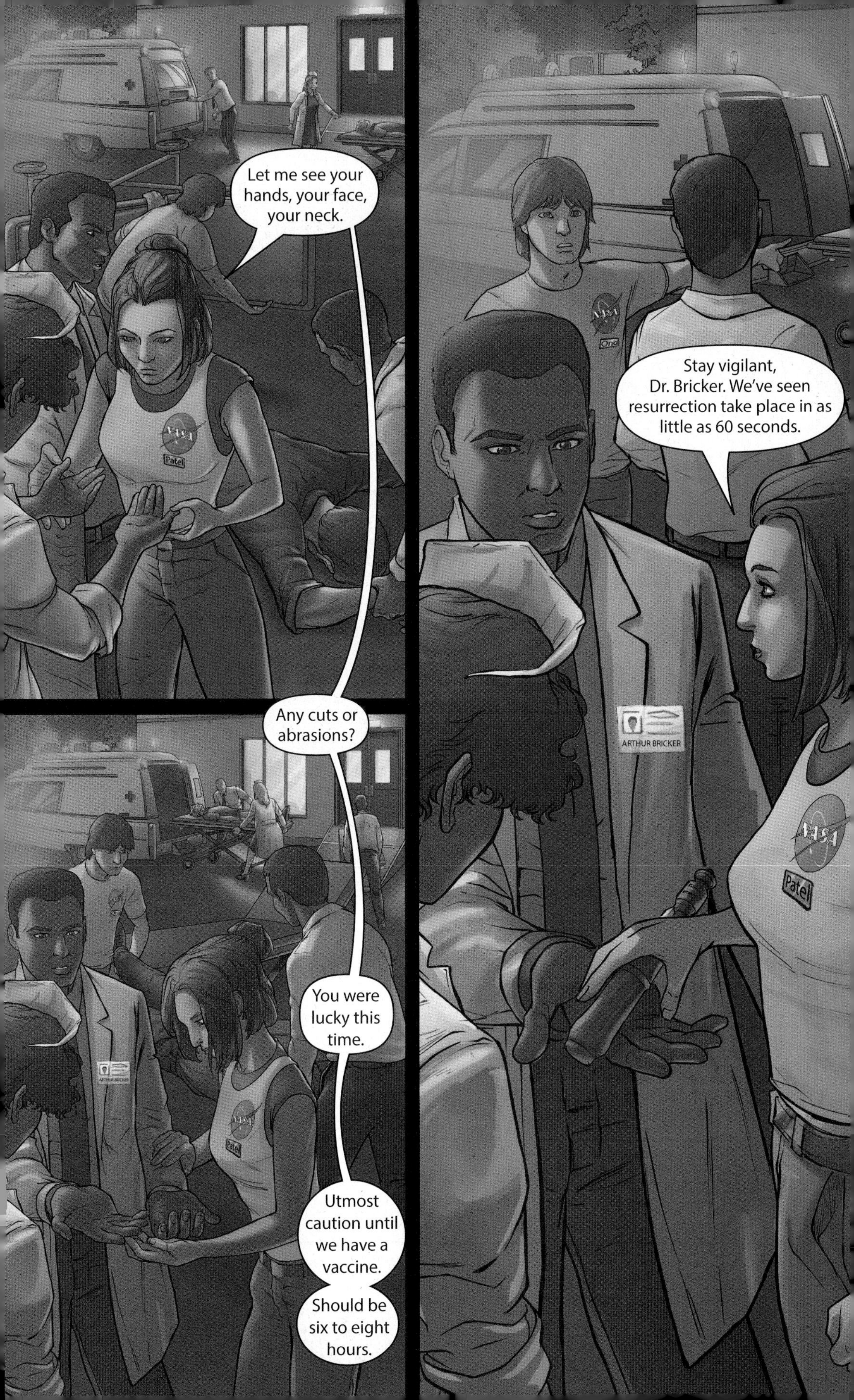
Let me see your hands, your face, your neck.
Any cuts or abrasions?
You were lucky this time.
Utmost caution until we have a vaccine.
Should be six to eight hours.
Stay vigilant, Dr. Bricker. We've seen resurrection take place in as little as 60 seconds.

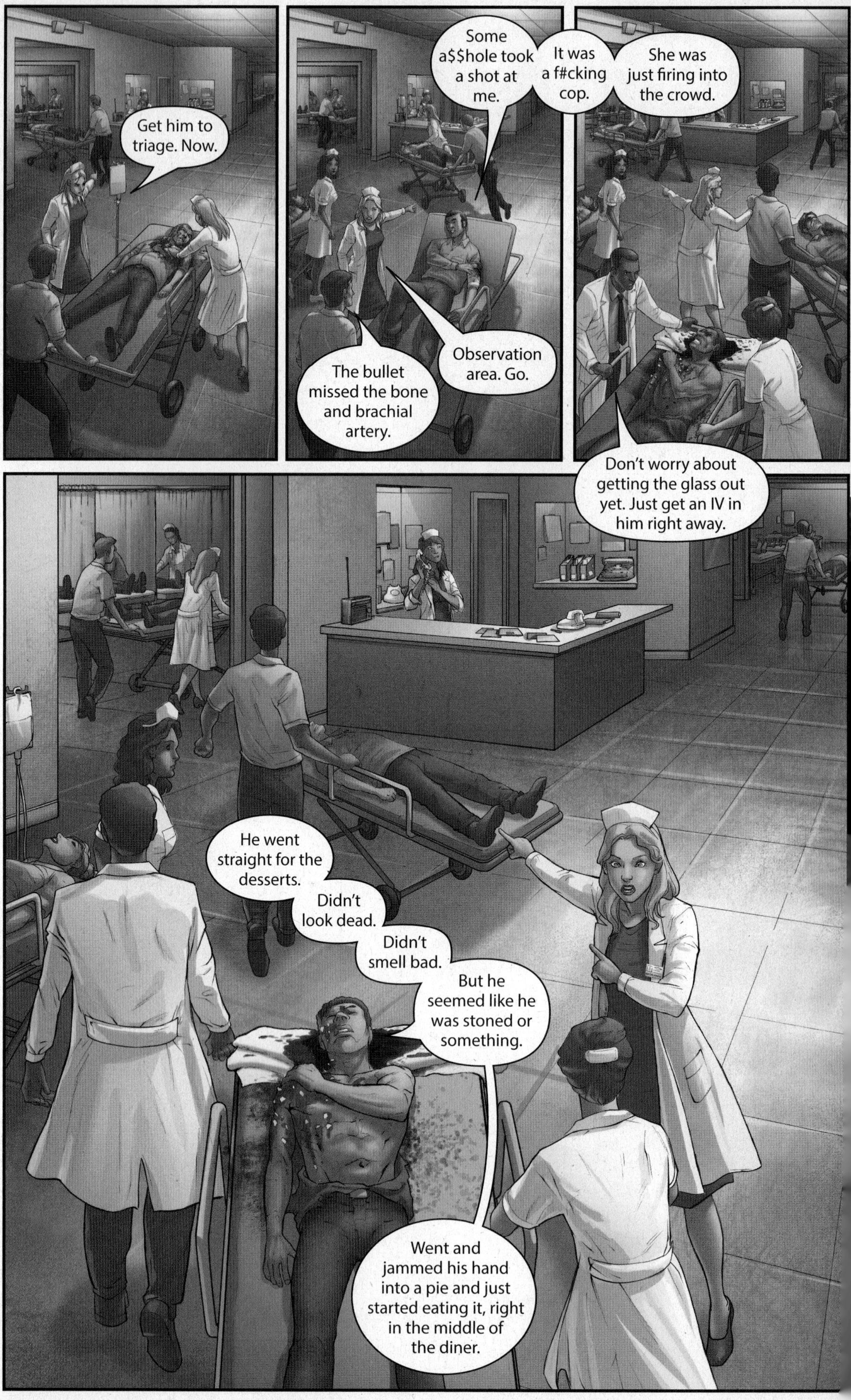
Get him to triage. Now.
Some a$$hole took a shot at me.
The bullet missed the bone and brachial artery.
Observation area. Go.
It was a f#cking cop.
She was just firing into the crowd.
Don't worry about getting the glass out yet. Just get an IV in him right away.
He went straight for the desserts.
Didn't look dead.
Didn't smell bad.
But he seemed like he was stoned or something.
Went and jammed his hand into a pie and just started eating it, right in the middle of the diner.

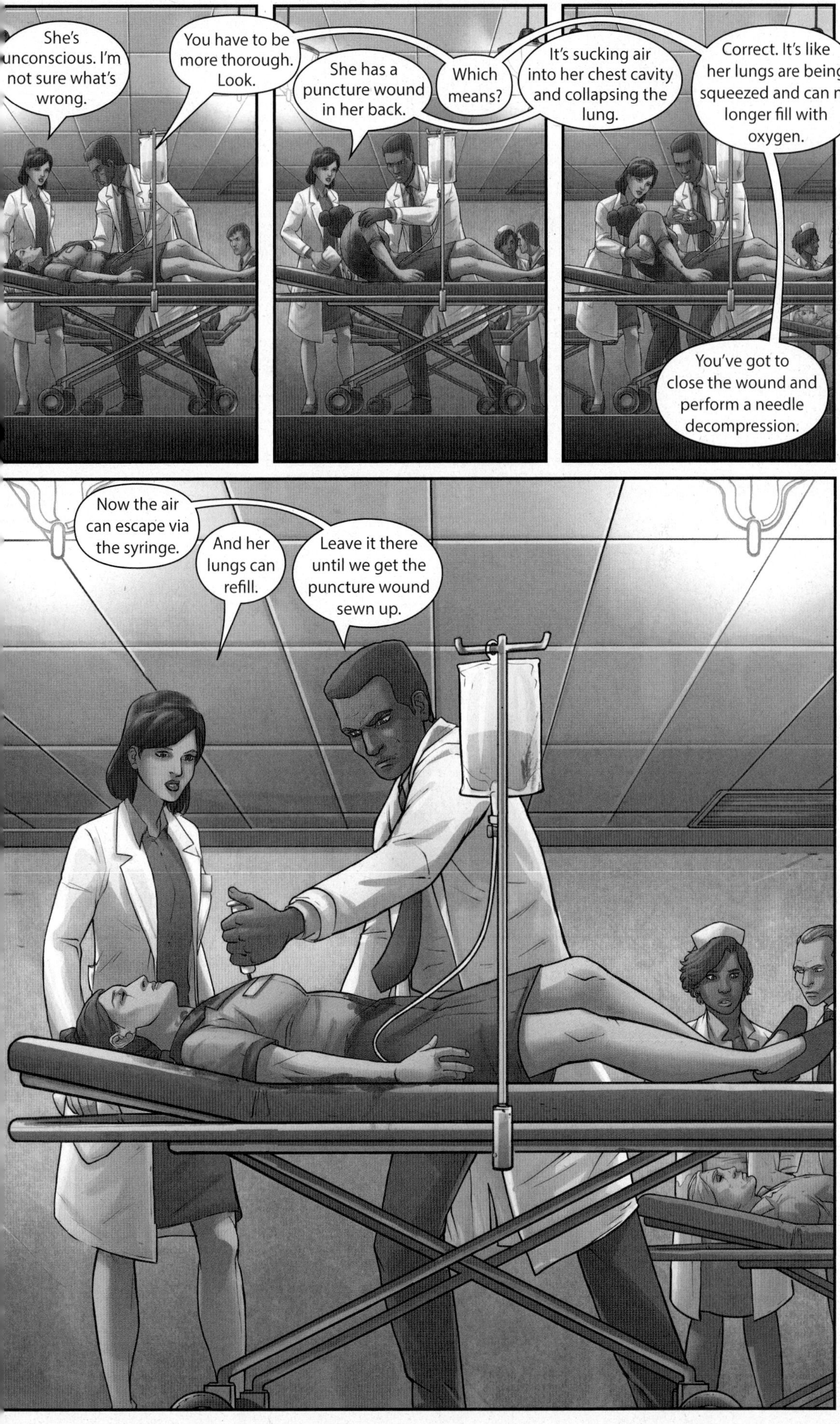
She's unconscious. I'm not sure what's wrong.
You have to be more thorough. Look.
She has a puncture wound in her back.
Which means?
It's sucking air into her chest cavity and collapsing the lung.
Correct. It's like her lungs are being squeezed and can no longer fill with oxygen.
You've got to close the wound and perform a needle decompression.
Now the air can escape via the syringe.
And her lungs can refill.
Leave it there until we get the puncture wound sewn up.

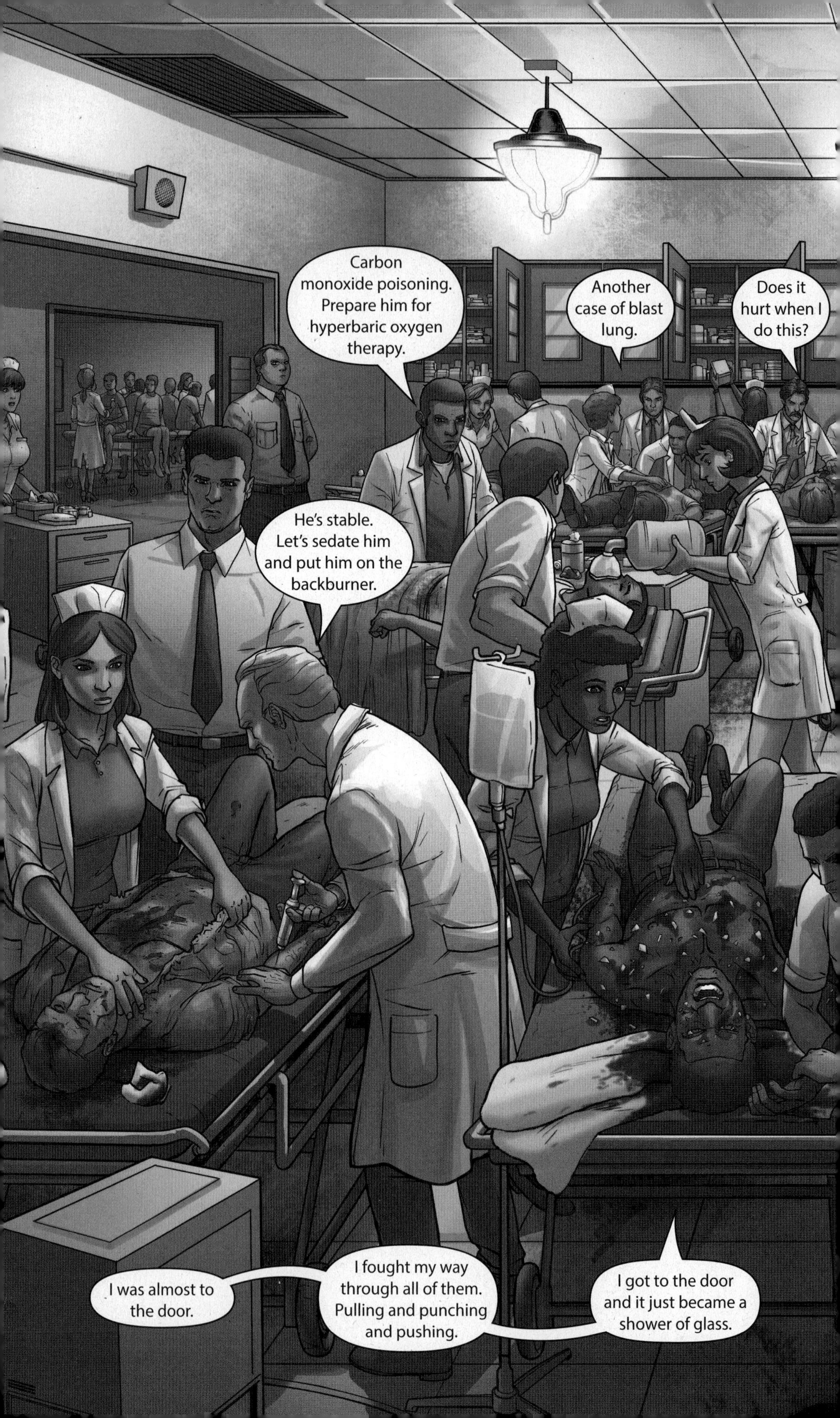
Carbon monoxide poisoning. Prepare him for hyperbaric oxygen therapy.
Another case of blast lung.
Does it hurt when I do this?
He's stable. Let's sedate him and put him on the backburner.
I was almost to the door.
I fought my way through all of them. Pulling and punching and pushing.
I got to the door and it just became a shower of glass.

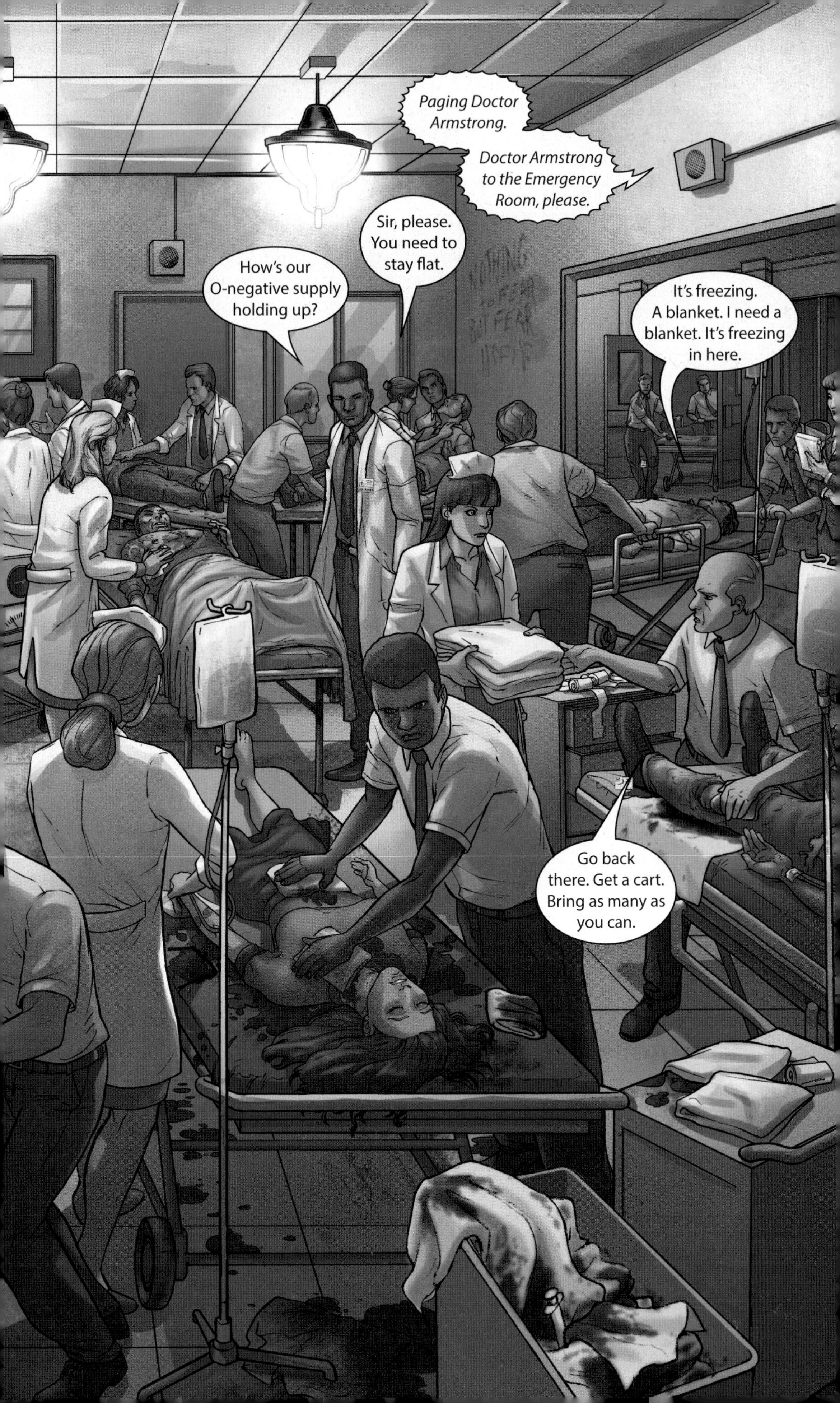
Paging Doctor Armstrong.
Doctor Armstrong to the Emergency Room, please.
Sir, please. You need to stay flat.
How's our O-negative supply holding up?
NOTHING to FEAR BUT FEAR ITSELF
It's freezing. A blanket. I need a blanket. It's freezing in here.
Go back there. Get a cart. Bring as many as you can.

Dr. Bricker, I need your help over here.
His skin is so burnt that it's tightening around his sternum.
He can barely breathe.
Should I prep for an escharotomy?
Too risky.
ARTHUR BRICKER
THUNKT

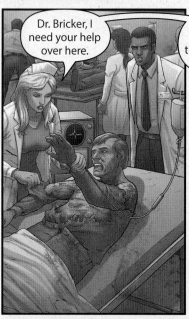

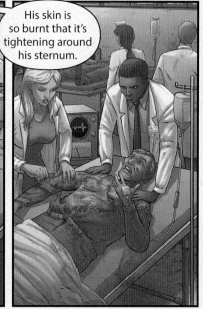

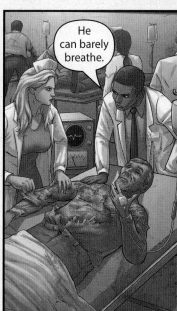

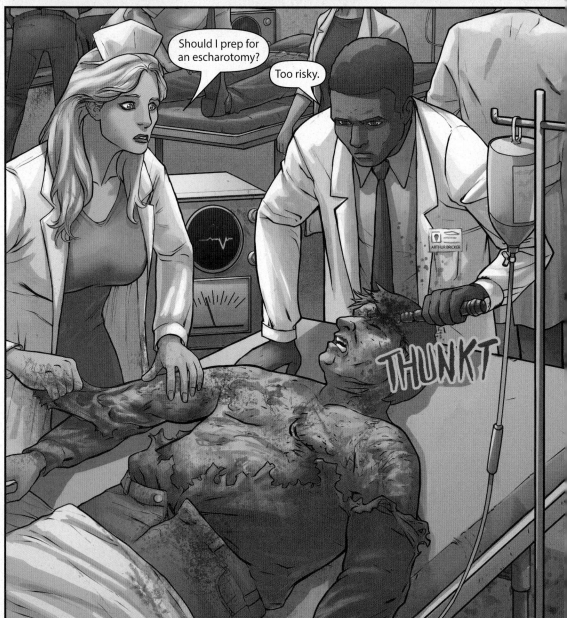

NATURAL RESOURCES

CUMULATIVE DEFORESTATION

WORLD FOREST COVER (in billion hectares)			
Pre-Industrial	1966	2016	2066*
5.9	4.3	4.0	3.7

etween the 1960s and today, humans have estroyed over 300 million hectares of forest. his is roughly the size of the contiguous estern United States.

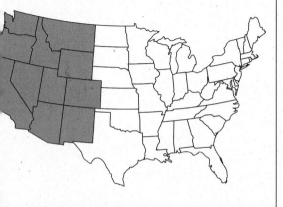

SOIL DEGRADATION

WORLD POPULATION		
1966	2016	2060*
3.1 billion	6.3 billion	9.6 billion
HECTARES OF ARABLE LAND PER CAPITA		
0.42	0.23	0.18

Forty percent of the soil used for agricuture around the world is degraded or seriously degraded from our modern farming practices. Soil is now being lost at between 10 and 40 times the rate at which it can be naturally replenished. Today, the world has a rough estimate of 60 years of topsoil left.

FRESH WATER DEPLETION

quifers around the world cannot keep up ith our consumption either. Today, 21 out of he 37 largest aquifers in the world are being apped at unsustainable rates. In the US, the igh Plains (HP) Aquifer system is one of the orld's largest, spanning portions of 8 states approximately 174,000 square miles).

DEPLETION OF SUPPLY IN THE HP AQUIFER		
1966	2016	2066*
3%	30%	69%

nce depleted, the HP Aquifer will take 500 1,300 years to completely refill.

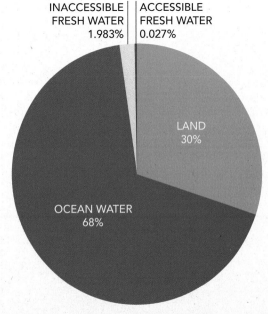

INACCESSIBLE FRESH WATER 1.983%

ACCESSIBLE FRESH WATER 0.027%

LAND 30%

OCEAN WATER 68%

*ESTIMATED DATA

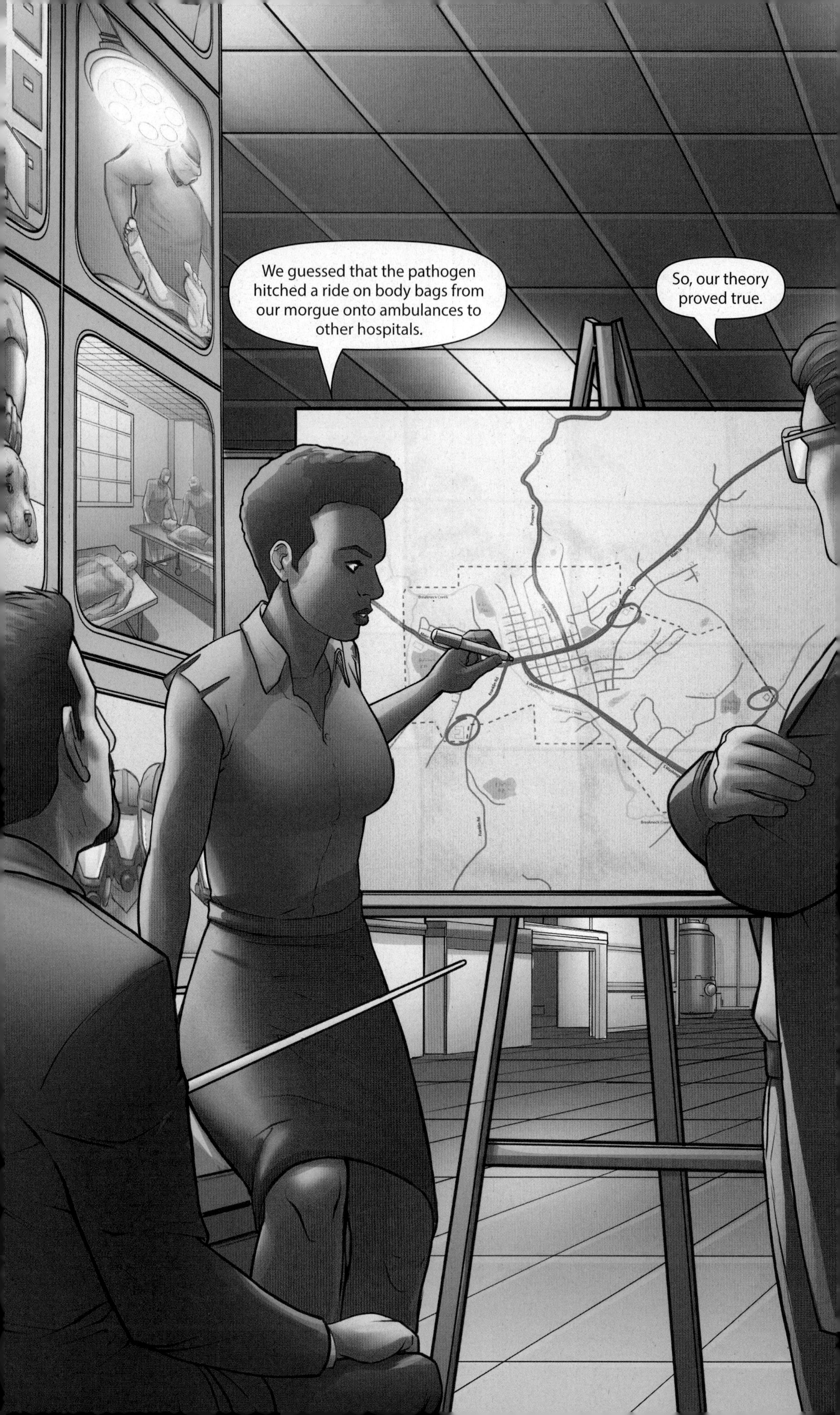
We guessed that the pathogen hitched a ride on body bags from our morgue onto ambulances to other hospitals.
So, our theory proved true.

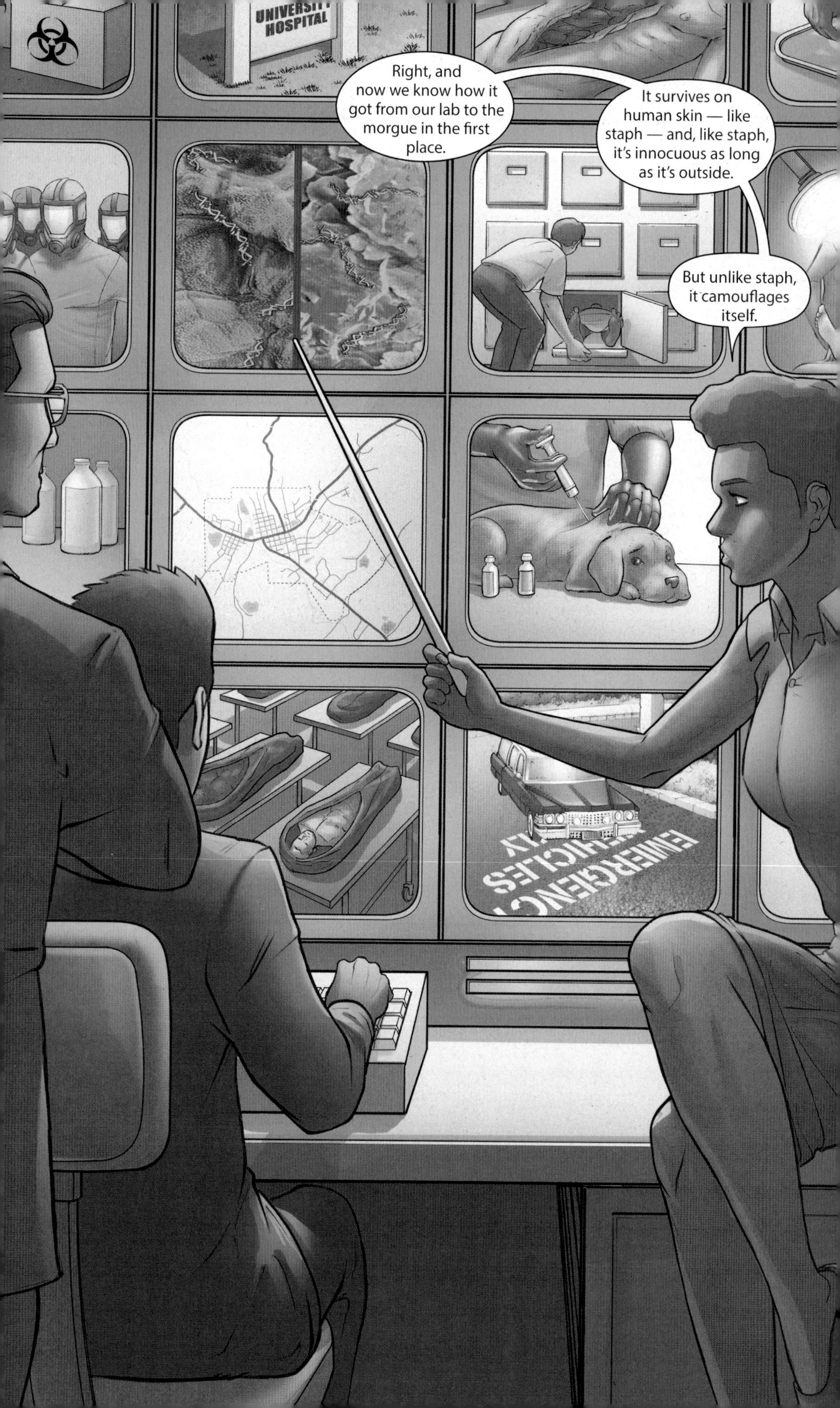

UNIVERSITY HOSPITAL
Right, and now we know how it got from our lab to the morgue in the first place.
It survives on human skin — like staph — and, like staph, it's innocuous as long as it's outside.
But unlike staph, it camouflages itself.

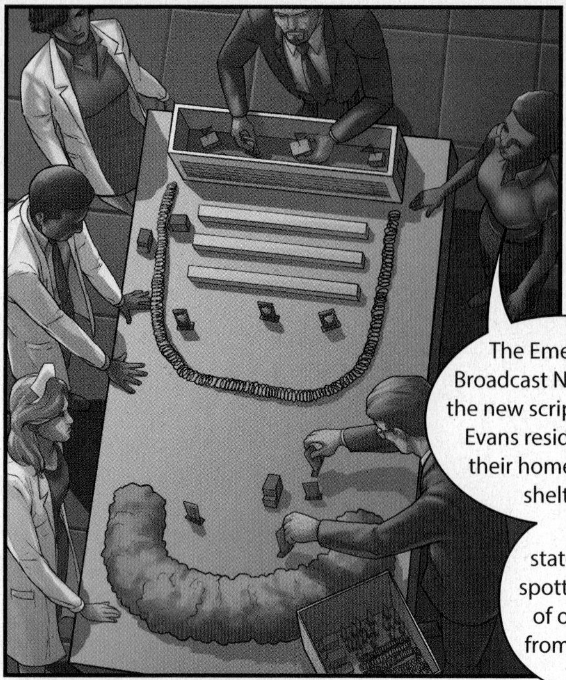
The Emergency Broadcast Network has the new script—it drives Evans residents from their homes to local shelters.
We have local and state police at every shelter, spotting people with any kind of open wound or abrasion from any source and herding them here.

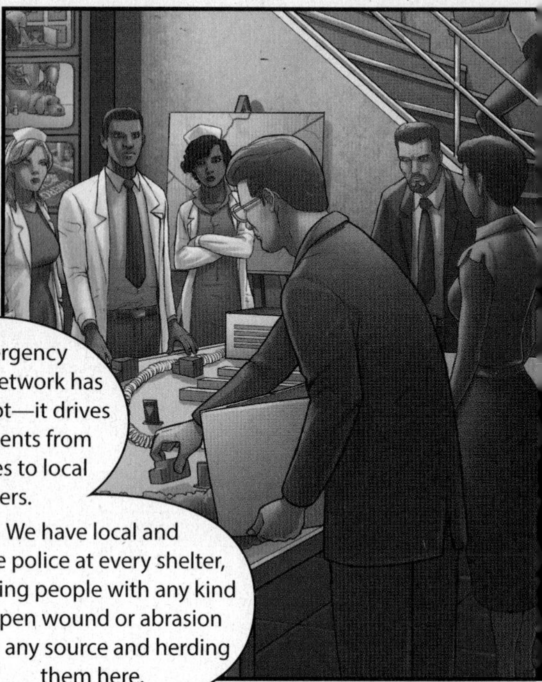

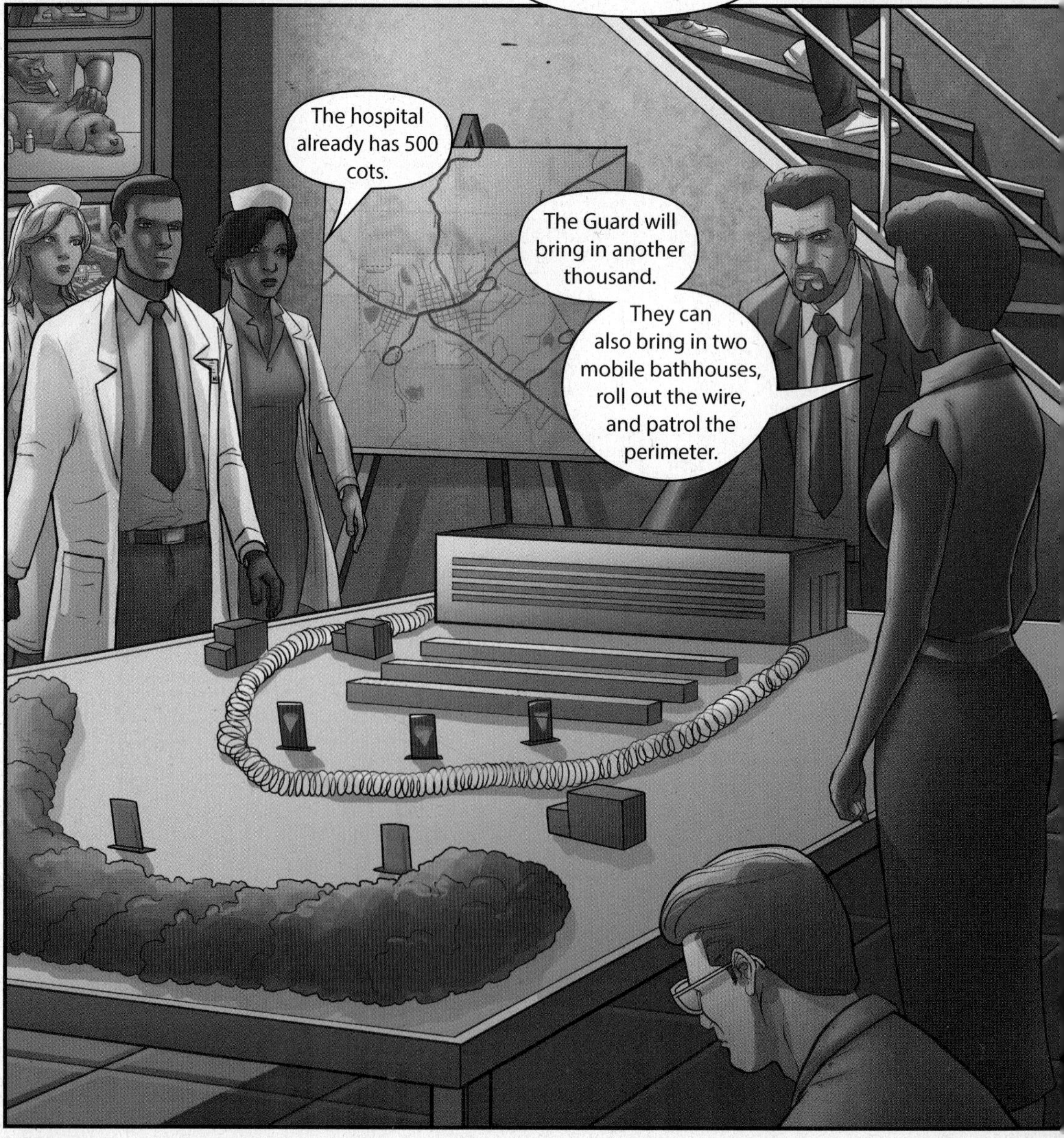
The hospital already has 500 cots.
The Guard will bring in another thousand.
They can also bring in two mobile bathhouses, roll out the wire, and patrol the perimeter.

THE NATIONAL AIR AND SPACE ADMINISTRATION

tober 4, 1957 – The Soviet Union launched *Sputnik*, world's first man-made satellite, into space.

vember 3, 1957 – The Soviet Union followed with *ıtnik 2*, which carried Laika, a canine. Laika survived trip into space but died when the oxygen supply out.

ıuary 31, 1958 – The United States launched its first ellite, *Explorer 1*.

gust 19, 1960 – The Soviet Union launched *Sputnik* ith a grey rabbit, 42 mice, two rats, flies, several nts, fungi, and two canines, Belka and Strelka; all sengers survived the trip to and from space.

ril 12, 1961 – Soviet cosmonaut Yuri Gagarin came the first human in space.

y 5, 1961 – Alan Shepard became the first American pace.

y 25, 1961 – President John F. Kennedy ied Congress and the nation to support the first nned mission to the moon, which became the ollo program.

ruary 3, 1966 – The Soviet Union landed the first cecraft on the moon; the United States followed n *Surveyor I* on June 2.

y 2, 1969 – American astronauts Neil Armstrong and ızz" Aldrin became the first men on the moon.

tember 1976 – American probe *Viking 2* covered water frost on Mars.

gust and September 1977 – *Voyagers 1* and *2* were nched; each would transmit images of the outer nets over the decades while on their (still ongoing) rneys.

ril 12, 1981 – The United States launched first space shuttle *Columbia*.

gust 6, 2012 – NASA's *iosity* rover landed Mars.

7 (8K71)
t vehicle
1957
8K71PS
Sputnik (PS) launcher
1957
8K72K
Vostok (3KA) launcher
1960
11A57
Voskhod (3KV) launcher
1963
11A511
Soyuz (7K-OK) launcher
1966

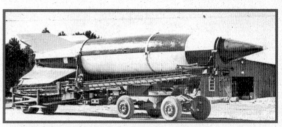

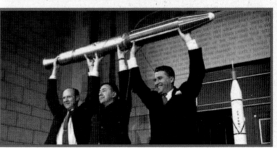

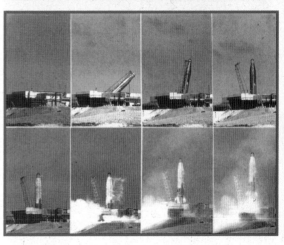

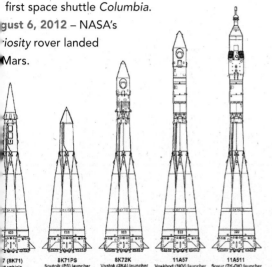

SINCE *SPUTNIK'S* LAUNCH IN 1957	
SATELLITES SENT INTO ORBIT	2,271
ACTIVE SATELLITES	1,381
UNITED STATES	568
RUSSIA	133
CHINA	177
ALL OTHER COUNTRIES	503
ACTIVE MILITARY SATELLITES	295
UNITED STATES	129
RUSSIA	75
CHINA	35
ALL OTHER COUNTRIES	56

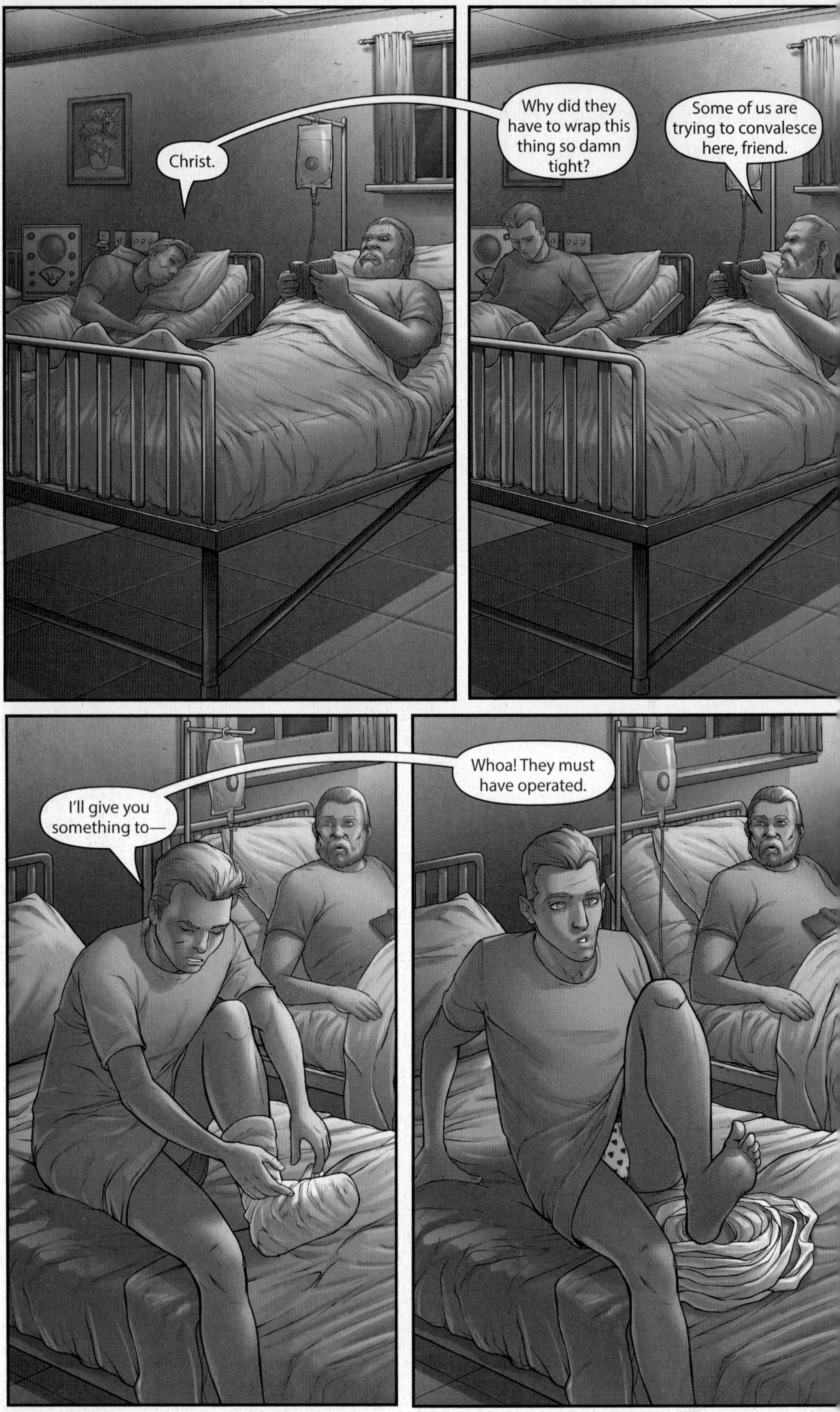
Christ.
Why did they have to wrap this thing so damn tight?
Some of us are trying to convalesce here, friend.
I'll give you something to—
Whoa! They must have operated.

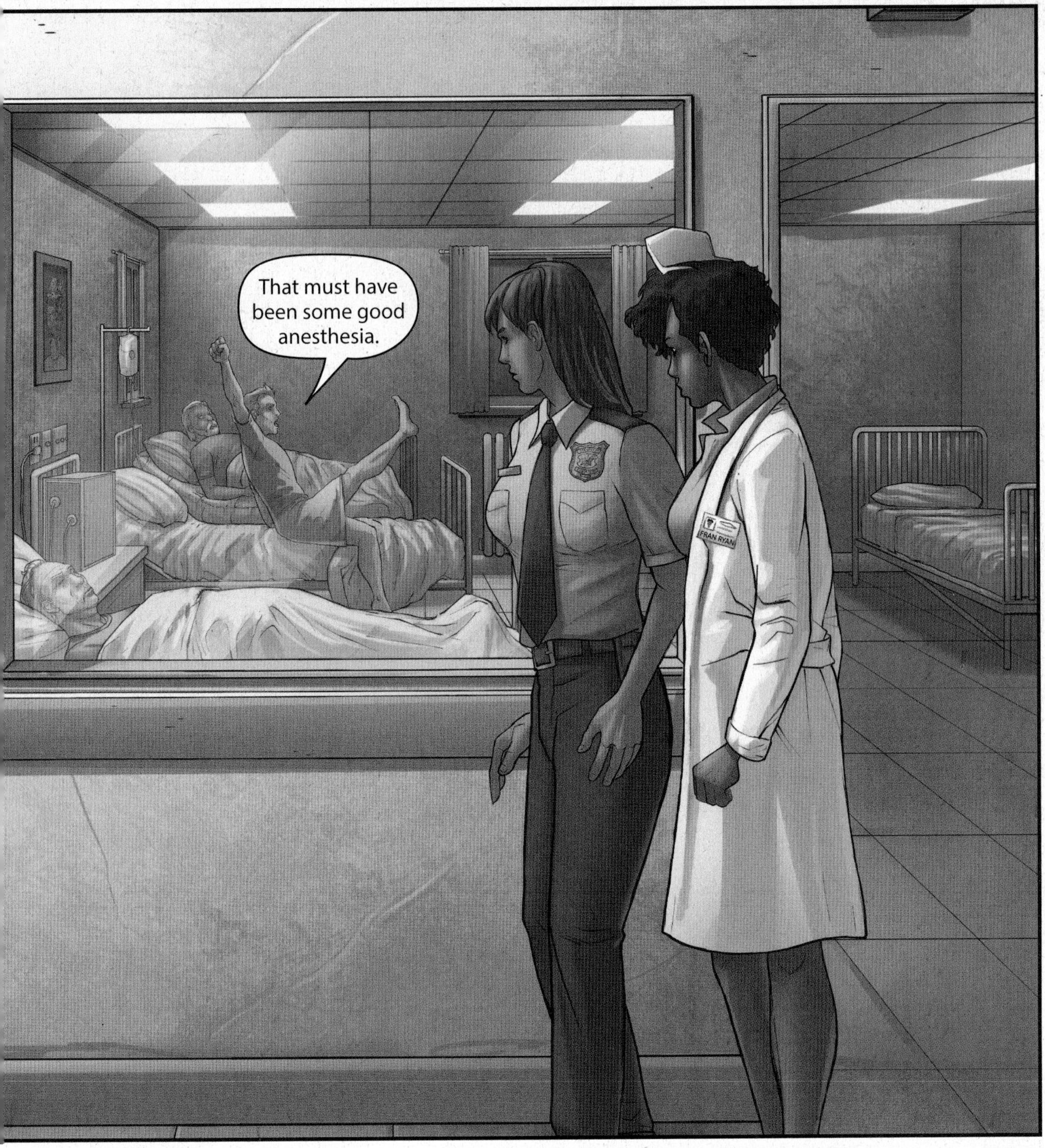
That must have been some good anesthesia.
FRAN RYAN

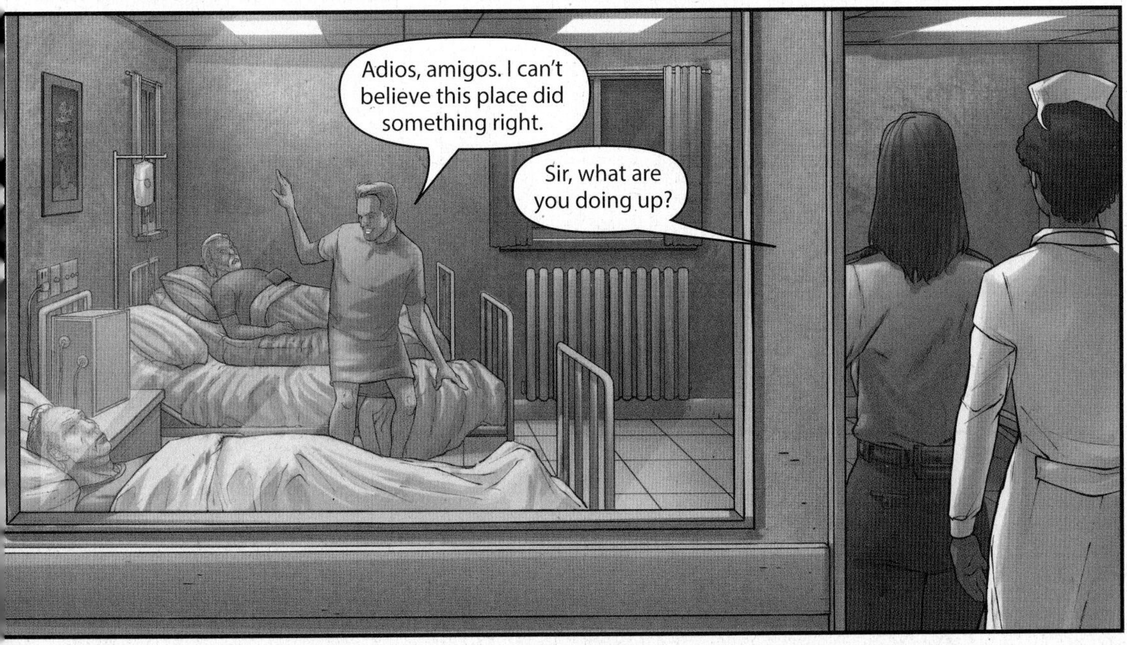
Adios, amigos. I can't believe this place did something right.
Sir, what are you doing up?

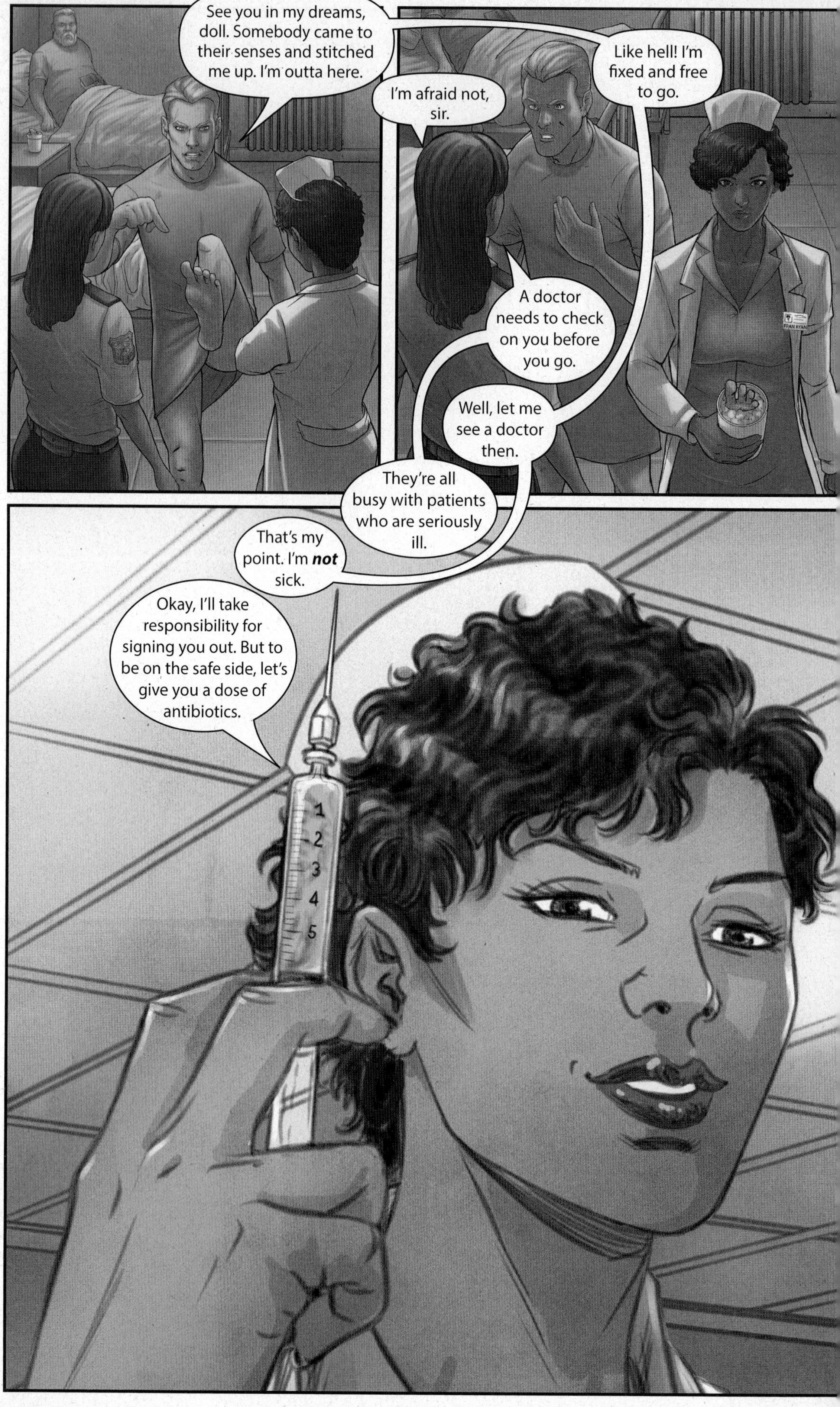

See you in my dreams, doll. Somebody came to their senses and stitched me up. I'm outta here.
Like hell! I'm fixed and free to go.
I'm afraid not, sir.
A doctor needs to check on you before you go.
Well, let me see a doctor then.
They're all busy with patients who are seriously ill.
That's my point. I'm ***not*** sick.
Okay, I'll take responsibility for signing you out. But to be on the safe side, let's give you a dose of antibiotics.

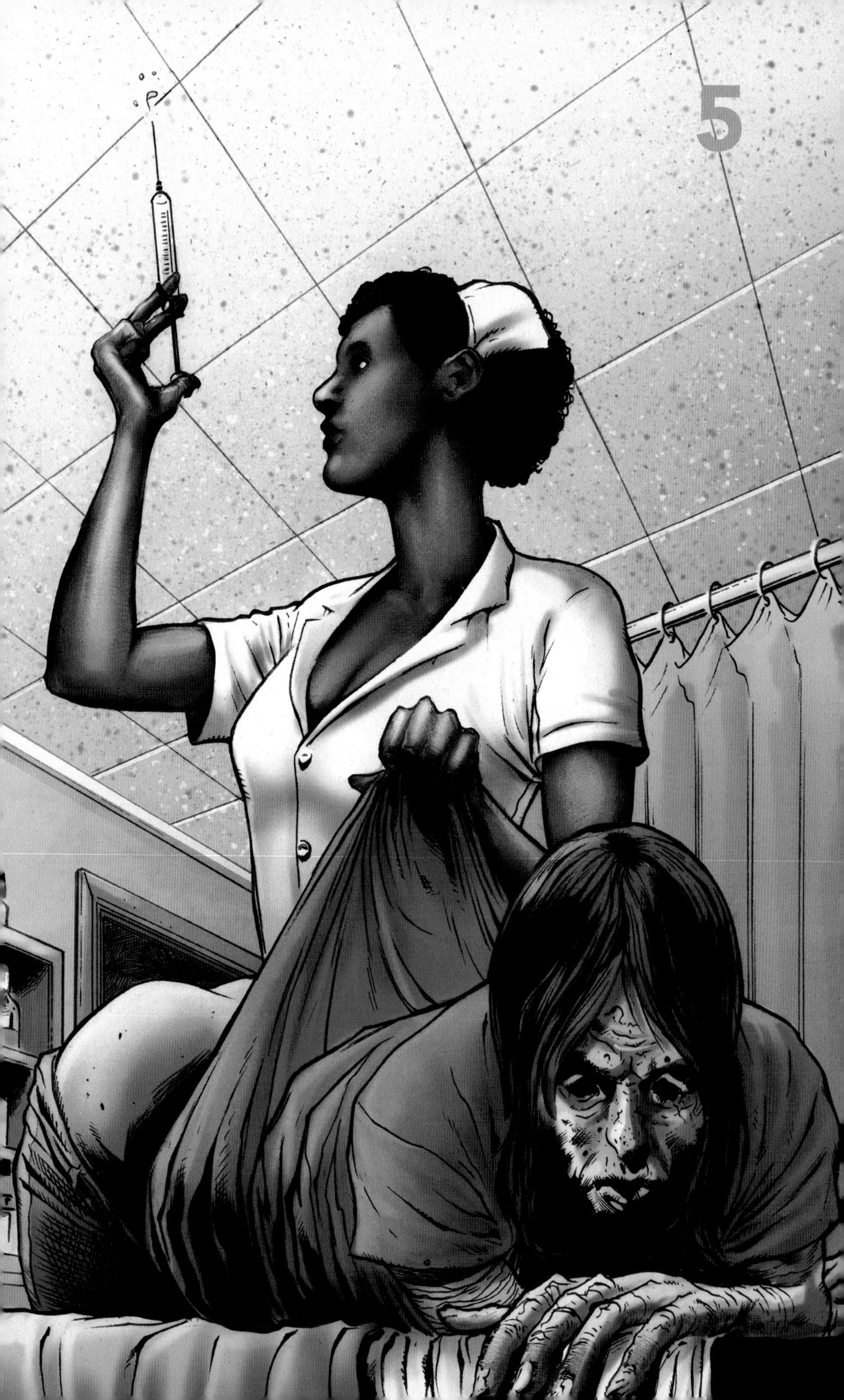
5

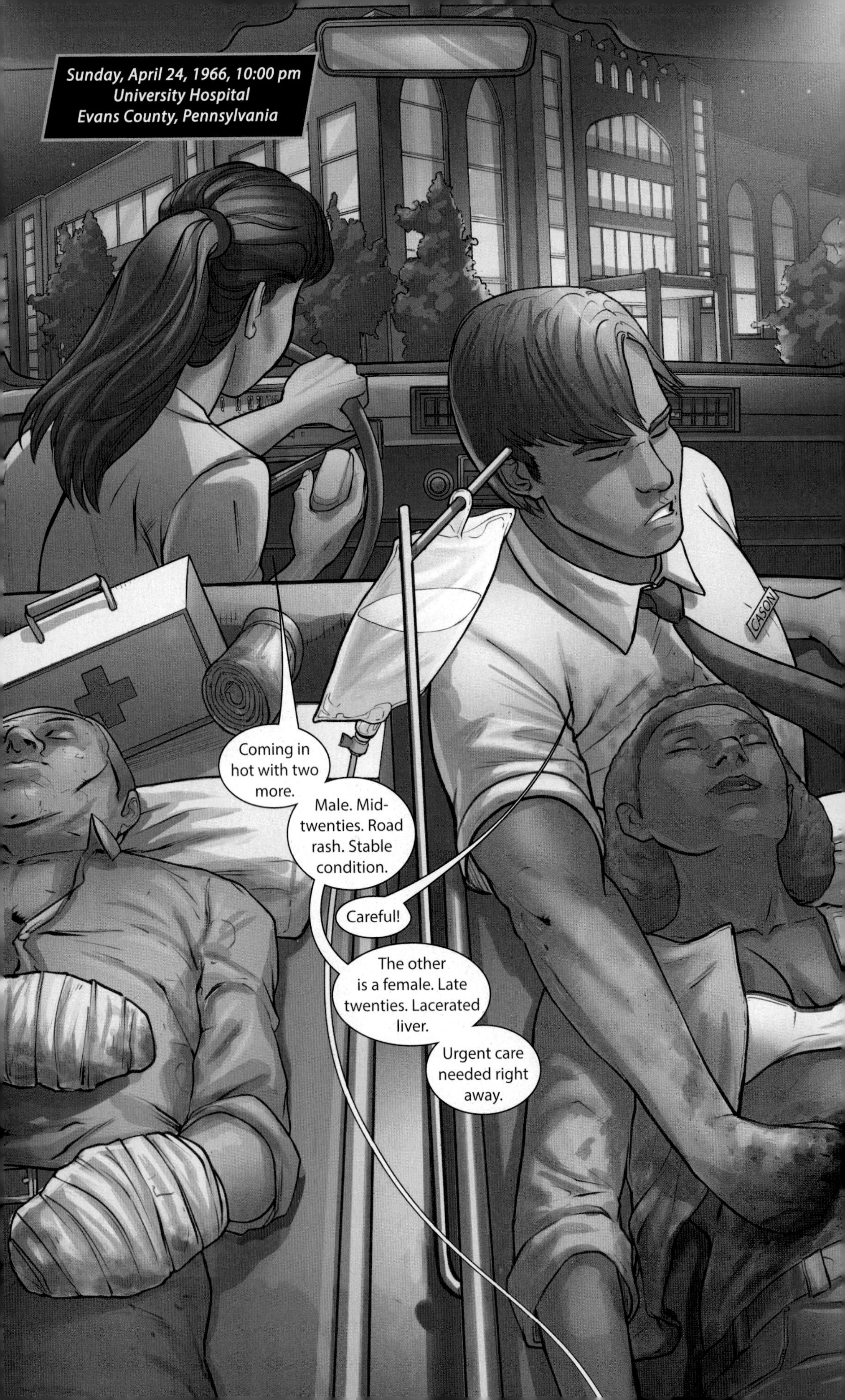
Sunday, April 24, 1966, 10:00 pm
University Hospital
Evans County, Pennsylvania
Coming in hot with two more.
Male. Mid-twenties. Road rash. Stable condition.
Careful!
The other is a female. Late twenties. Lacerated liver.
Urgent care needed right away.
CASON

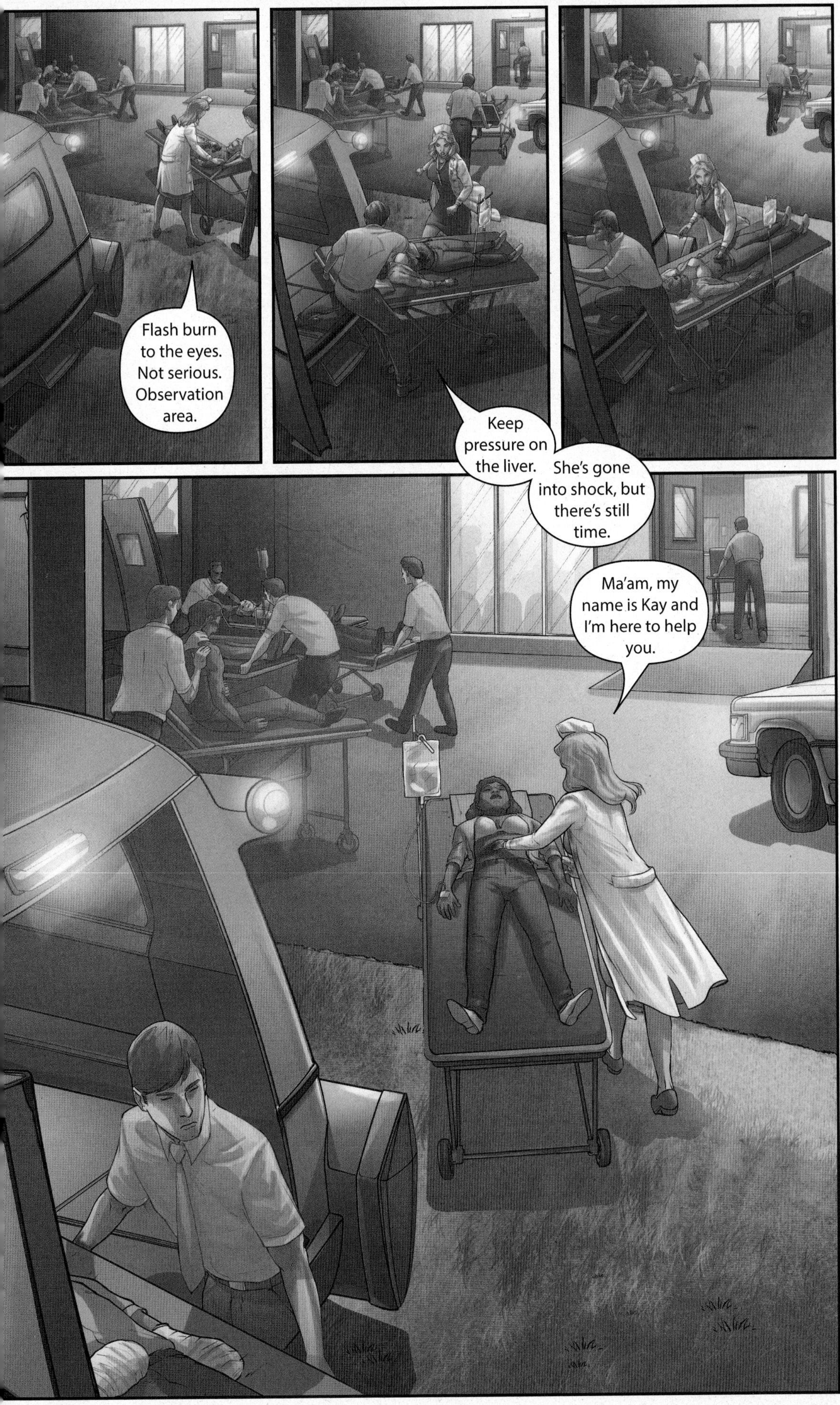
Flash burn to the eyes. Not serious. Observation area.
Keep pressure on the liver.
She's gone into shock, but there's still time.
Ma'am, my name is Kay and I'm here to help you.

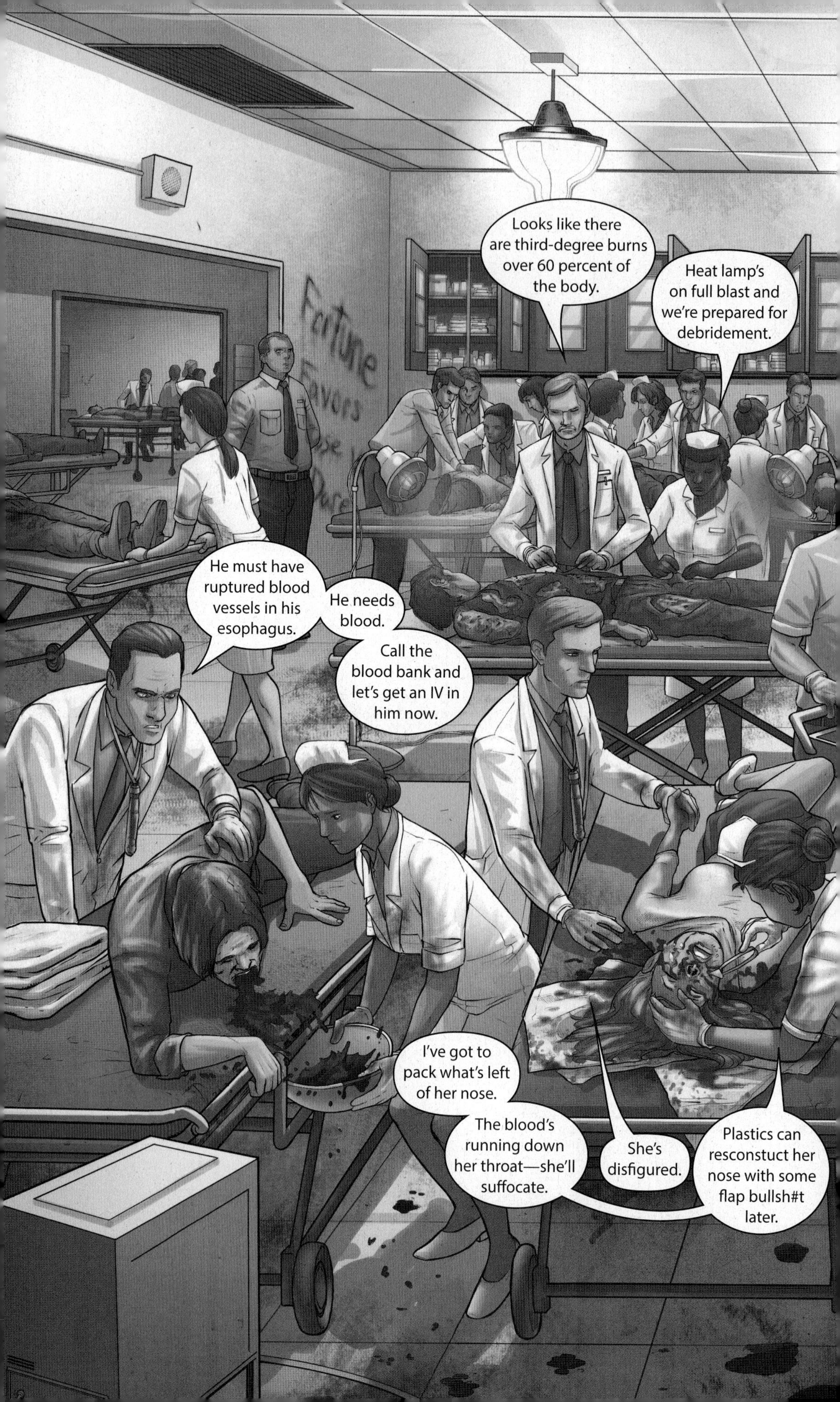

Fortune Favors
Looks like there are third-degree burns over 60 percent of the body.
Heat lamp's on full blast and we're prepared for debridement.
He must have ruptured blood vessels in his esophagus.
He needs blood.
Call the blood bank and let's get an IV in him now.
I've got to pack what's left of her nose.
The blood's running down her throat—she'll suffocate.
She's disfigured.
Plastics can resconstuct her nose with some flap bullsh#t later.

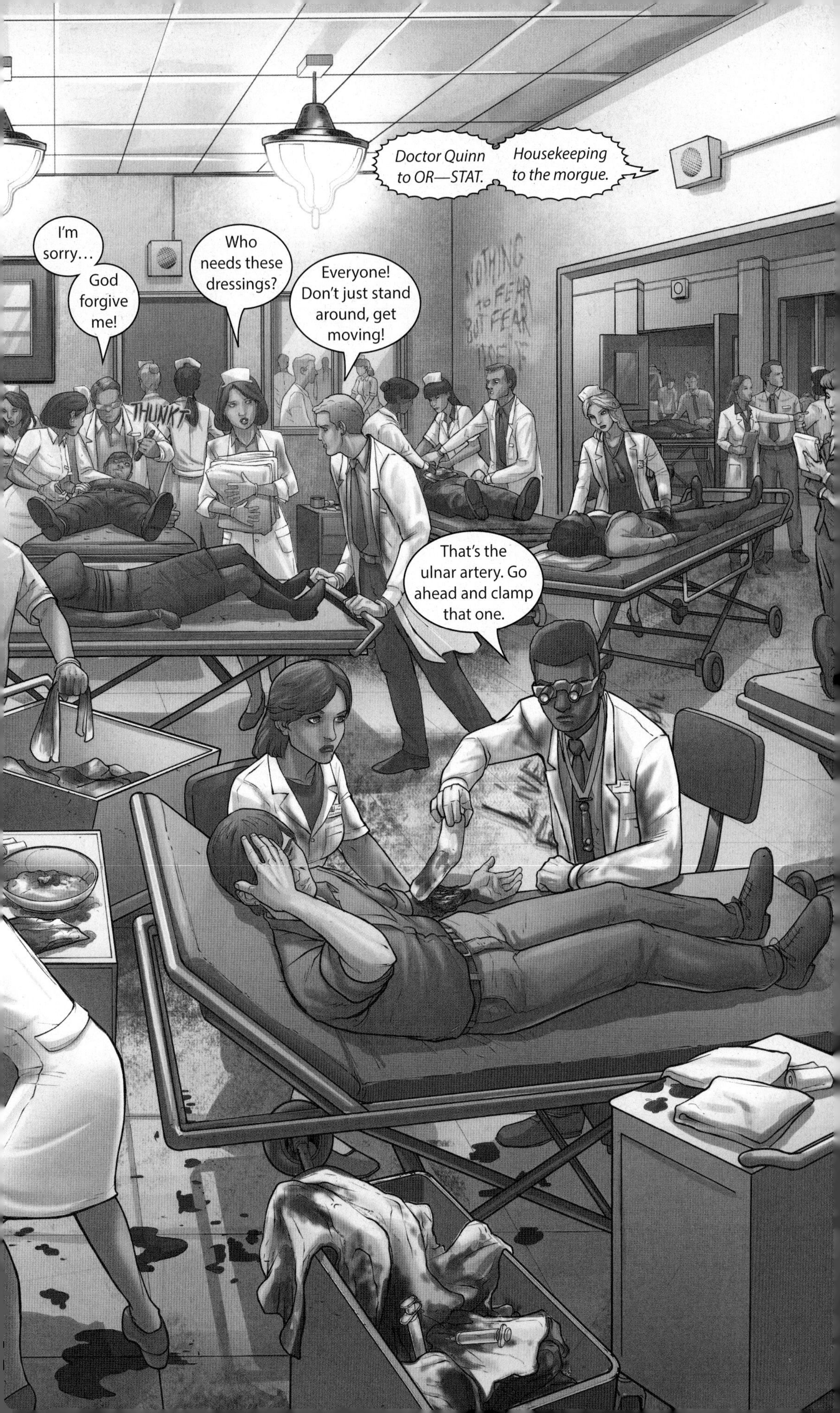
Doctor Quinn to OR—STAT.
Housekeeping to the morgue.
I'm sorry…
God forgive me!
Who needs these dressings?
Everyone! Don't just stand around, get moving!
NOTHING to FEAR BUT FEAR ITSELF
THUNK!
That's the ulnar artery. Go ahead and clamp that one.

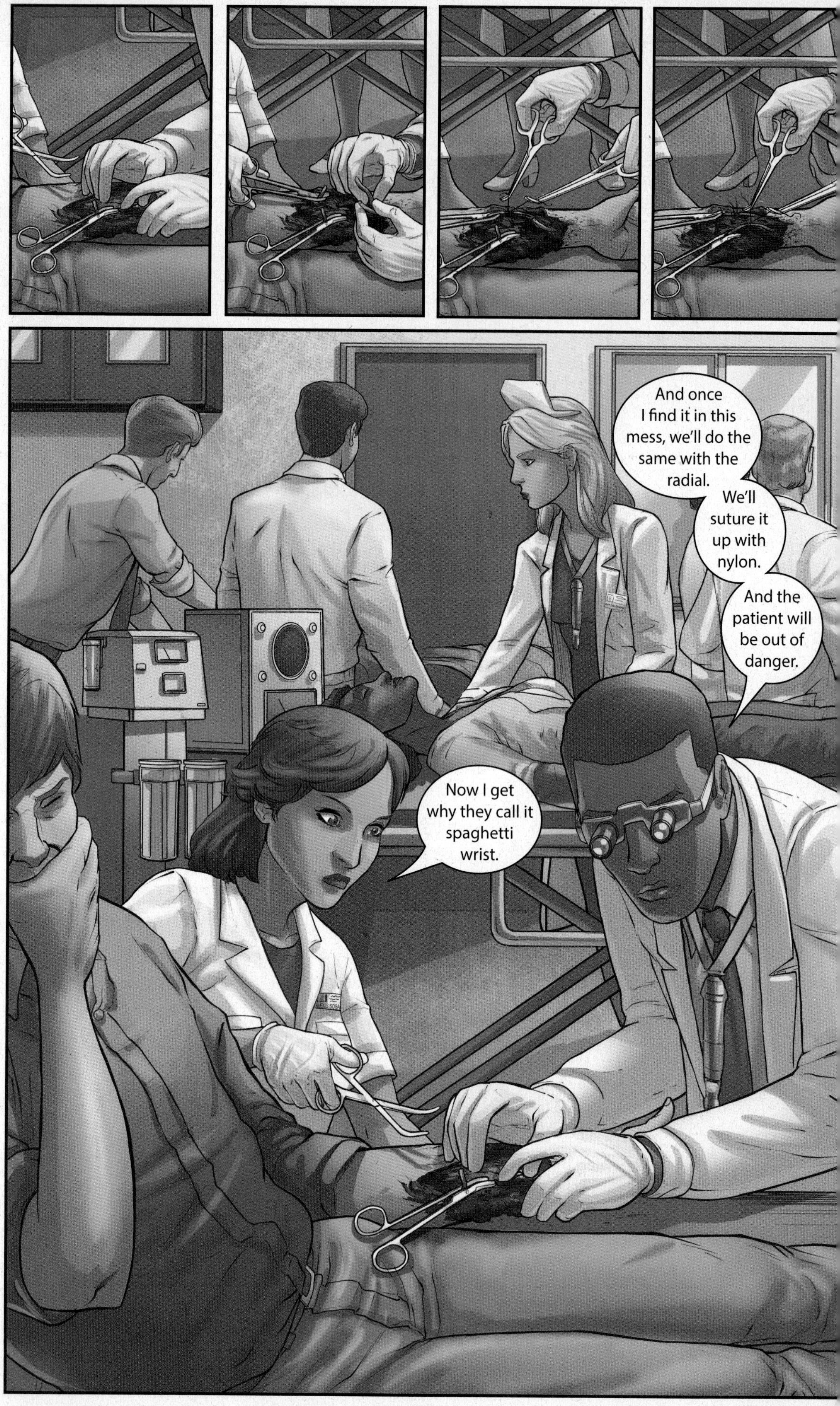
And once I find it in this mess, we'll do the same with the radial.
We'll suture it up with nylon.
And the patient will be out of danger.
Now I get why they call it spaghetti wrist.

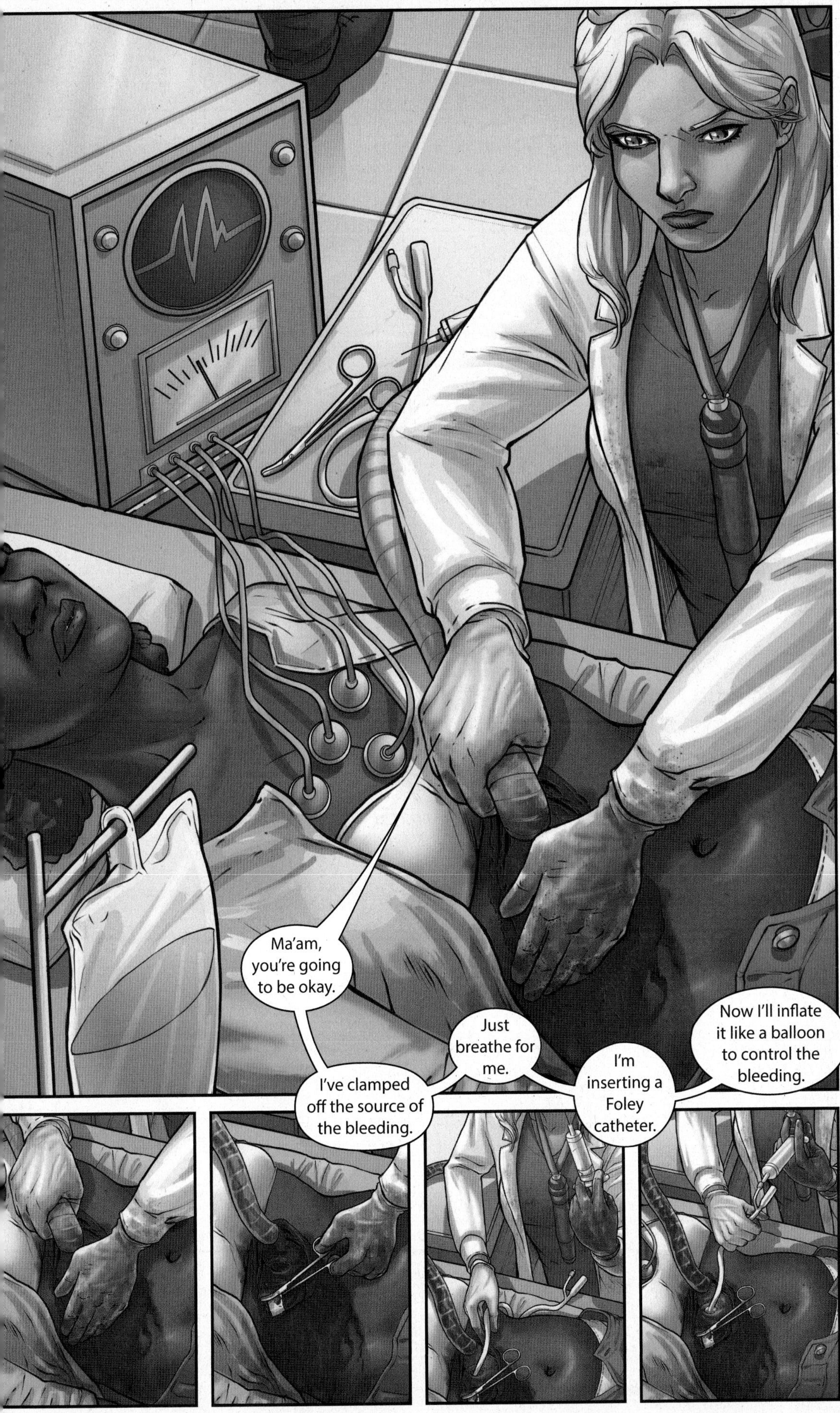

Ma'am, you're going to be okay.
Just breathe for me.
I've clamped off the source of the bleeding.
I'm inserting a Foley catheter.
Now I'll inflate it like a balloon to control the bleeding.

BEEEEEEEEE
No no no no…
One minute. If I had just one more minute…
Please…
Thank…

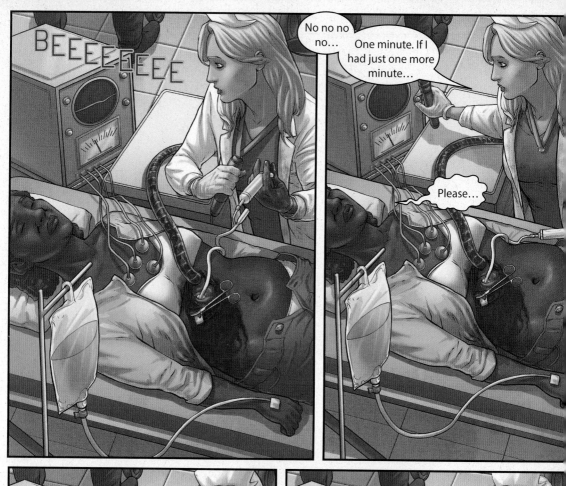

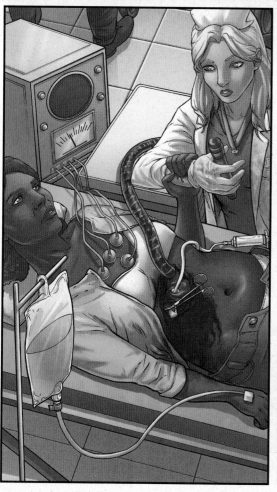

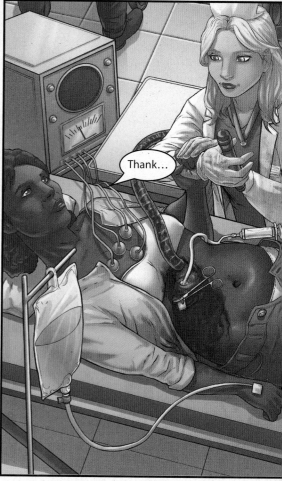

LGBT IN HISTORY

ergefell v. Hodges, June 26, 2015

the most recent landmark case r lesbian, gay, bisexual and ansgender (LGBT) rights, the US preme Court decides marriage uality for same sex couples is a nstitutional right.

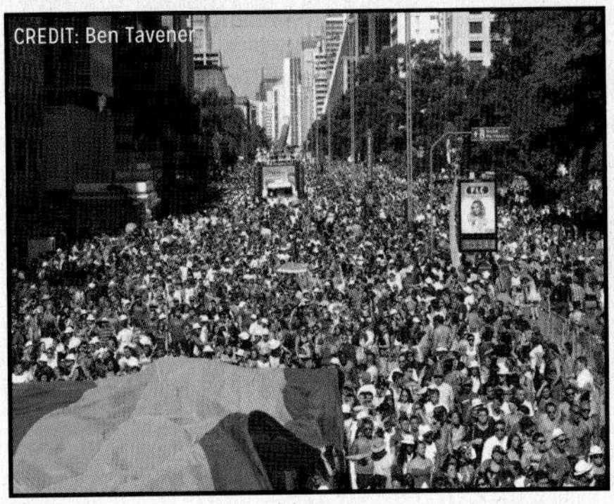
CREDIT: Ben Tavener

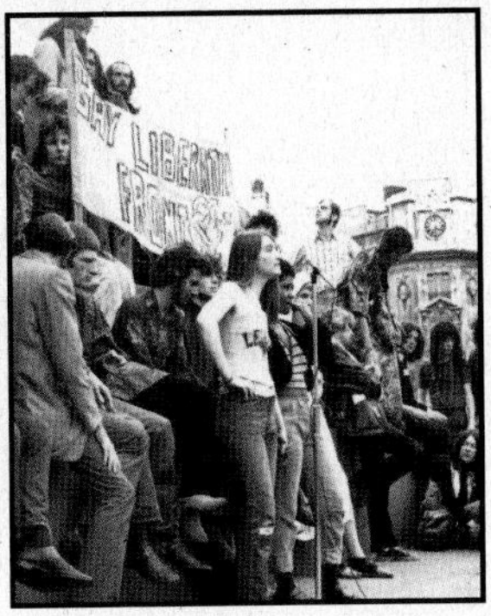

of April 2016, 19 countries recognize same-sex marriage. But 73 countries still criminalize homosexuality; and about lf of the Member States in the United Nations oppose, or still do not officially support, LGBT rights.

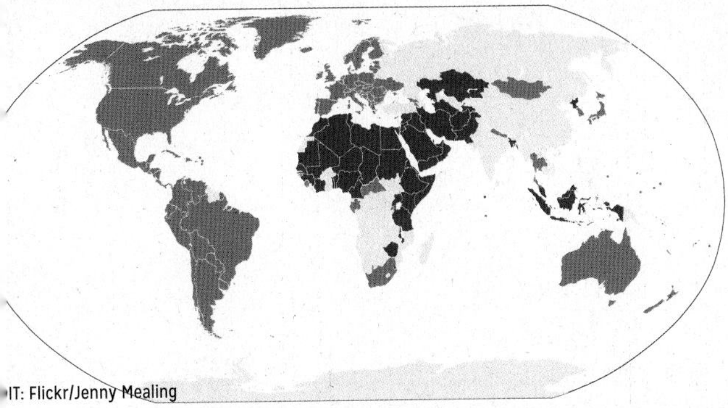
IT: Flickr/Jenny Mealing

Green = Countries that have signed a declaration supporting LGBT rights (94 members)

Red = Countries that oppose LGBT rights (54 members)

Grey = Countries that have expressed neither official support or opposition to LGBT rights (46 members)

he term "homophobia" is relatively new: coined in the 1960s by George Weinberg, an American clinical psychol-gist. But intolerance towards homosexuality dates back to the Middle Ages. Many ancient cultures, though, enerated love between two men:

ncient Celts – Their men openly preferred male lovers. Greek historian Diodorus Siculus recorded in the 1st Century .C. that the young men would offer themselves to strangers and would be insulted if their offer was refused.

ncient India – In the Hindu and Vedic texts, Lords Vishnu and Shiva manifested themselves as a woman and a ermaphrodite, respectively. Lord Vishnu takes the form of Mohini, an enchantress; Lord Shiva appears as Ardhanar-hvara, a half male and half female form. The Kamasutra, an ancient treatise on love and sex, also covered the topic f same-sex attraction.

ncient Rome – Ancient Roman sexuality did not recognize the binary concepts of homosexuality and heterosexuality. man playing the penetrative role in a same-sex relationship was considered acceptable and natural. On the flipside, he Romans looked down upon a man who willfully performed oral or received anal sex.

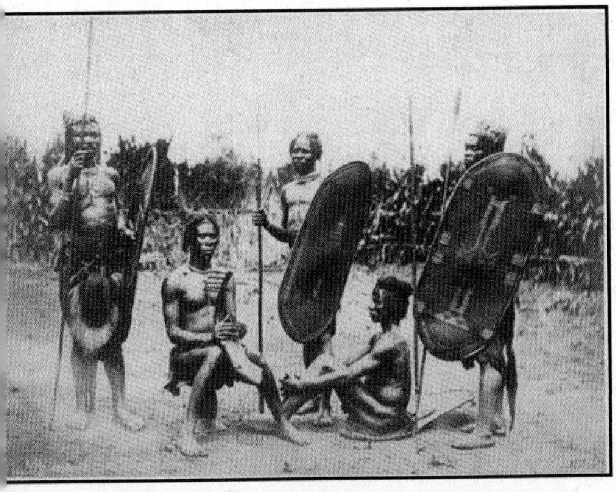

Feudal Japan – In the 16th Century A.D., during the Tokugawa shogunate, samurais took on their young male apprentices as lovers in a "brotherhood contract," an exclusive homosexual relationship that was received as positive.

Ancient Persia – Homosexuality was tolerated in public places, from monasteries to taverns. Male prostitution houses were legally recognized and paid taxes between the 16th and 18th Centuries A.D.

Congo – A 20th Century English anthropologist wrote that the male Azande warriors in the northern Congo routinely had young male lovers.

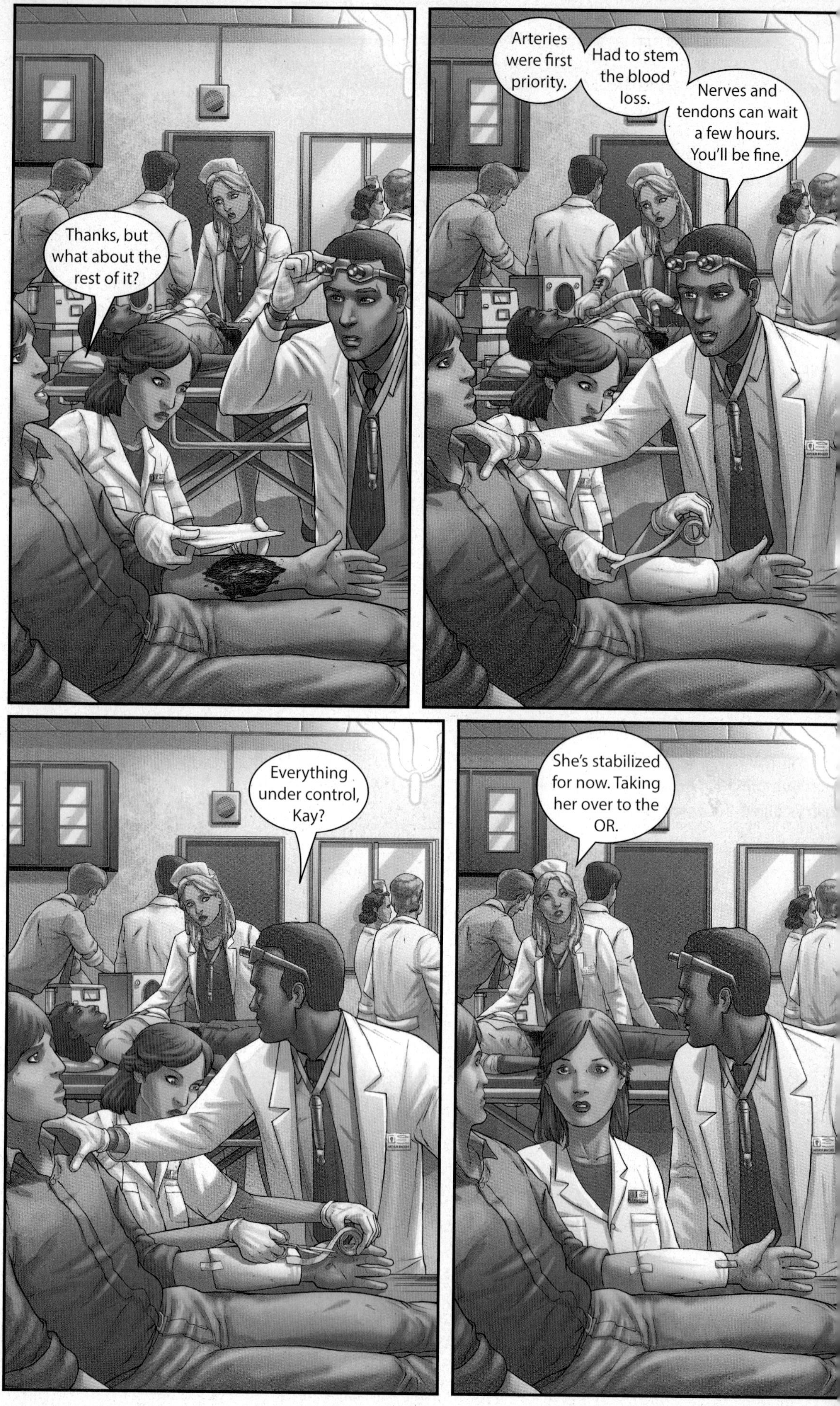
Thanks, but what about the rest of it?
Arteries were first priority.
Had to stem the blood loss.
Nerves and tendons can wait a few hours. You'll be fine.
Everything under control, Kay?
She's stabilized for now. Taking her over to the OR.

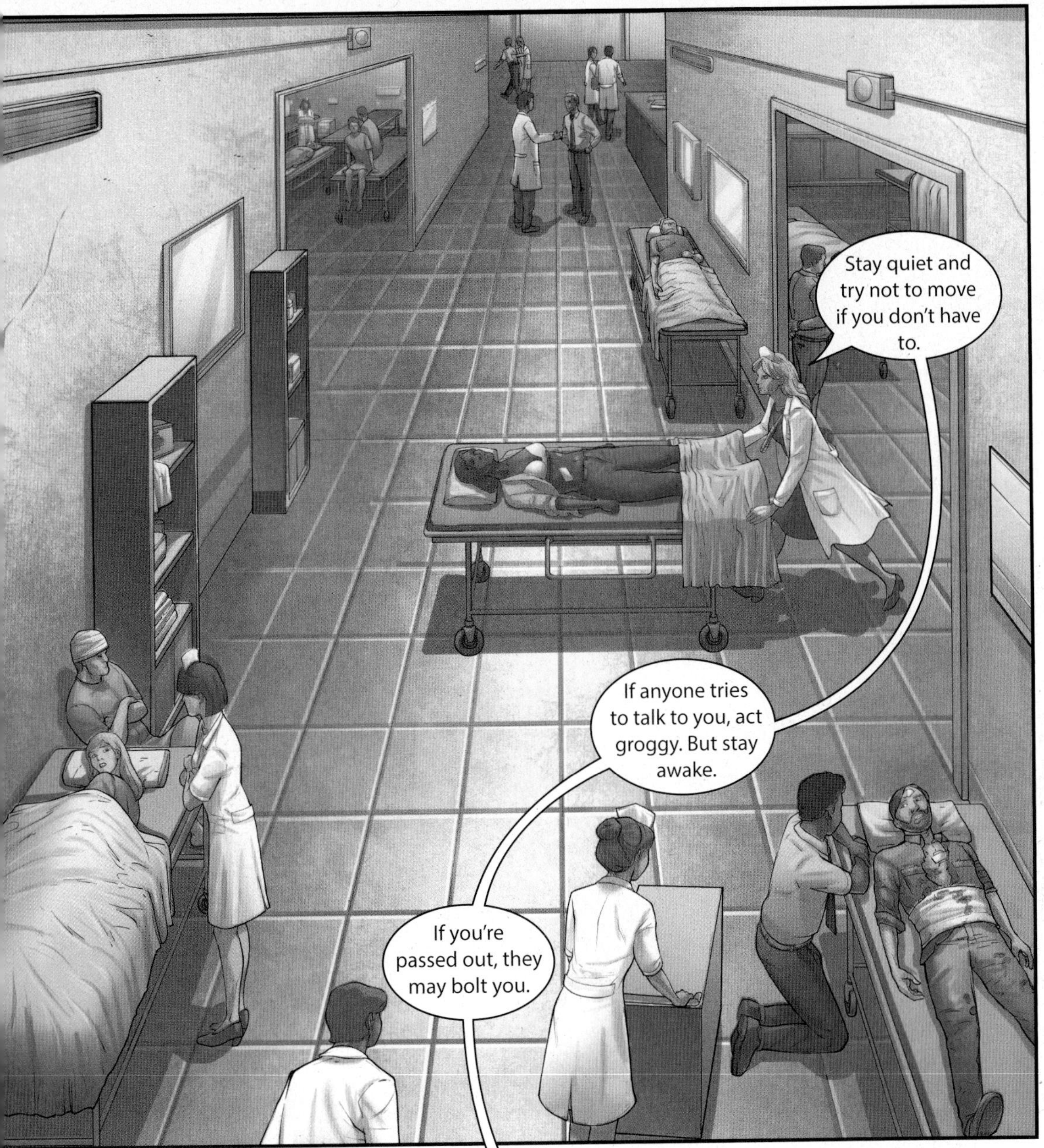
Stay quiet and try not to move if you don't have to.
If anyone tries to talk to you, act groggy. But stay awake.
If you're passed out, they may bolt you.

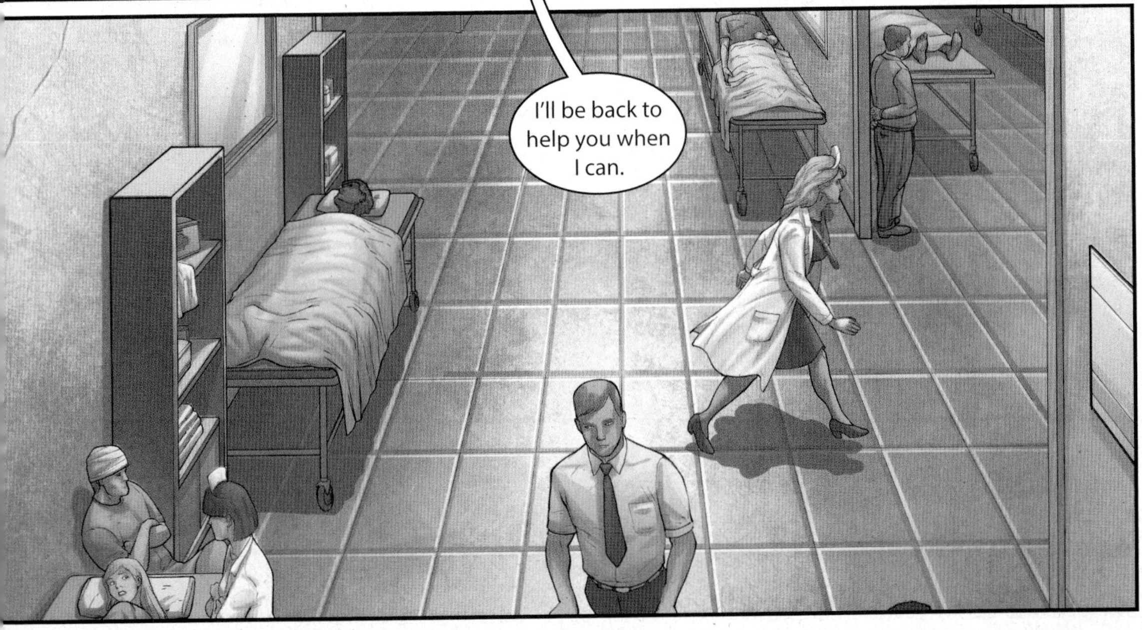
I'll be back to help you when I can.

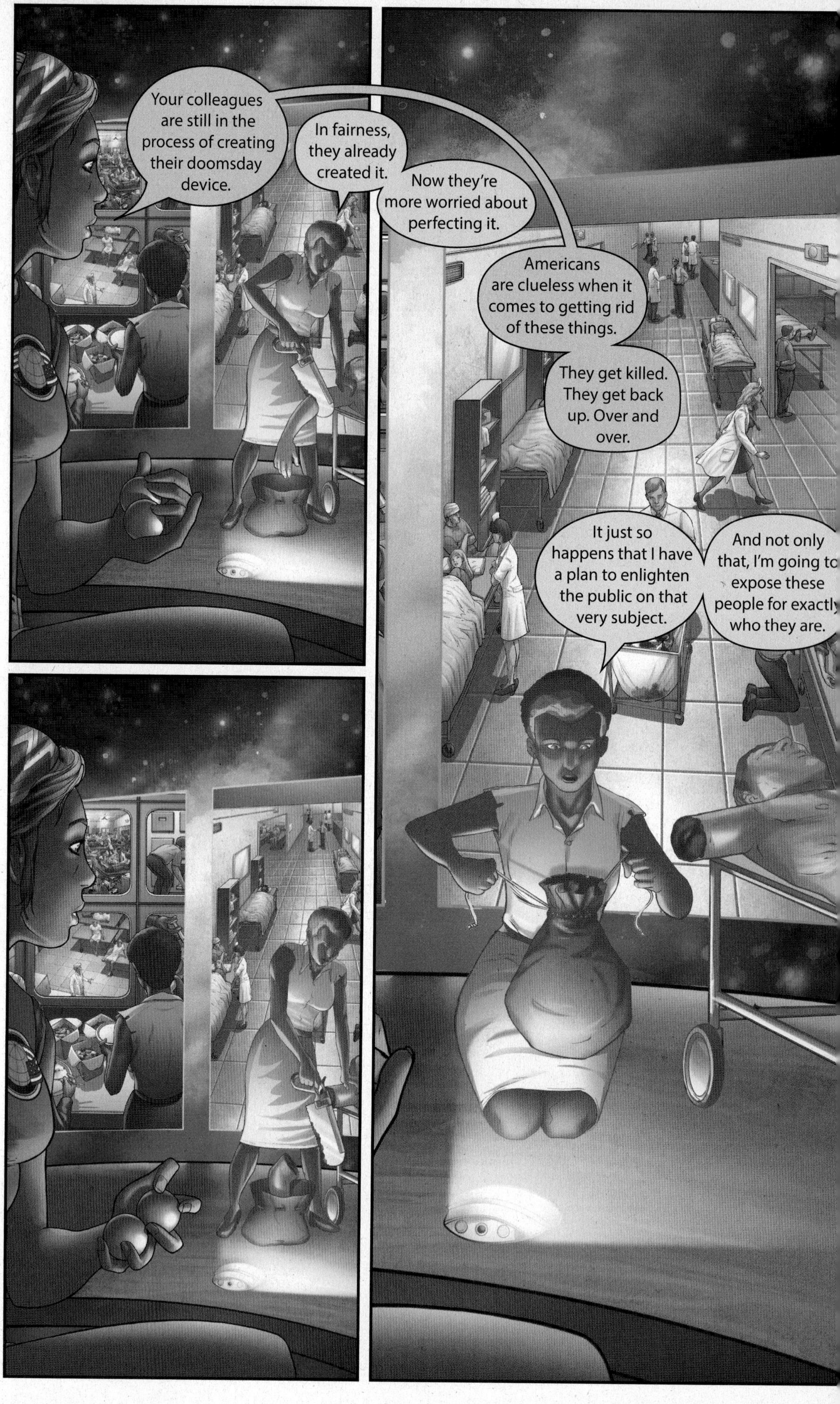
Your colleagues are still in the process of creating their doomsday device.
In fairness, they already created it.
Now they're more worried about perfecting it.
Americans are clueless when it comes to getting rid of these things.
They get killed. They get back up. Over and over.
It just so happens that I have a plan to enlighten the public on that very subject.
And not only that, I'm going to expose these people for exactly who they are.

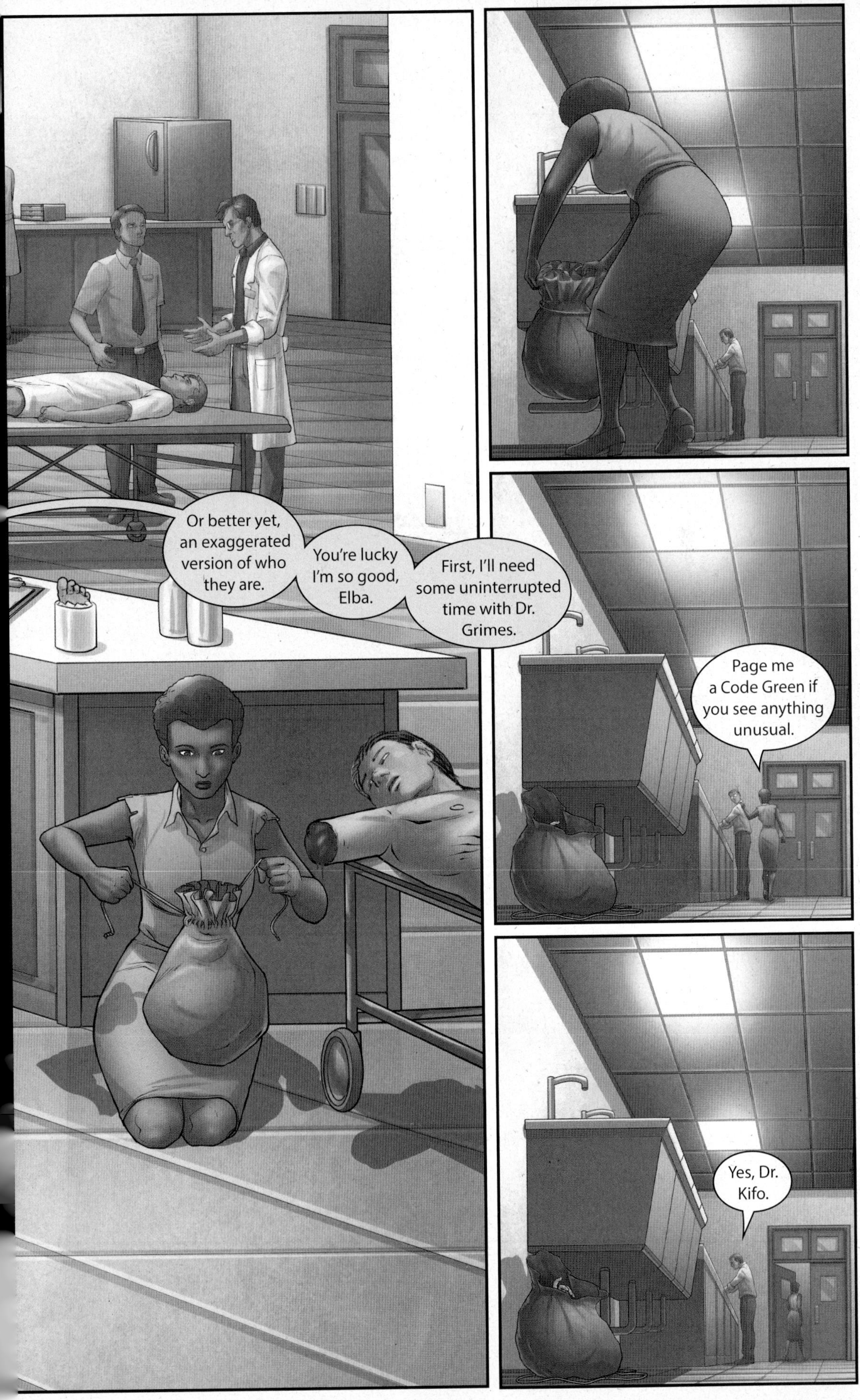
Or better yet, an exaggerated version of who they are.
You're lucky I'm so good, Elba.
First, I'll need some uninterrupted time with Dr. Grimes.
Page me a Code Green if you see anything unusual.
Yes, Dr. Kifo.

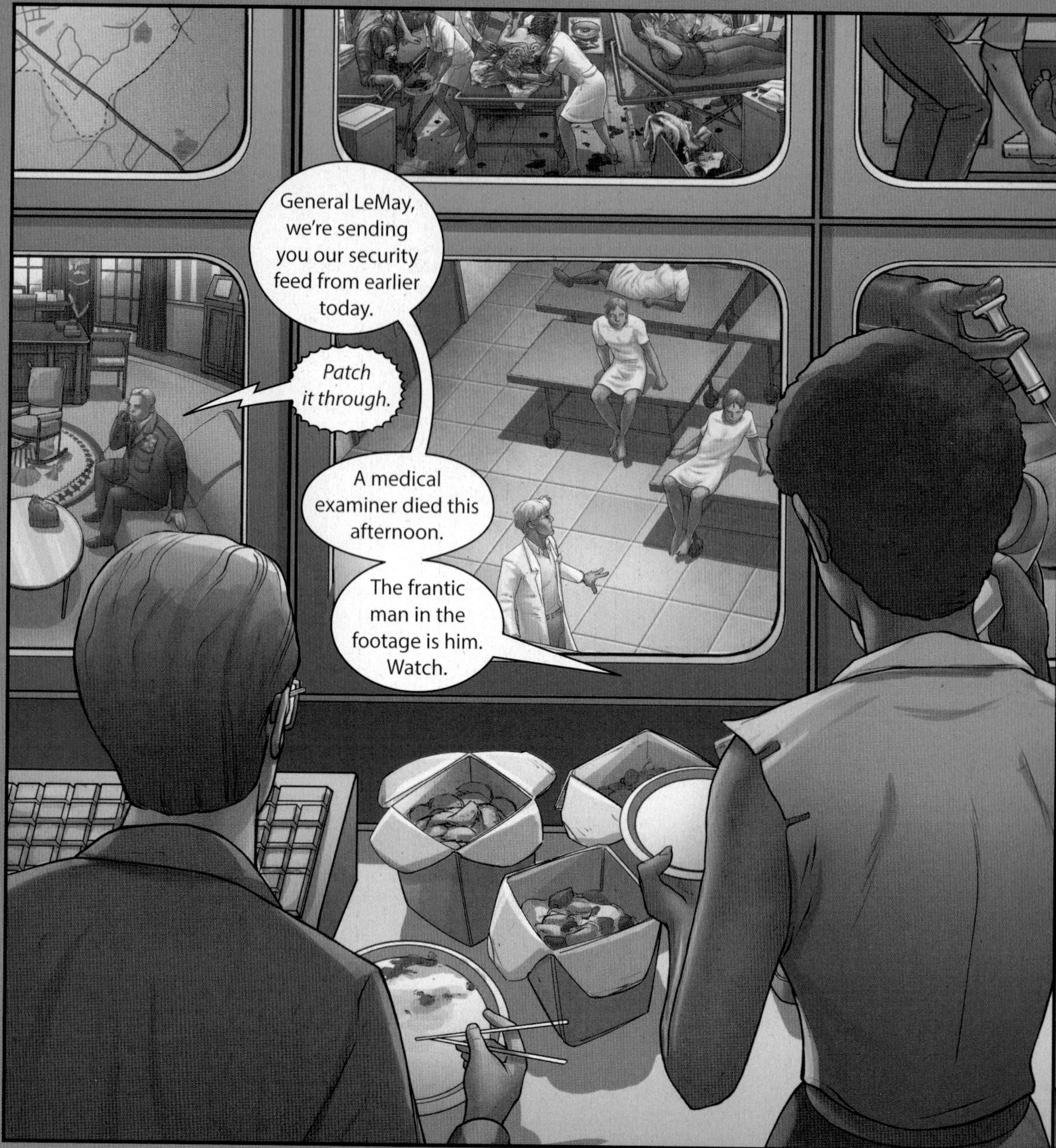
General LeMay, we're sending you our security feed from earlier today.
Patch it through.
A medical examiner died this afternoon.
The frantic man in the footage is him. Watch.

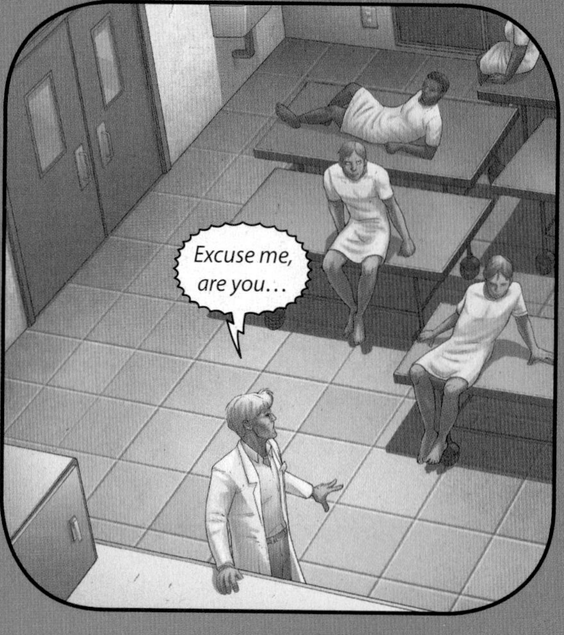
Excuse me, are you…

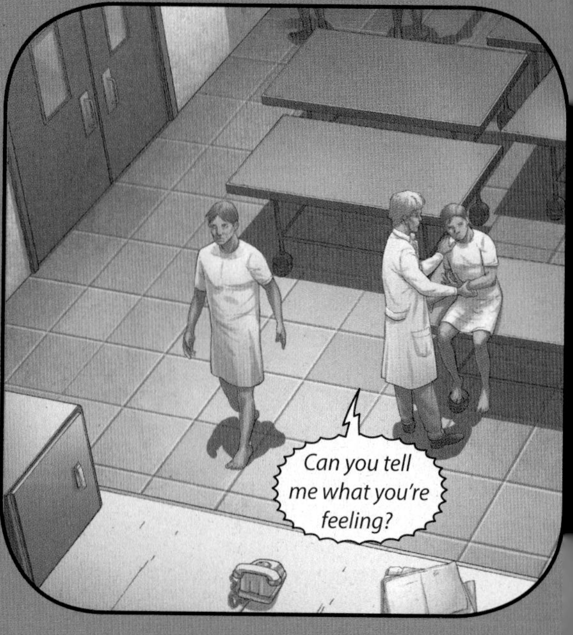
Can you tell me what you're feeling?

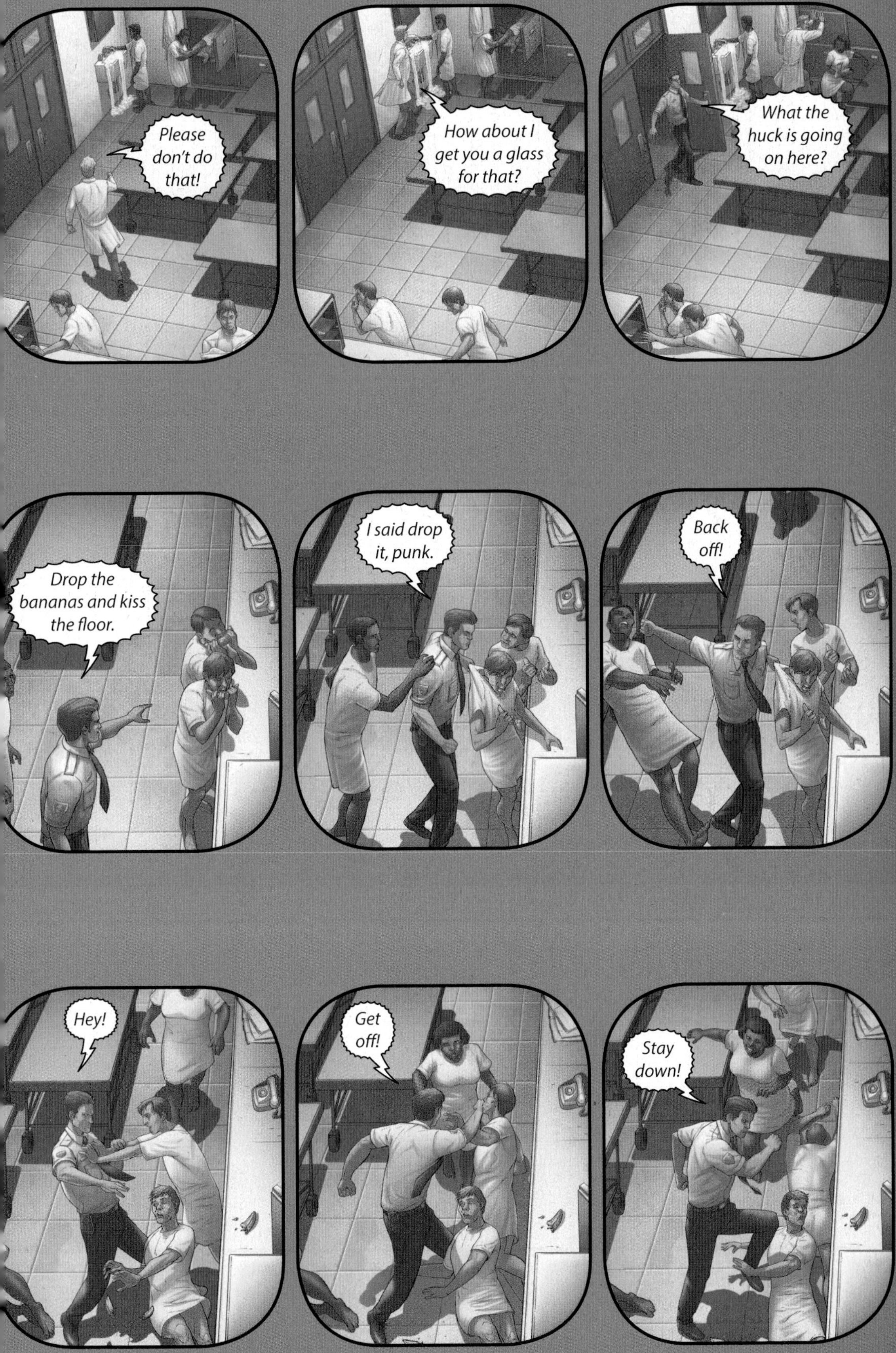
Please don't do that!
How about I get you a glass for that?
What the huck is going on here?
Drop the bananas and kiss the floor.
I said drop it, punk.
Back off!
Hey!
Get off!
Stay down!

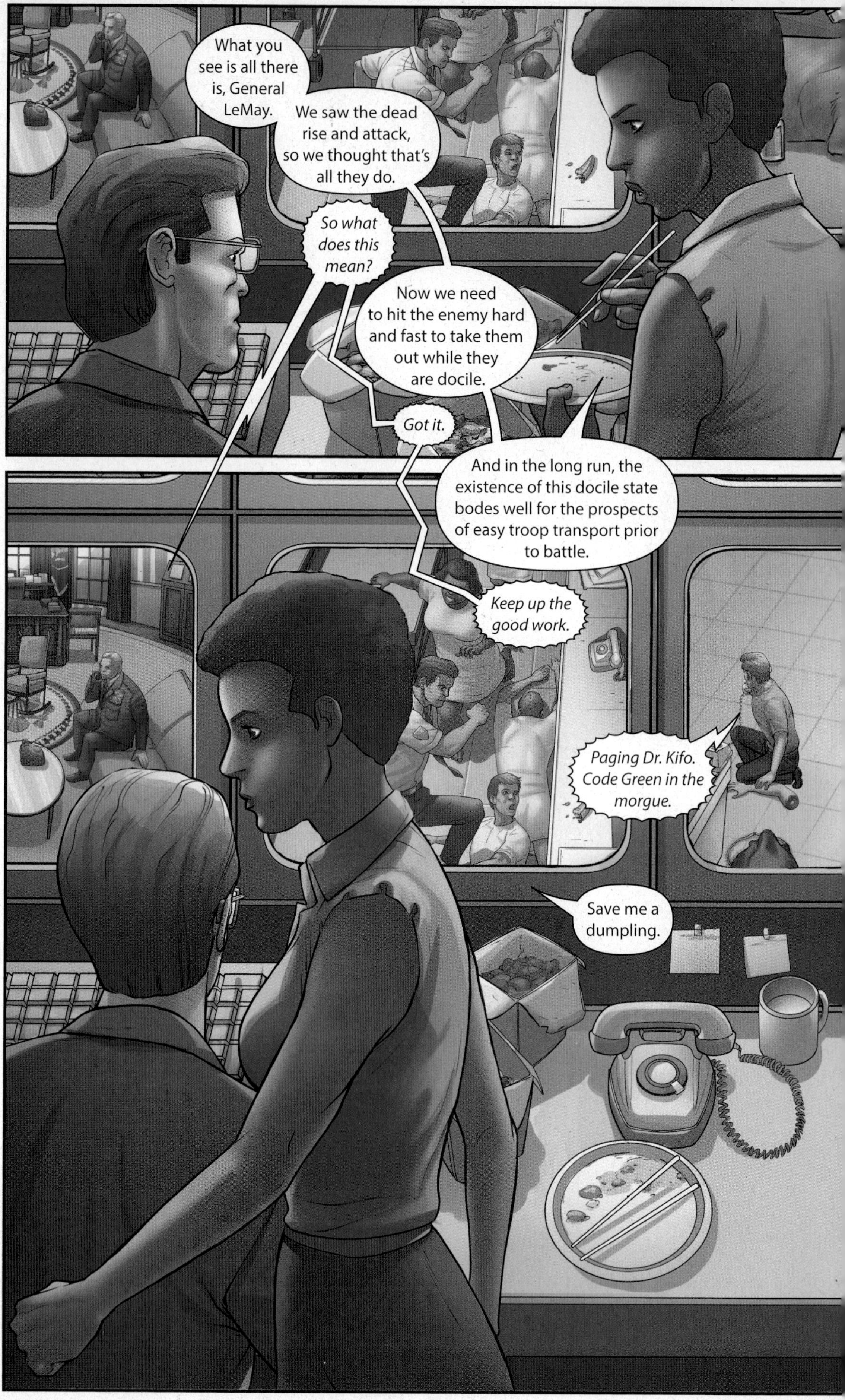
What you see is all there is, General LeMay.
We saw the dead rise and attack, so we thought that's all they do.
So what does this mean?
Now we need to hit the enemy hard and fast to take them out while they are docile.
Got it.
And in the long run, the existence of this docile state bodes well for the prospects of easy troop transport prior to battle.
Keep up the good work.
Paging Dr. Kifo. Code Green in the morgue.
Save me a dumpling.

NATURE'S ZOMBIES

The modern zombie is usually a cadaver or living human infected with a virus that alters the host's behavior. Our zombie fiction may be closer to reality than imagined. From protozoans to wasps, these parasites manipulate their hosts' behaviors for their benefit (and to their hosts' detriment).

Credit: Flickr / Stig Nygaard

JEWEL WASP OR EMERALD COCKROACH WASP

TOXOPLASMA GONDII: A mouse finds itself in the cat's territory; it should be wary from the scent of cat urine. But this mouse is not behaving normally: it is less averse, having been infected with a parasitic protozoan called *T. gondii*. The cat easily snatches up the infected prey. The parasite ends up exactly where it wants to be: in the cat's intestinal tract, which is the only place where it's known to reproduce, and it will spread through feline excrement. While *T. gondii* seems to primarily alter behavior in mice, the parasite can infect almost all warm-blooded animals. An estimated 30 to 50 percent of the global human population may be chronically infected with *T. gondii* after exposure. While infection in humans is mostly asymptomatic, some studies suggest that the parasite may be associated with a number of neurological disorders in humans (e.g., schizophrenia).

AMPULEX COMPRESSA: Located in South Asia, Africa, and the Pacific Islands, the female jewel wasp uses a cockroach as its living nursery. First, she paralyzes the roach's front legs; then, she stings the roach's head with a venom disabling the roach's escape reflexes. Instead of running, the roach will groom extensively, and become sluggish. Next, the wasp leads the roach to its burrow by pulling on one of the roach's antennae (much like a leash). Over the next eight days, her larva consumes the roach's organs. The roach stays alive until the larva pupates.

Credit: Brett A. Goodman, Pieter T.J. Johnson

PARASITIC FLATWORM - RIBEIROIA ONDATRAE: The *R. ondatrae* is a microscopic flatworm that first attacks a snail's reproductive organs, turning it into a vehicle to release thousands of larvae that burrow into tadpoles' budding limbs. As infected tadpoles develop, cysts from the flatworm larvae cause deformities, such as extra limbs. These frogs are crippled and easy prey for waterbirds. Once consumed, the waterbirds carry the parasites in their stomach to another body of water.

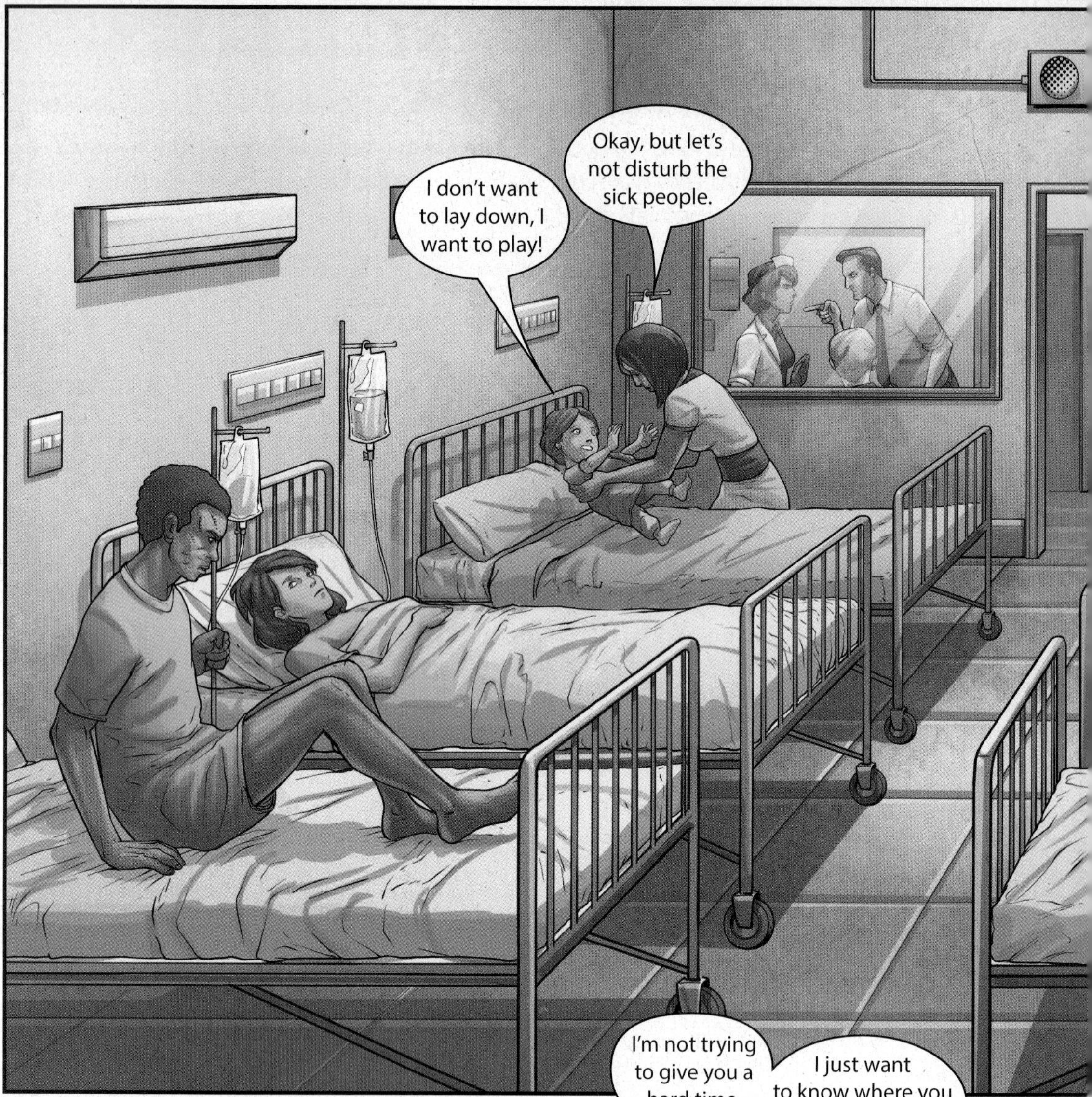
I don't want to lay down, I want to play!
Okay, but let's not disturb the sick people.

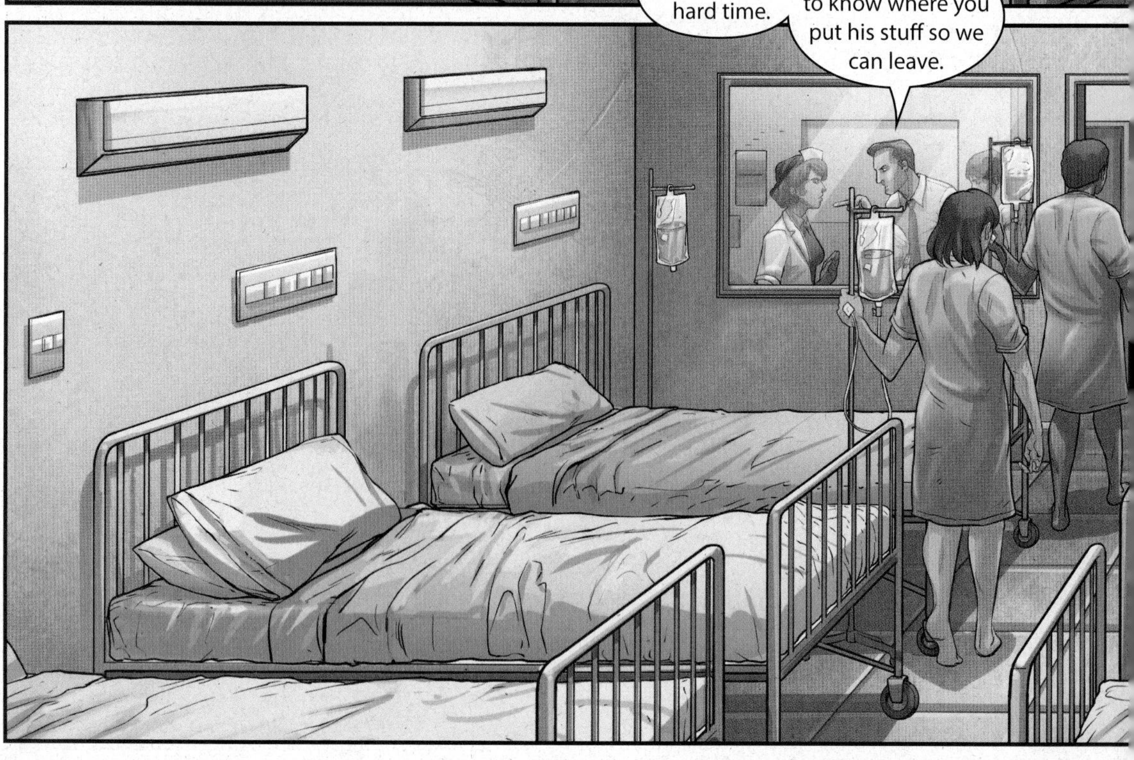
I'm not trying to give you a hard time.
I just want to know where you put his stuff so we can leave.

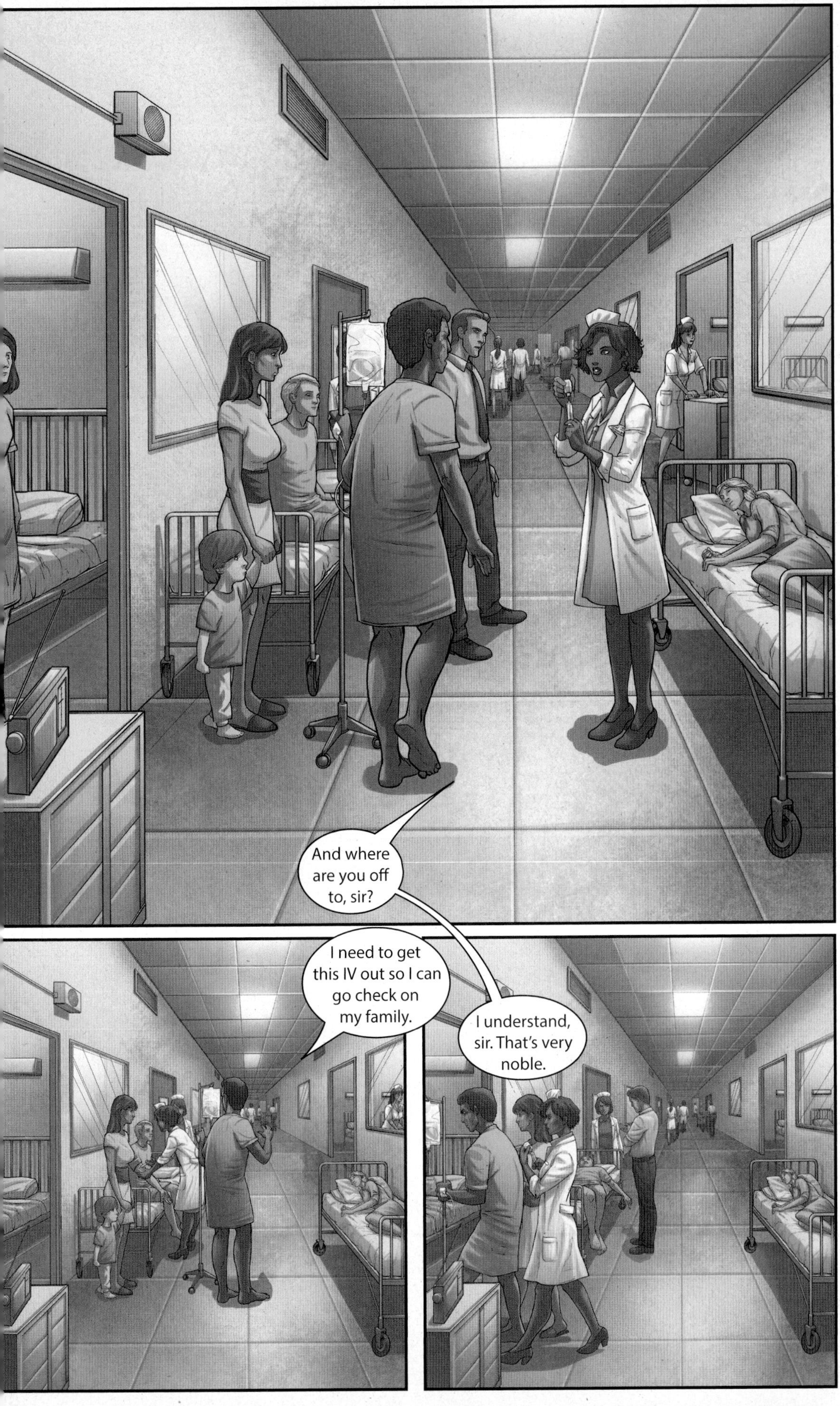
And where are you off to, sir?
I need to get this IV out so I can go check on my family.
I understand, sir. That's very noble.

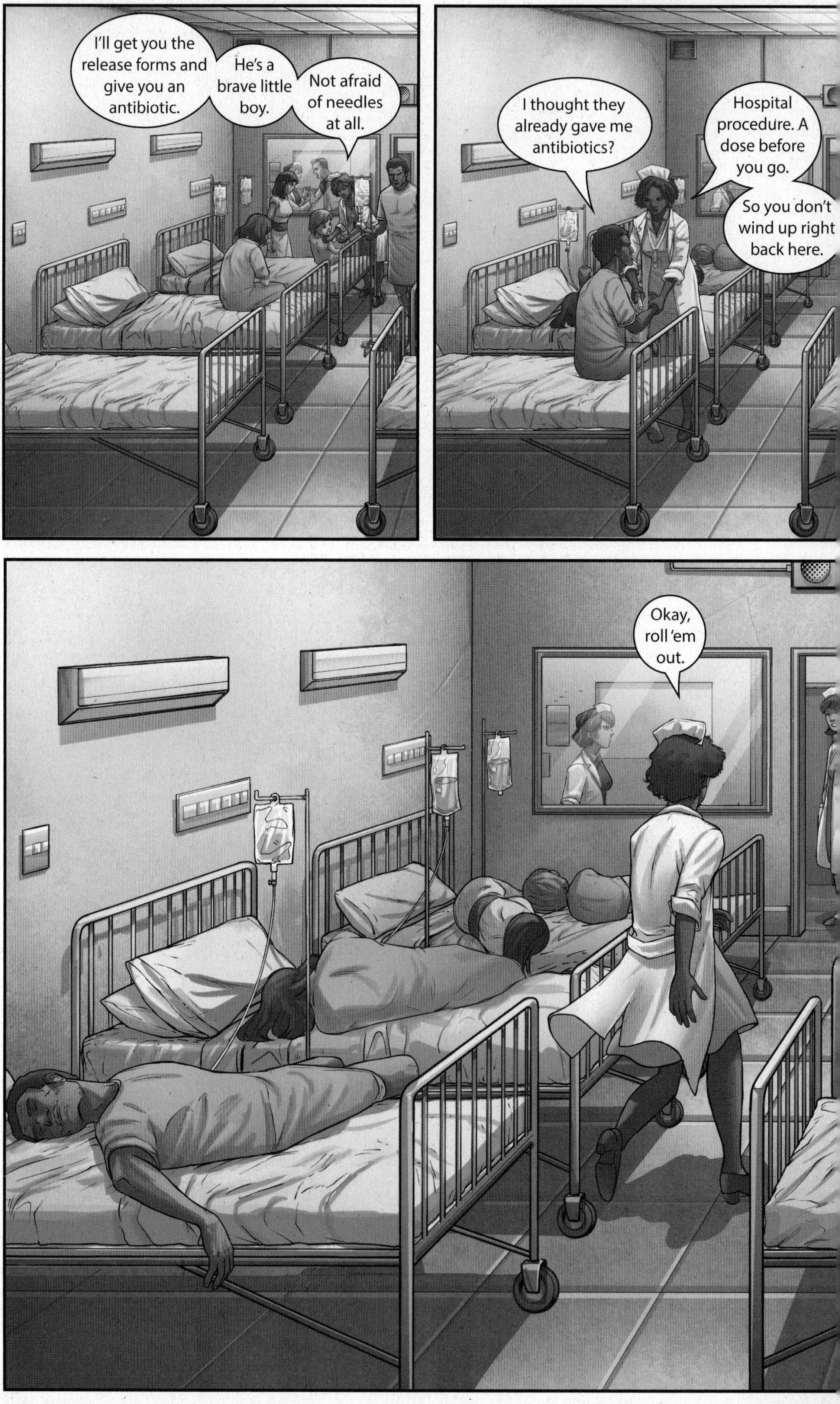
I'll get you the release forms and give you an antibiotic.
He's a brave little boy.
Not afraid of needles at all.
I thought they already gave me antibiotics?
Hospital procedure. A dose before you go.
So you don't wind up right back here.
Okay, roll 'em out.

THE AMERICAN STUDENT DEBT CRISIS

	1960s*	2010s	DIFFERENCE
Median Family Income	$45,700	$51,939	14%
Total Annual Student Loans	$891.4 million	$260 billion	29,068%
Federal	$891.4 million	$178 billion	19,869%
Non-federal	$0	$81 billion	0%
Average Public College Tuition	$7,432	$14,500	103%
Average Private College Tuition	$15,348	$34,000	130%
Average Income for Male Grad	$91,100	$36,000	-61%
Average Income for Female Grad	$25,000	$36,000	44%
Bachelor Degrees Conferred	5,200,000	19,000,000	265%
Public Law School Tuition	$3,664	$42,000	1,046%
Private Law School Tuition	$1,661	$24,000	1,345%

As of late 2014, federal-owned student loans totaled $850 billion, jumping up 750% from $100 billion in the mid-1990s; student loans now make up almost half of the federal portfolio (not including assets owned by the Federal reserve and land).

*IN 2016 DOLLARS

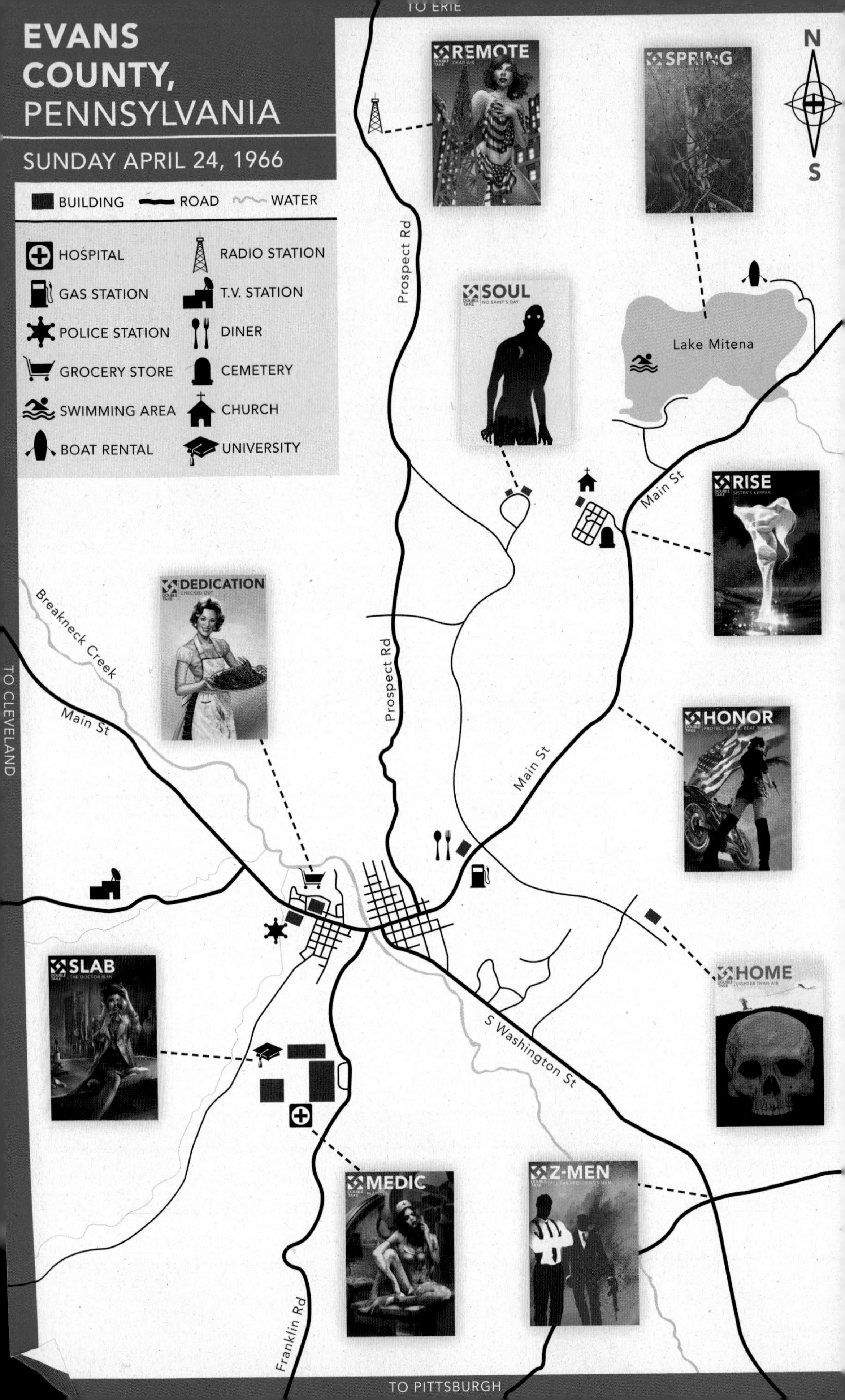

EVANS COUNTY, PENNSYLVANIA
SUNDAY APRIL 24, 1966
BUILDING
ROAD
WATER
HOSPITAL
GAS STATION
POLICE STATION
GROCERY STORE
SWIMMING AREA
BOAT RENTAL
RADIO STATION
T.V. STATION
DINER
CEMETERY
CHURCH
UNIVERSITY
N
S
TO ERIE
TO CLEVELAND
TO PITTSBURGH
REMOTE
DEAD AIR
SPRING
SOUL
NO SAINT'S DAY
Lake Mitena
RISE
SISTER'S KEEPER
DEDICATION
CHECKED OUT
HONOR
PROTECT. SERVE. BEAT. BURN.
HOME
LIGHTER THAN AIR
SLAB
THE DOCTOR IS IN
MEDIC
Z-MEN
ALL THE PRESIDENT'S MEN
Prospect Rd
Prospect Rd
Main St
Main St
Main St
Breakneck Creek
S Washington St
Franklin Rd

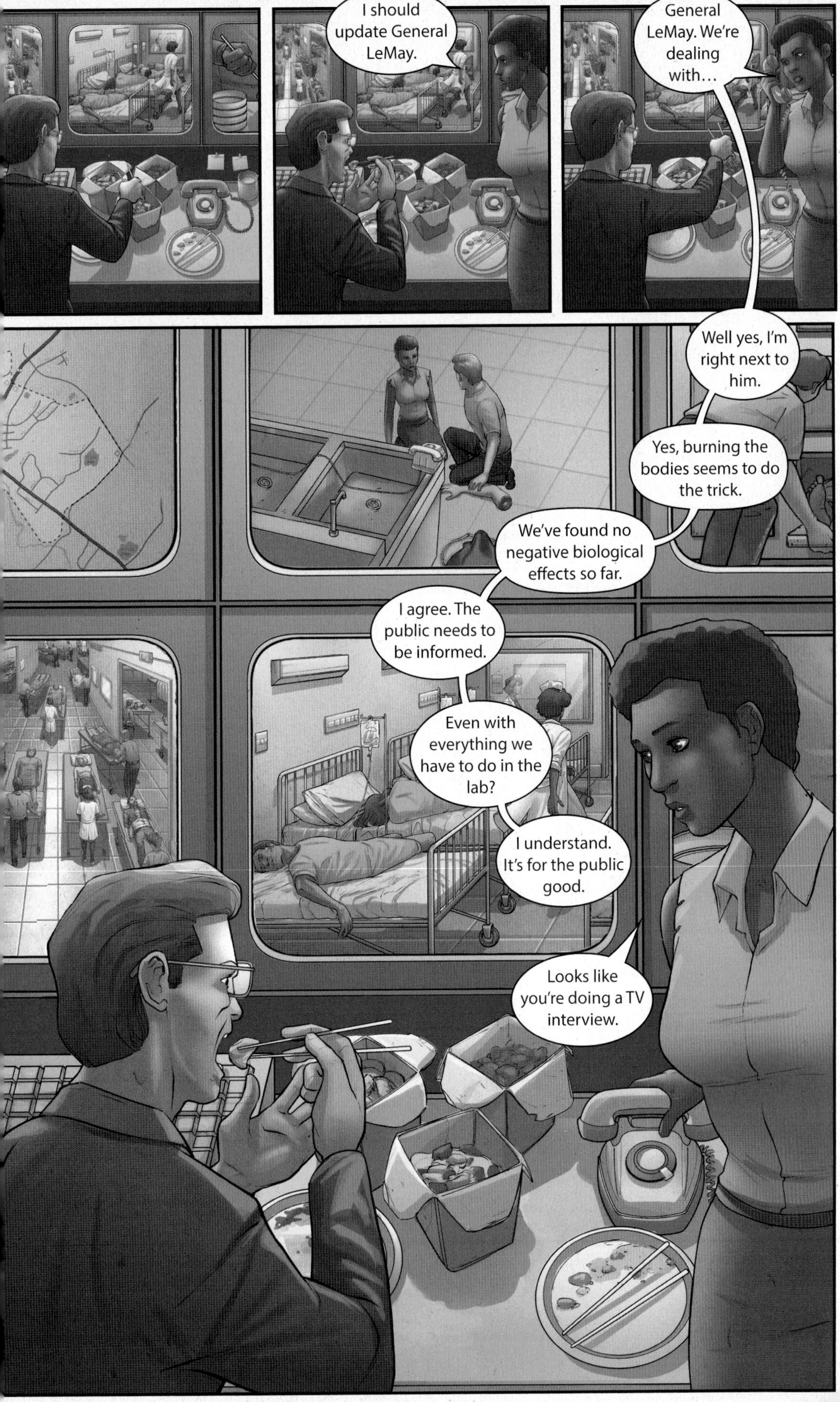
I should update General LeMay.
General LeMay. We're dealing with…
Well yes, I'm right next to him.
Yes, burning the bodies seems to do the trick.
We've found no negative biological effects so far.
I agree. The public needs to be informed.
Even with everything we have to do in the lab?
I understand. It's for the public good.
Looks like you're doing a TV interview.

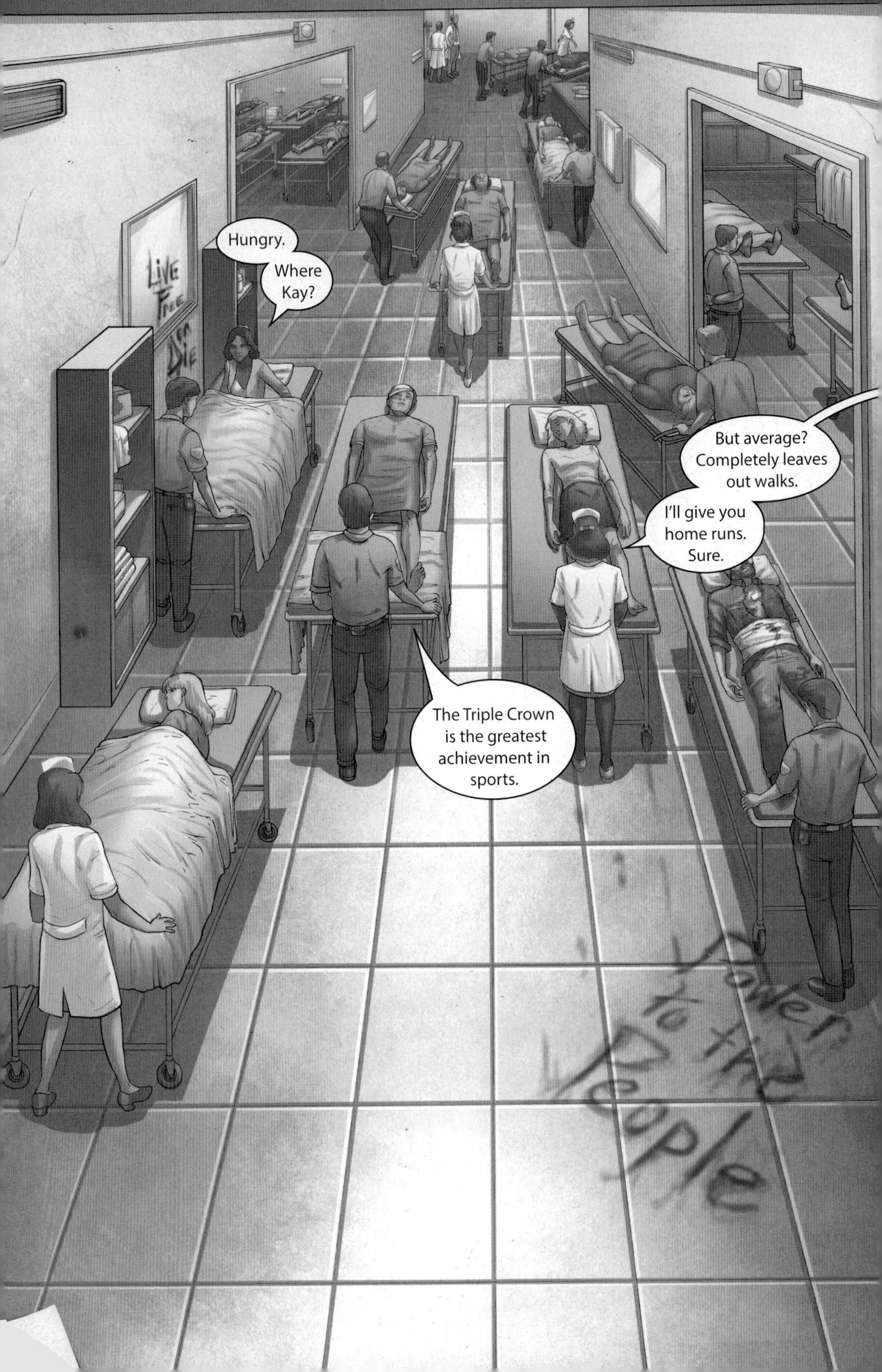
Hungry.
Where Kay?
The Triple Crown is the greatest achievement in sports.
I'll give you home runs. Sure.
But average? Completely leaves out walks.
Power to the People

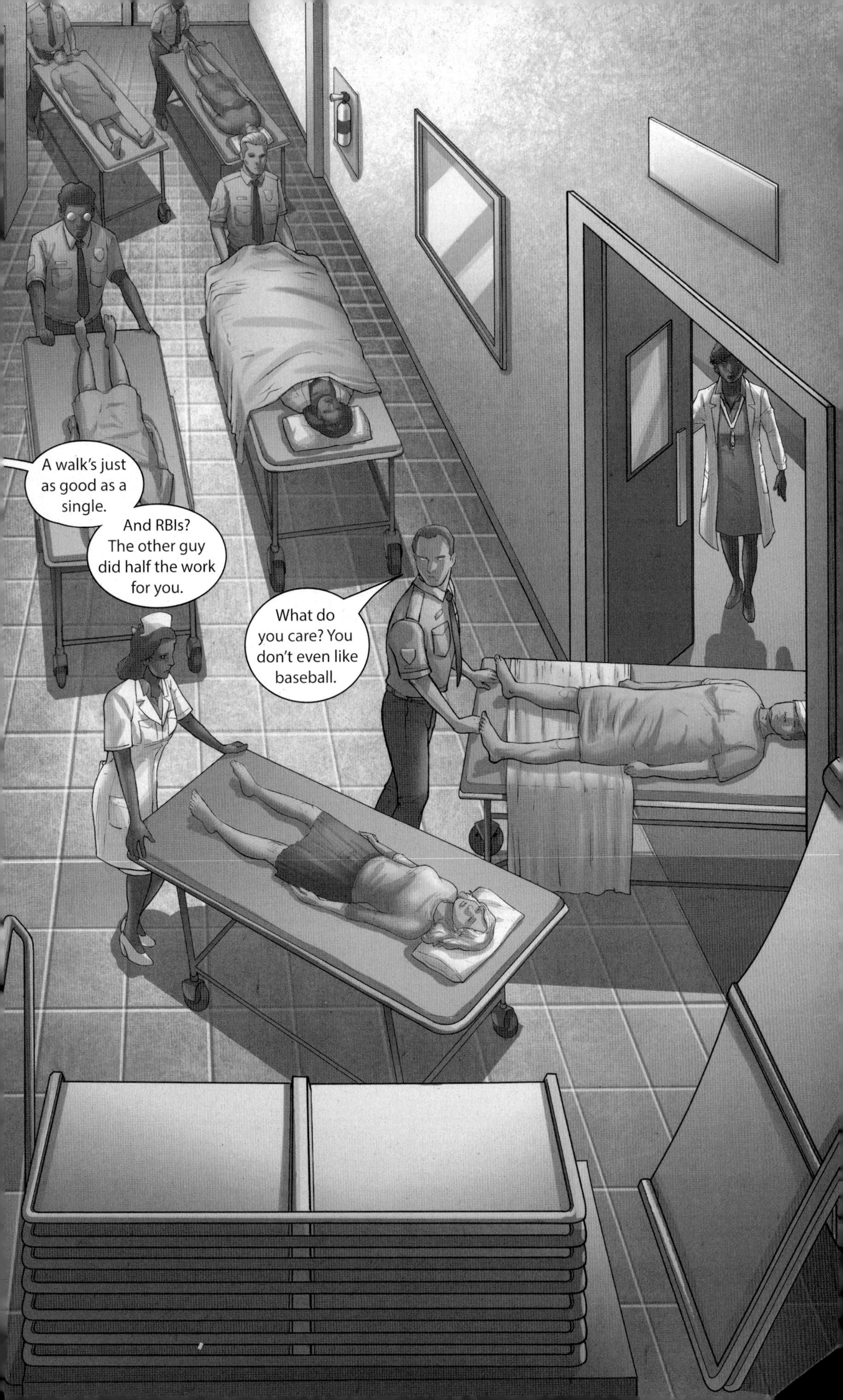
A walk's just as good as a single.
And RBIs? The other guy did half the work for you.
What do you care? You don't even like baseball.

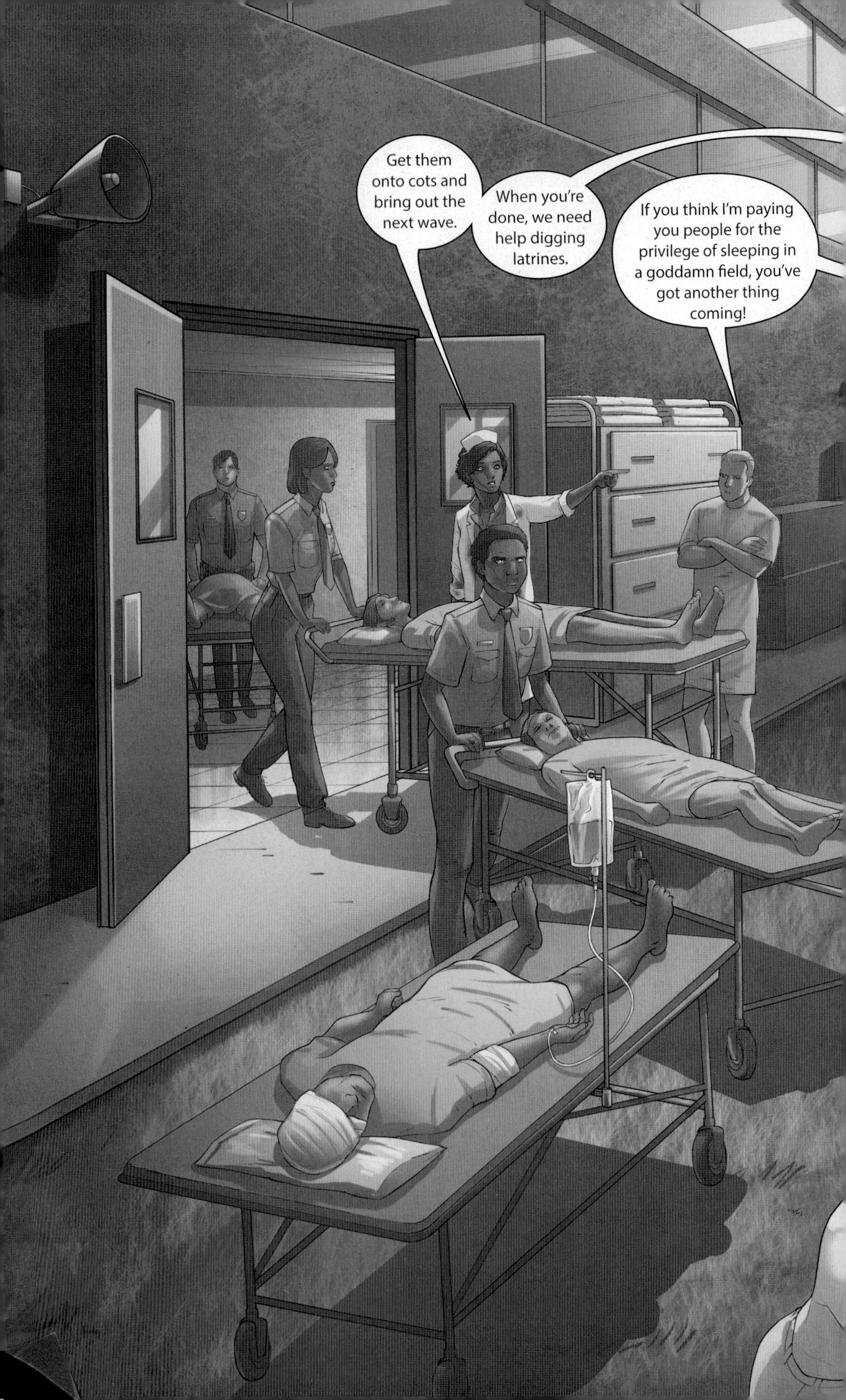
Get them onto cots and bring out the next wave.
When you're done, we need help digging latrines.
If you think I'm paying you people for the privilege of sleeping in a goddamn field, you've got another thing coming!

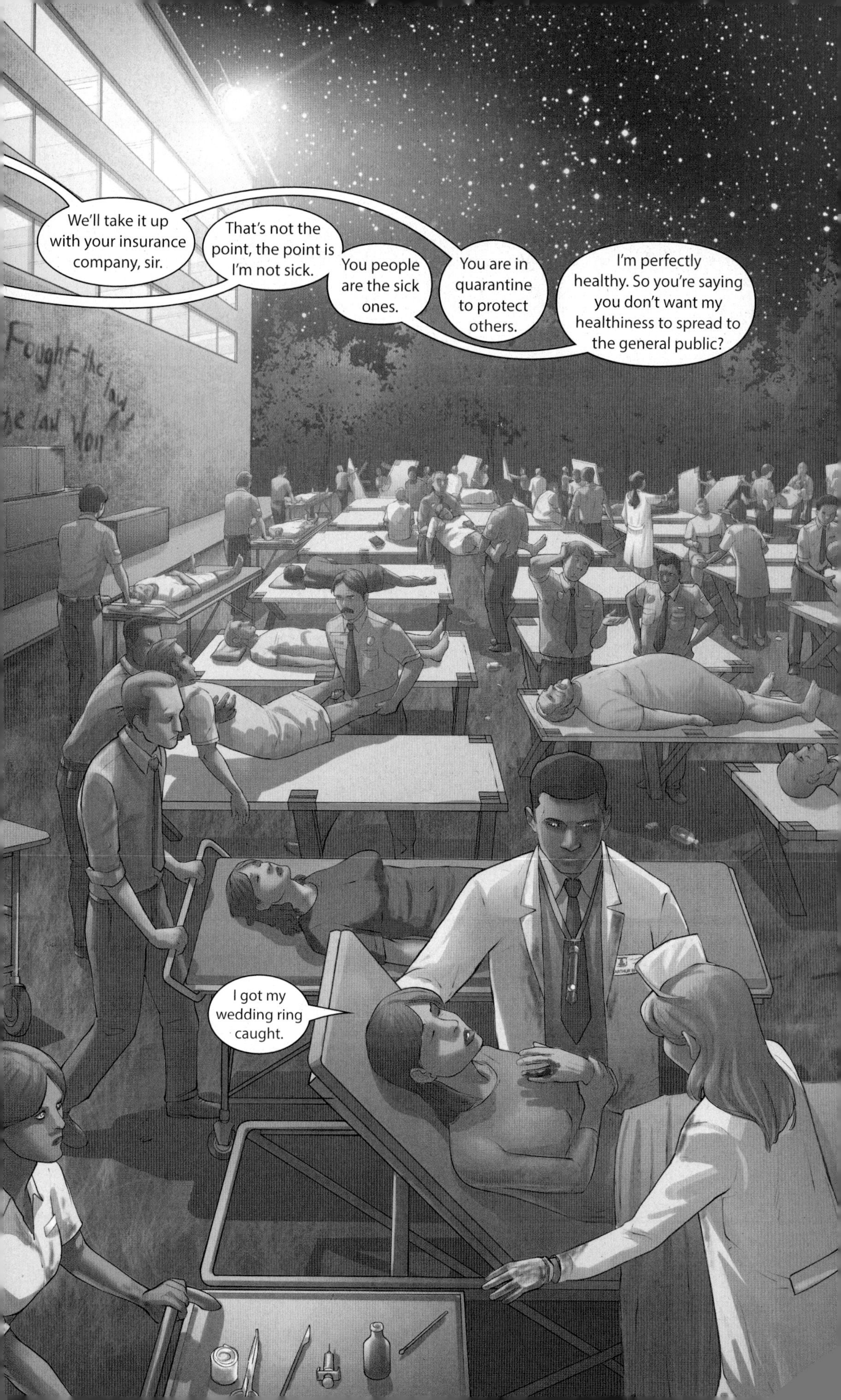

We'll take it up with your insurance company, sir.
That's not the point, the point is I'm not sick.
You people are the sick ones.
You are in quarantine to protect others.
I'm perfectly healthy. So you're saying you don't want my healthiness to spread to the general public?
I got my wedding ring caught.

It pulled the skin off like it was nothing.

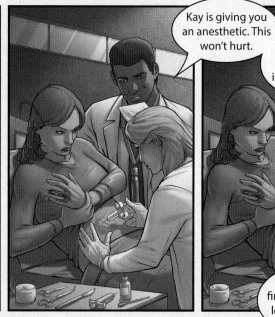

Kay is giving you an anesthetic. This won't hurt.

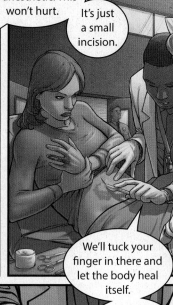

It's just a small incision.

We'll tuck your finger in there and let the body heal itself.

In a week you won't be able to tell it ever happened.

Just don't pull the cake out of the oven too soon, okay?

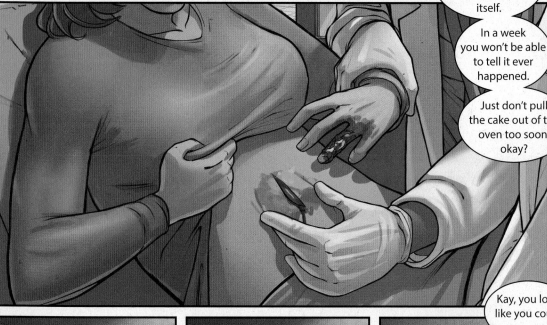

Kay, you loo[k] like you cou[ld] use a—

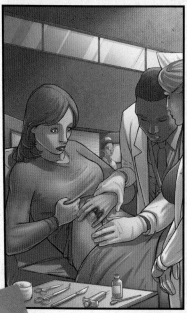

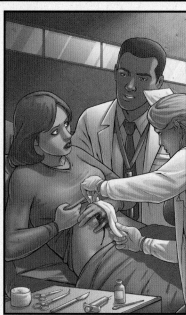

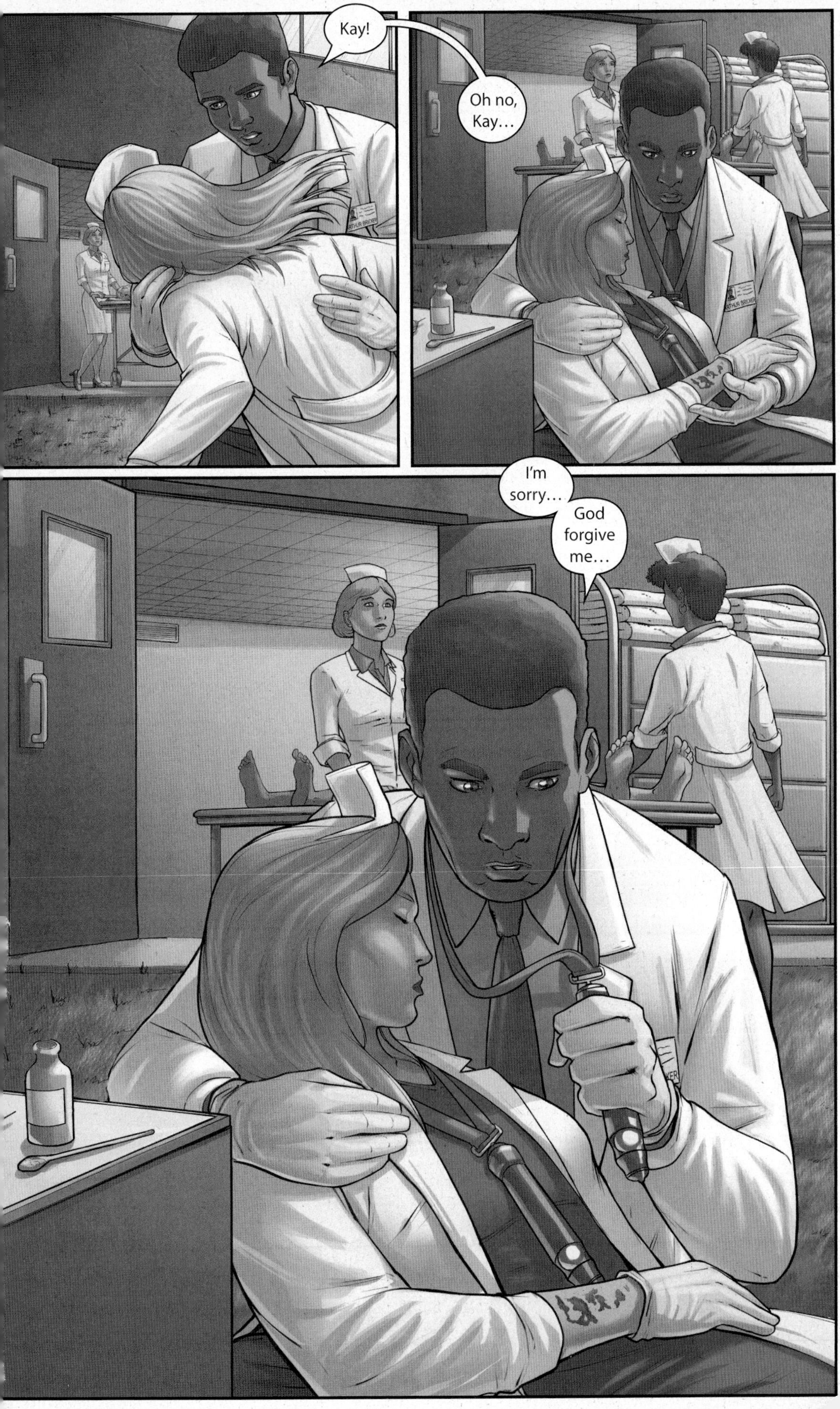
Kay!
Oh no, Kay…
I'm sorry…
God forgive me…
ARTHUR BRICKER